SCAM ME IF YOU CAN

Portfolio / Penguin
An imprint of Penguin Random House LLC
penguinrandomhouse.com

Most Portfolio books are available at a discount when purchased in quantity for sales promotions or corporate use. Special editions, which include personalized covers, excerpts, and corporate imprints, can be created when purchased in large quantities. For more information, please call (212) 572-2232 or e-mail specialmarkets@penguinrandomhouse.com. Your local bookstore can also assist with discounted bulk purchases using the Penguin Random House corporate Business-to-Business program. For assistance in locating a participating retailer, e-mail B2B@penguinrandomhouse.com.

ISBN 9780525538967 (hardcover)
ISBN 9780525538974 (ebook)

Printed in the United States of America
1   2   3   4   5   6   7   8   9   10

Book design by Amanda Dewey

SCAM ME IF YOU CAN

Simple Strategies to Outsmart
Today's Rip-off Artists

FRANK ABAGNALE

PORTFOLIO | PENGUIN

This book is dedicated to my grandchildren.

Contents

RULE #3 | PRESERVE YOUR DIGITAL PRESENCE

RULE #4 | SAFEGUARD YOUR HOME AND HEARTH

RULE #5 | SHELTER YOUR HEART

Foreword by Keith Slotter

first arrived at FBI headquarters in early 1995, eager to kick off the management portion of my career as a newly appointed supervisor in the Financial Institution Fraud Unit, part of the global financial crimes enforcement team. Placed in charge of the Bureau's check fraud initiative, my first directive was to host a series of national conferences bringing our field managers up to speed on the latest scams and how we might defeat them, or at least gain some traction on the problem.

While searching possible expert speakers, an associate referred me to Frank Abagnale. I had never heard of him, nor his criminal and FBI past. Though Steven Spielberg already possessed the rights to Frank's life story, this was years before *Catch Me If You Can* was written, cast, or filmed. Of course, the movie would eventually become a mega-hit, with a spin-off Broadway show, but in those pre-Internet days, all I could do was scrape together a few basics, including some material Frank sent me. It was thoroughly impressive and quickly confirmed that this guy was truly an expert in bank fraud and its prevention. There was a good chance he'd do quite well for my upcoming conferences. How little did I know.

Well, he killed it at our first warm-up session in Salt Lake City and then again to a much larger audience in Boston six months later. Frank was witty, clever, and incredibly knowledge-able, and his fraud experience and expertise were unmatched. He even showed me how to wash checks, erasing handwritten ink using simple nail polish remover, so I could muddle through similar demonstrations on my own. And he was freely available! I tried to at least pay for his travel and expenses, but he'd insist that I only tell him where to be and when.

Time went on, I'd request another presentation, and there he'd be at the appointed time and location. He was busy with paying gigs but would always find a way to carve out space for us. Amazingly, I still didn't know much about Frank. His primary pursuer during those youthful days on the run, Special Agent Joe Shea (the inspiration for Carl Hanratty in the movie), had long since retired, and most folks in the Bureau by then simply didn't know who Frank was. Meanwhile, he was barnstorming the country as a speaker, consultant, and general adviser, winning over clients with his anti-fraud messaging and amazing con-man past. Then, at a conference in San Diego, he gave me a copy of his book, *Catch Me If You Can*, and an audiocassette by the same name recounting his life story. I can't count how many times I listened to that tape, but each time the message was incredibly authentic and mesmerizing, and a mere prelude to what the movie would become.

Frank's commitment to providing these presentations never ceased. He conveyed his wisdom in fighting fraud—in ways only he could convey—to thousands of FBI and other federal agents. Everyone wanted to learn from him; even Leonardo DiCaprio and Tom Hanks attended a session in preparation for their upcoming film roles. Then the movie came out, and his popularity and demand skyrocketed to the stratosphere. At home and internationally, companies, banks, protection groups—everyone—wanted a piece of Frank. But still, he was always there whenever I called asking for another favor.

Of course, the criminal landscape has changed dramatically since our check fraud days, and Frank has continued to change and adapt to the new challenges as well. He was one of the first to anticipate the acceleration and personal devastation caused by identity theft and, ultimately, the many cyber risks attached to so many white-collar crimes we see today, which you'll read much more about in these pages.

People see the film, the antics, the cons, and the jail time and ask, "What is the real Frank Abagnale like?" Well, I can tell you that he's certainly brilliant to have pulled off all those capers, but more important, he's one of the most gracious, humble, and soft-spoken people you'll ever meet. Case in point: A decade or so after first meeting Frank, I'd risen to the position of assistant director of training, including heading the FBI Academy, in Quantico, Virginia. One morning, I headed upstairs to greet the latest batch of new recruits on their first day and officially swear them in as new FBI agents in training.

The classrooms are tiered, and the new agent hires sit in alphabetical order. After reciting the oath, they sat back down, and I glanced at the name card of the first new agent to my left. Scott Abagnale. At the time, I knew Frank had three sons, but I didn't remember their names and jokingly asked if he was related to Frank. "He's my dad," came the reply, and the room burst into laughter. Obviously, the joke was on me. "Wait till I talk to him," I warned, head shaking. But of course, that was Frank, not wanting any special treatment or recognition for his son. Sixteen weeks later, I'd have the honor of being on the graduation stage with Scott and his classmates as then-Director Robert Mueller gave them their official Special Agent oath of office. It was one of the proudest days of Frank's life.

One can walk into any bookstore and find entire sections on investment strategies, building wealth, and climbing the ladder to financial success. It's a cottage industry and very profitable for the more renowned authors who write those books. But before climbing that next rung, how about properly securing what's already been accumulated? Nobody really talks about that, but believe me, the scammers and thieves are out there. Every day. This is where Frank comes in, and this is his gift. He's not just a financial consultant or adviser, but actually provokes thought and causes people to change their behavioral acumen. By following *Scam Me If You Can*'s suggestions, you'll find your financial health and risk exposure improving because you'll eliminate some bad fiscal habits and institute better practices, lowering your exposure to fraud and abuse. This isn't a complex series of equations and financial strategies, but commonsense practices, easily implemented, to help keep us more secure.

I've known Frank now for longer than I can remember, and I'm honored to call him my friend. He truly did bolster my career, and in turn changed my life, but I have never really understood why he's done all this, and nor have I ever pushed him for an explanation. Those who have seen him present in person know how powerful and prescient his guidance can be. For those who haven't, it's a definite bucket list item, whether you're savvy about scams but want to hone your knowledge, or you know next to nothing about cons and want to learn how to protect yourself, or you're somewhere in between. Either way, enjoy the read and keep *Scam Me If You Can* on hand for future reference. Stay alert, remain diligent, and we can all stay a step ahead of the never-ending con game.

Keith Slotter
Former FBI Assistant Director,
Training Division, Retired

Smart People Get Scammed

Scam [skăm] *n.* *(informal)*: a dishonest scheme; a fraud.

Fraud [frôd] *n.*: a person or group of people or thing(s) used by a person or group intended to unethically or criminally deceive other people for personal gain, usually by unjustifiably claiming to provide something of desire, value, or necessity, or by claiming to have certain advantageous qualities or accomplishments.

I just wanted to die," said Helen Anderson. "I wanted to go to sleep and not wake up, because I was so tired of it never ending and I didn't know what to do."

Helen, sixty-four, was a victim of identity theft. She had worked in the operating room of a Seattle hospital and, like many nurses, had developed back problems because of the long hours she spent on her feet and the labor involved in maneuvering and lifting patients. By 2011 her legs had started to hurt so badly that she required back surgery, which prevented her from returning to work. Helen wasn't worried about the loss of income. She had planned wisely for her retirement, enjoyed a solid credit rating, paid her bills on time, and owned her house outright.

Soon after she'd recovered from surgery, her daughter in Portland, Oregon, started to suffer from health problems. Since Helen was now retired, she had time to travel to see her. She left her home and her dog in the care of her niece, Samantha. Helen asked Samantha to promise not to allow anyone else to stay in the house. She had had a bad experience fifteen years earlier, when the sister of one of her hospital coworkers stayed with her for a week. Using information she had found in Helen's home, the woman opened a credit card in Helen's name. After discovering the crime, Helen confronted the woman, who then paid off the debt and closed the account. But the event left an impression on Helen, and she didn't want any strangers in her house, especially not while she was away.

When Helen returned home from visiting her daughter, she was understandably upset to see another woman staying there. When Helen asked Samantha about the stranger, she explained that the woman, Alice Lipski, was a friend who had had a fight with her boyfriend and needed a place to stay. It would just be for a few days, and Samantha didn't think Helen would mind. Well, Helen did mind, and asked that Alice be out of the house by the end of the week. She was right to feel uneasy. That feeling intensified when the branch manager of Helen's credit union called her to tell her someone had charged $300 on a debit card that Helen had never used before. Now her account was overdrawn.

Helen went to her credit union office to fill out a fraud

affidavit, and the lost money was restored. But the problems continued. A few days later, she received another phone call, this one from Wells Fargo. Had she just made $5,000 in charges on a credit card she'd never used before? No, she hadn't. The card had apparently been activated from her home the week before, and the balance had been paid off with one of her own credit union checks. What was happening? Helen went back to her credit union. While looking over her account, the manager asked, "Did you just pay $500 from this checking account toward your American Express card bill online?" No, she hadn't. Helen didn't pay bills online. The manager told her to file a police report.

This was just the beginning of Helen's identity nightmare. While Helen was trying to plug up the widening hole in her credit problems, Alice Lipski was methodically *becoming* Helen Anderson. On top of what Alice had stolen from paperwork at the house, she had also found Helen's mother's birthday through some basic social media sleuthing and an Internet background check. This information allowed Alice to negotiate the security questions and reactivate a canceled store card from Costco, setting new security answers that only Alice knew. In doing so, she effectively locked Helen out of her own account. She also signed Helen up for a credit-monitoring service. But instead of protecting Helen against ID theft, it gave Alice access to Helen's complete credit history.

The credit report contained a great deal of information about Helen's bank and store credit cards. Alice reported each card as lost or stolen and opened new replacement cards, each with a new and unique username and password. And then she started to use them. Next, she had photo IDs made up with her photo but Helen's info, so she could effectively impersonate Helen in real life, not just online. Then Alice instructed the U.S. Postal Service to forward Helen's mail to a post office box. Naturally, Alice used one of Helen's credit cards to pay the monthly fee. She also had a valid-looking driver's license made, and she had Helen's Social Security number, thanks to the new Medicare card Alice had received in the mail. (At the time, Medicare cards still listed Social Security numbers on them.)

It took a while for Helen to notice that she was no longer receiving checks and bills in the mail. And then more calls came in from credit card companies asking about suspicious transactions. "I would call a card company and they would ask for the account number and password, and I couldn't give them either one," Helen said. She felt as if she were disappearing. She had to go to banks and stores in person and show them her driver's license in an effort to convince them she was who she said she was. "I couldn't prove who I was, because [Alice] could prove it easier than I could," she said. Helen would cancel cards and reset information when she could, and there would be peace . . . for a while. But then a whole new set of charges would appear. Helen believes that more than $30,000 was spent in her name—at stores, restaurants, casinos, gas stations, and other places.

What Helen didn't know at the time was that Alice was spinning out of control. She was a methamphetamine addict. Law enforcement experts say there is a discernible link between meth addiction and ID theft. But eventually an addict's drug use escalates, making her more prone to make mistakes. Alice was writing bad checks on other stolen accounts to keep Helen's accounts from exceeding their limits. After Alice's boyfriend was arrested, she needed $10,000 to bail him out of jail. To get it, she drained Helen's credit union account, along with three other accounts stolen from other people. She also pledged equity in Helen's home to spring him from jail. Helen had no idea that her house, which she had lived in for forty years and owned outright, was in jeopardy until she received an angry call from a bail bond company.

"I felt like I was a nonhuman being," said Helen.

The devastation that Helen felt is often the most damaging aspect of identity theft—or any type of fraud. Even if you can get your money back and restore your credit ratings, what may never leave is the sense of violation that comes with the knowledge that your home, family, and personal information have been compromised. Experts say the effects of fraud on individuals are similar to the psychological aftermath experienced by victims of violent crimes and war, ranging from anxiety to emotional volatility, depression to post-traumatic stress disorder (PTSD).

One night, Alice racked up $2,000 on one of Helen's accounts on a Macy's shopping spree. She was high, and in her haste to get out of the store, she left her purse on a chair. That handbag contained a meth pipe and all the tools of Alice's trade—and proof of her deceit: a tablet computer with information about her victims, fraudulent credit cards, and ten Washington State driver's licenses in nine different names. Each one had Alice's picture on it. When she realized she had left her purse behind and went back to retrieve it, it was too late. The police had been called and were already trying to track her down, but she was able to flee the store before they arrived.

Ultimately, it took six weeks for officers to find and arrest Alice. They learned she had accumulated these tools of her trade over the span of a few months, and with the help of a small team of accomplices, including a man named Dino, who crafted fake IDs so authentic-looking they fooled experienced bank tellers, and another named Brian, who had the skills to calculate algorithms used to determine driver's license numbers, Alice was charged with ten counts of identity theft. She and her colleagues had stolen close to $1 million from Helen and other victims. Alice was successfully prosecuted but cut a deal that would limit her jail time if she successfully completed drug rehab.

The funds Alice had stolen were restored, because Helen filed the appropriate police reports, but her life will never be the same. Her financial future remains uncertain as she struggles to clean up her damaged credit. After this ordeal, she sold the house that she had called home for forty years and moved in with her elderly mother. Helen is often stymied by the arduous paperwork she needs to fill out to get credit bureaus to correct her record and is fatalistic about the possibility of future fraud. "My information is out there for another scammer to use," she said. Unfortunately, this will always be the case.

Every year, millions of American consumers—nearly 7 percent of the population—are victims of scams and fraud. Criminals everywhere, from people in your own community to international rings, are looking for opportunities to take advantage of you. In 2017, the number of fraud victims in the United States reached 16.7 million, with $16.8 billion lost. Victims lose not just money; they can spend hours trying to resolve scams. And worse: Scams can alter and ruin lives.

In this book, I reveal the truth behind the methods used by the world's most skillful con artists to steal billions of dollars each year from unsuspecting consumers. And I give you very specific steps to protect yourself and your family.

I'm writing this book now because in my anti-fraud work I see how quickly scams and scammers are advancing. It's frightening. I also see firsthand how devastating fraud can be.

Scam Me If You Can draws on my own expertise working on the front lines to combat fraud. For more than forty-five years, I've worked with, advised, and consulted with the FBI and hundreds of financial institutions, corporations, and government agencies around the world to help them in their fight against fraud. I also serve as the Fraud Watch Network Ambassador for AARP, a nonprofit with thirty-seven million members. But my unusual blend of knowledge and expertise began more than fifty years ago, in an unusual way: I was one of the world's most famous con men.

I became a con artist in 1964, at the age of sixteen, and continued until I was caught and brought to justice in 1969, when I was just twenty-one. In those intervening years, even though I was very young, I was able to don a variety of professional disguises and professions, including airline pilot, doctor, lawyer, sociology professor, FBI agent, and Federal Bureau of Prisons agent. This is the story depicted in my 1980 book *Catch Me If You Can*, which in 2002 became a Steven Spielberg film of the same name, featuring Leonardo DiCaprio as me. (If you watch closely, you'll see me make an appearance as a French cop!) I traveled the world, cashing more than $2.5 million in forged checks, and as a result I financed a lifestyle that included bespoke suits, luxury cars, and world travel. I dated beautiful women. It was thrilling.

First I assumed the identity of a Pan Am copilot. I created a fake pilot's license and posed as an off-duty pro, allowing me to fly in the cockpit anywhere I wanted for free. (Rest assured, I never actually flew a plane.)

I was pretty audacious. Picture a sixteen-year-old decked out in a Pan Am uniform, impersonating an airline pilot. I was tall, which made me appear older, nicely dressed, and very polite. I knew that certain kinds of people were more apt to come under my spell than others. Pretty young women, older people, and those who felt I represented authority were all good targets. Young women because, well . . . I liked them and they liked me. Older people were always impressed with a well-spoken and courteous young man. And all sorts of people—airline and airport staff, people in banks and other institutions—respected someone in a pilot's uniform. After all, we trust a pilot to fly a giant machine and get us to our destination safely.

When I became tired of constant travel, I moved to a luxury apartment outside Atlanta, where I assumed the identity of a doctor. I was even hired as a supervising resident at a local hospital. (Again, you can breathe easy: I never practiced medicine on patients.) Next I pretended to be a Harvard-educated lawyer and a Columbia-educated sociology professor. After a while, I decided to return to my pretense as a pilot and went to Europe, where I printed and cashed more fake checks. It was an elaborate hoax that involved operating my girlfriend's father's massive Heidelberg printing press—one of the fun scenes in the movie. Finally, I was apprehended (a stewardess and former girlfriend recognized my face on a WANTED poster and alerted the authorities) and imprisoned by French police, was extradited to Sweden, and eventually landed in a U.S. prison (although I managed to escape police custody twice, once from a taxiing airliner and once from a federal penitentiary). Eventually, though, I was sent to prison and served four years.

After I was released—still in my twenties—the FBI asked me

if I wanted to use my expertise (so to speak) to fight the bad guys. I said yes, believing that devoting myself to fighting fraud was a good way to continue to repay a debt I owed to society. While I am ashamed of what I did as a young man, cheating and stealing and, along the way, deceiving and hurting people, I was grateful for the opportunity to turn myself around. The release of the *Catch Me If You Can* film gave me a wider audience to talk about fraud prevention.

I've now been a security and anti-fraud consultant for more than forty-three years. I have a consulting company, Abagnale & Associates. My fraud prevention programs are used by more than fourteen thousand financial institutions, corporations, and law enforcement agencies. I've met and talked to thousands of everyday people who have been harmed by scams—from small business owners to CEOs, from students to retirees, and everyone in between, people of all ages and from all backgrounds, around the world—hearing their stories and offering advice. This has allowed me to cover a wide variety of scams, investigate where they come from, and find ways to fight back against this worldwide scourge.

I don't want it to happen to anyone else. That's why I wrote this book.

My goal with *Scam Me If You Can* is to arm as many people as I can with the information and tools you need to put a shield between you and the scammers. The book is part of AARP's efforts to educate and arm readers of every age about as many scam techniques and prevention strategies as possible.

Many of the stories I've heard and all the advice I've given is packed into this book. It's such important information to have on hand, because we are living in a unique time. At no other point in history has it been easier to be a con artist—or to be victimized by one. In the past decade, technology has completely transformed the landscape of scams, making them quicker, more global, more anonymous, and more interconnected than ever before. Each week seems to bring new, ever more dismaying headlines about the use of technology for nefarious purposes, whether it's such Orwellian acts as the use of social media to disseminate fraudulent news stories for political purposes during the 2016 election cycle or the widespread use of scams targeting vulnerable veterans. (Sixteen percent of vets lost money to scams between 2012 and 2017, and the number continues to grow.)

The good news is that fraud is preventable. Vigilance is your weapon, and it is always at your disposal. Protection and prevention are your personal responsibility and can be achieved by taking easy, practical steps. *Scam Me If You Can* will empower you with information and proactive tips and strategies to defend yourself. Even small changes in habits, recommendations for which I provide here, allow you to stay a step ahead of the multitude of illegal schemes bombarding you constantly in a multitude of ways—via your front door, your mailbox, your telephone, and, of course, your electronic devices. Reading this book can make a world of difference in your life.

WHO GETS SCAMMED

Who is likely to experience certain scams? It turns out that demographics—gender, socioeconomic status, age—differ based on the type of scam. The 2011 AARP Foundation National Fraud Victim Study of 723 fraud victims and 1,509 respondents from the general public found that victims of investment fraud, for instance, were more likely than the general population to be male, be married, have some college education, and make $50,000 or more. Lottery victims were more likely to be single, to have less than a college education, and to be less likely to make $50,000 or more. Victims of identity theft to obtain prescription drugs were more likely to be female and single, have less than some college education, report an annual income of less than $50,000, and have a higher average age than the general population.

Are some of us more prone to becoming victims than others? Yes and no. Research shows you can be vulnerable to a scam whether you're seventy-five or five—yes, children can be victims, too. I've also heard from business executives, doctors, lawyers, and other highly educated individuals who have been victims. So let's take a moment now to examine who gets scammed most often— and why. If you see yourself in any of these categories, you may have to be more vigilant in making yourself un-scammable.

- **Active in more sales situations:** Victims tend to be more engaged in the marketplace—whether that is the consumer marketplace (such as shopping or investing in the stock market) or the marketplace of ideas (social media). They are more likely to report attending sales presentations when offered a free meal or hotel stay in return; entering their name in drawings to win a prize; allowing salespeople into their homes to make a presentation; and opening and reading every piece of mail they receive—catalogs, advertising circulars, contests offerings, and promotional come-ons.

- **Slow to take preventative actions:** Victims are less likely than the general population to report taking prevention measures such as signing up for the National Do Not Call Registry or checking the references of businesses before hiring them.

- **Under more stress:** We have to be especially cautious in our decision-making during stressful events or when life is putting great demands on us. That's because stress takes up cognitive capacity, which means we may not be thinking about how to defend ourselves against scams. Moreover, when we're under stress, we give more weight to positive outcomes and we tend to discount negative effects of decisions.

IN THIS BOOK

The quiz that starts on p.15 will help you determine how knowledgeable you are about scams. But there are so many scams even the most vigilant people may not have heard of. The topics I discuss throughout this book range from identity theft and investment scams to digital safety and romance scams. To provide a framework for the wide swath of scams covered, I've organized the book around the five simple steps you can take to scam-proof your life.

1. Protect your identity
2. Secure your finances
3. Preserve your digital presence

4. Safeguard your home and hearth
5. Shelter your heart

Within each of these categories, chapters take you through what the related scams are, how they work, and what you can do to prevent them. Read the book straight through, or dip into the section or chapter that serves your immediate needs. It's a reference you can look to again and again, since the index makes it easy to find specific topics. This is a solutions-oriented book; for every scam, I provide succinct ways you can protect yourself and your family as well as what to do if you become a victim.

You'll find fascinating detours into what I call our Hall of Shame, stories of notorious scammers and their scams; the psychology behind scams; and hundreds of in-depth, comprehensive tips to help keep you one step ahead of clever scammers and their rip-offs.

So get ready. Today is a brave new world in which *anyone*—regardless of education or intelligence, age, gender, or class—can fall prey to a new, highly sophisticated breed of criminal. No matter how savvy or how old you are, it could be you! It's a sad fact that scams continually evolve and become more insidious and convincing as scammers learn more about ways to thwart the latest anti-fraud and security efforts. So what can you do? Know where you fit into the profile. Be aware of, and guard yourself against, persuasion tactics. Take action to protect yourself. Be skeptical. Know the likely cons, and keep up with the latest scams by signing up for AARP's Fraud Watch Network.

I invite you to join me on this journey to make yourself "scam-wise." Share this information with your relatives and friends.

There is power in numbers, and an army of vigilant, informed citizens connected through community makes us *all* safer. Working together, we can make a difference and reduce the number of scams. And, more important, we can protect you and your family.

—*Frank W. Abagnale Jr.*

What's Your Scam Quotient?

The following quiz can help test and identify your vulnerability to scams—what I call your Scam Quotient, or SQ. The results give you a general idea of how prone you are to becoming a fraud victim. No matter how you score, the good news is that the information, tips, and strategies in this book show you how to up your scam-proofing skills and raise your SQ. I recommend that you take this test again when you've finished reading, to see how much your SQ has improved. The quiz is simple: Read the statement and then decide whether you think it's true or false. When you're done, add up your score and read your assessment.

1. Fraudsters use psychology more than technology to successfully run their scams.
   True
   False

2. Always wait at least twenty-four hours before making any important financial decision.
   True
   False

3. Identity theft is not a problem if you don't use social media or do online shopping.
True
False

4. The IRS is allowed by law to call you about back taxes you may owe without sending you written notice first.
True
False

5. Medical ID theft is a serious issue only for people on Medicare.
True
False

6. Banks never send their customers emails that ask them to click on a link wanting them to verify their information.
True
False

7. State lotteries charge a fee in order to collect large winnings.
True
False

8. Houses of worship, sororities and fraternities, alumni organizations, and other membership groups are a good way to learn about investment opportunities and meet financial professionals you can trust.
True
False

9. The Social Security Administration might call and ask for confirmation of your Social Security number.

True

False

10. Pop-up windows warning you of a computer virus are a handy way to identify a problem on your computer, and you should click on them to solve the problem.

True

False

11. Long, complex passwords are one of the best ways to secure accounts online.

True

False

12. Sharing vacation photos on social media while you're away is a great way to keep family and friends up to date on your adventures.

True

False

13. It is illegal for telemarketers to call you if you've never done business with them.

True

False

14. It's fine to buy medications from Canadian online store-fronts or small pharmacies that don't require a prescription or that offer deep discounts.
True
False

15. It's okay to buy a pre-owned or new designer bag online as long as it comes with a guarantee of authenticity and offers buyer protection.
True
False

16. Up-front fees are legitimate and necessary to secure a lease on an apartment.
True
False

17. Selling a timeshare requires numerous up-front fees.
True
False

18. Dating apps are always a safe way to meet potential significant others.
True
False

19. It's difficult to get a copy of a birth certificate.
True
False

ANSWER KEY

Check your answers using the key below. Give yourself 0 points for every wrong answer and 10 points for every right answer.

1. **True.** Psychology is the most important tool scammers use to defraud victims (see page 29).
2. **True.** It's a good idea to give yourself time to gather your thoughts and emotions to make a sensible decision (see page 30).
3. **False.** Your identity can be stolen even if you don't own a single digital device (see Protect Your Identity).
4. **False.** The IRS will always send written notices before taking the rare step of calling you (see page 77).
5. **False.** In fact, children are some of the most vulnerable people when it comes to medical ID theft (see page 88).
6. **True.** Banks never send their customers emails that ask them to click on a link to verify personal information (see Secure Your Finances).
7. **False.** There is never a fee to collect legitimate lottery winnings (although you may have to pay taxes on them!) (see page 36).
8. **False.** Some scammers use what's called "affinity" to seek out targets in religious organizations or volunteer and school groups. Just because someone is a member of your house of worship, volunteer group, or school group is not a guarantee that they will give you credible legal advice (see page 115).
9. **False.** The SSA knows your Social Security number—they don't need to ask you what it is (see page 118).

10. **False.** Pop-up windows telling you that your computer has a virus are scams to get money and/or infect your computer with malicious and destructive software programs (see page 143).

11. **False.** Most passwords used by scammers are stolen—not guessed. Long, complex passwords are as easy to steal as short, simple ones (see page 194).

12. **False.** Share your photos after you come back—don't signal on social media that you're not home! (see page 66).

13. **True.** Of course, this doesn't stop illegal robocalls from interrupting your day (see page 217).

14. **False.** Pharmacies that do not require prescriptions for prescription drugs are often selling out-of-date, tainted medicine or fake pharmaceuticals.

15. **True.** There are reputable sellers online in the business of selling genuine articles—as long as they offer buyer protection and proof of authenticity, you can shop till you drop.

16. **False.** Avoid rental companies that require up-front fees and monthly membership dues to access listings of low-cost rentals, pre-foreclosure rentals, or rent-to-own properties. Most are scams. Moreover, if the landlord or agent wants a fee to show you the property, it's a scam (see page 233).

17. **False.** Selling a timeshare should not require any fees other than closing costs, which are paid at the closing table (see page 238).

18. **False.** While you can meet honest people via digital dating, many scammers troll these sites to find potential victims (see page 290).

19. **False.** It's very easy to order any birth certificate from a county clerk's office (see page 310).

Add up the total to get your SQ score:

0 to 50 points: You are at a higher risk of becoming a victim of a scam than higher-scoring readers. You may have already been scammed. Keep calm and know that you're in good hands. You're ready to read this book cover to cover—and your Scam Quotient will go way up.

60 to 100 points: You are at average risk for becoming the victim of a scam, but you do have some knowledge of various schemes and how they work. You may have been a victim in the past, but you've learned from it. The good news is that you are poised to become scam-proof if you read this book.

110 to 150 points: You're well on your way to becoming scam-proof. You have knowledge and great instincts. If you've been tempted by a scam in the past, you likely were able to resist it.

160 to 190 points: You are pretty close to being a scam-proof rock star. Keep reading to take yourself over the top.

1

The Playbook Exposed: Recognize—and Beat— the Con Artist's Game

In this chapter, I shine a bright light on the common strategies scammers use and offer strategies to defend against their tricks, which should become part of your everyday scam-proofing tool kit. I've seen scammers use these methods for all the years I've worked with law enforcement, and I used them myself as a young man when impersonating an airline pilot and doctor, opening fake accounts at banks and cashing fake checks. As I relate examples of real-life scammers and how they operate in this chapter, I'll point out the consistent strategies they use so you can spot them and stay safe.

Let's start with the story of Kevin, a scammer working out of a large "boiler room," a space where workers gather to make high-pressure calls, looking for customers—or, in fraudulent boiler rooms, victims. Kevin comes from a long line of scammers, and no, I'm not talking about his actual family, but a tradition of scammers that goes far back in time and that I was a member of, too, for a while. Kevin's job was to call people he found on timeshare resale websites, using a set of methods common to all scammers to win the confidence of those frustrated with owning a timeshare and eager to sell it.

Con men like Kevin are well trained in the techniques to get targets "under the ether." Ether is a condition of trust and even infatuation with what is being presented. Getting a victim under the ether is crucial to all cons, no matter where or how they are perpetrated. This heightened emotional state makes it hard for the victim to think clearly or make rational decisions. To get their victims under the ether, fraudsters hit their fear, panic, and urgency buttons.

Kevin found the perfect targets when he reached out to Florida natives Nancy Adams and her sister, Edith. The siblings had gotten swept up in the pitch from a timeshare company that had offered them a free weekend in April 2012 at one of its properties, in Charleston, South Carolina. Nancy, then in her early seventies, had grown up working at her grandfather's Florida resort; she wanted to be the pampered guest for a change. Before the weekend was over, the sisters had bought a unit.

But two years later, Nancy was starting to regret the purchase. The sisters had used the unit several times over the past twenty-four months and had even accumulated "points" that could be used to stay at another one of the resort's properties. But expensive membership upgrades meant their total investment in the timeshare was now more than $20,000, so Nancy wanted to sell. She posted a for-sale ad on a website called BuyATimeshare.com. That was where Kevin saw the ad, and he reached out to her.

Nancy answered Kevin's call because it looked like it came from a local Florida area code, not an 800 number, like many previous calls she'd received (and hadn't answered). The area code made her feel that the call was legitimate. On the phone, Kevin identified himself as a buyer's agent from a firm called International Marketing Solutions. He told Nancy he represented a couple from Montreal who wanted to buy her unit. He even provided the buyers' contact information so Nancy could speak to them directly, which made her feel more secure. She called the number provided, and the woman on the other end confirmed everything Kevin had said. The sisters were reassured. They could off-load the timeshare—right now! Kevin and his colleague posing as the potential buyer knew exactly what to say to make them feel confident.

Kevin faxed Nancy and Edith documents signed by the phony buyers, and Nancy wrote a check for $2,250 (to be refunded later, Kevin assured the sisters) to set up an escrow account and title services. But then, as the weeks passed, and then months, Nancy never heard from Kevin or "the buyers" again. Kevin, it turned out, had moved on to more timeshare scams—for which he was eventually caught, arrested, and jailed. When Nancy realized what had happened, she filed a report, and eventually the state reimbursed her for most of what she had lost, and the resort bought her unit back. But she could have saved herself a lot of pain and money if she had known how to protect herself from fraud.

GETTING TARGETS UNDER THE ETHER

The best con artists know how to use a comforting and confident tone of voice to get people under the ether. They prey on vulnerabilities and seduce their victims into revealing their personal information. I perfected this technique while running scams as a young man. I knew how to modulate my voice and speak in a calm and reassuring manner to all my targets. The effect was almost hypnotic—before I was finished explaining why I had to cash a check or catch a free ride on an airplane, I had the target in the palm of my hand, under the ether. As Rocky, a con artist who worked as a consultant to numerous fraudulent boiler rooms in the 1980s and '90s, explains, a good con should always try "to keep the victim up in the altitude of the ether, because once they drop into the valley of logic, [you've] lost them."

Establishing a level of trust provides the con with a valuable tool for accumulating data that he can use to lead targets into making less than ideal decisions that, under normal circumstances, they would not make. To induce the ether, the con artist asks questions that trigger emotional responses. In Nancy's timeshare sale, for example, the con was straightforward and earnest, calm and professional, asking Nancy about her concerns about the cost of the unit and whether she would be able to carve out enough time to use it that it would be worthwhile in the future. But the questions vary depending on the scam. In a dating scam, for example, the con might ask his fake love interest what she likes to do in her spare time. In a home improvement scam, the con might ask the victim if it has been frustrating to deal with needed repairs.

Once a con identifies your triggers, he uses them as part of the pitch to drive you to a heightened emotional state. The questions he asks help him create a target profile that contains information he can use in follow-up calls, to keep you under the ether until you seal the deal.

Jimmy Edwards, a scammer who for eight years worked in thirty fraudulent boiler rooms before being arrested and convicted of fraud, explained how it works on a personal level. "The con gathers an arsenal of information by being personable and being friendly," he said. "They are making notes: two children, one with a mental illness, one brother lost in Vietnam. They're using all that information to put together their arsenal . . . so they know which buttons to push to bring the emotion up in that person. When I wrap that in tons of emotion . . . the logic goes out the window. . . . Now I've endeared you to me, now I'm no longer the predator on the phone. I'm Jim from New York."

This layer of trust gives the con an opening to ask more personal questions, the kinds of questions a close friend might ask. And the con knows how to ask them in the right way, with a softness and friendly curiosity that sets the target at ease. Instead of asking, "What's your monthly mortgage payment?" which would put the target on edge, the con might gently say, "Let me ask you something. It sounds like you have a wonderful home there. How much is that mortgage each month?" Instead of "When did your spouse die?" he said, "I know you loved your husband very much and miss him terribly. If you don't mind my asking, how long has he been gone?" Once the emotions and memories come flooding into the target's mind, the target connects those feelings to the person on the other end of the phone. The con has become a "friend," so the target opens up, answering personal questions and, more important, starting to trust the con. Now the con has established an important layer of trust with his victim.

HOW TO AVOID TRUSTING SOMEONE YOU SHOULDN'T

- Never engage a stranger in dialogue about your personal life.
- Don't reveal any personal information—not just account information but also names of family, friends, and even pets.
- Every time a stranger asks you a personal question, ask this question in return: *Why do you need to know?*
- Remember that you don't owe anything to a stranger—not information, consent to buy what they are selling, or anything else.

HITTING YOUR SCARCITY AND URGENCY BUTTONS, WITH A TOUCH OF FLATTERY THROWN IN

Once a con identifies your triggers, he'll up the ante by using a series of other strategies to further convince you that you must act—and act now! Scarcity, urgency, and flattery are three hot buttons often used together by scammers, unscrupulous salespeople, and others who want to talk their victims into agreeing to unfavorable deals.

Psychology professor Robert Cialdini popularized the term "scarcity principle" to explain how people are enticed by opportunities that seem finite or fleeting. Scarcity is often paired with urgency (*You must act now!*) and flattery (*You're too smart to let a deal this great get away!*). This strategy is used by legitimate businesses, including retail stores, to try to get customers to buy things. They'll use advertisements like "Special sale! Last day!" or "Only two in stock! Order now!" This is a tried-and-true sales technique that manipulates our natural psychological tendency to want to get in on a rare opportunity. And it works: People are more likely to purchase something if they think a great deal will be available for only a short time.

Scammers also take advantage of this, using scarcity, urgency, and flattery together to pressure you. While it is true that there are legitimate offers for things that exist in small quantities (for example, a unique piece of art for sale at an auction), when someone puts pressure on you to make a snap decision, a red flag should pop up. Boiler-room scams use the powerful combination of scarcity, urgency, and flattery to seduce investors into participating in phony financial schemes. In one instance, a man sold phony rare coins to collectors by making claims such as "Back in 1860 from the Philadelphia mint, there were 22,625 of these coins minted. Of those 22,625, only four have survived." This established scarcity. Then he'd create a sense of urgency with phrases like "There are only twenty-four hours left before this offer will expire" and "There are only three units left, so you'd better decide soon" to arouse panic in the buyer, making him afraid he'll miss out if he doesn't act immediately. And finally, the con artist would add flattery, complimenting the target to seal the deal: "You're very astute. You won't have to check with your family, will you?" Or: "You're really smart to be thinking of this opportunity right now. It's really unique." By claiming that there are only four coins (or condos) left, or only hours left to get in on an investment opportunity, the con is trying to make you believe that if you don't act now, you may never have a similar opportunity again. The con is pressing your panic buttons to get you under the ether.

While there may be some "once-in-a-lifetime" opportunities out there, there aren't many. Remember that there will always be another coin, another house, or another investment. The terms may change, prices can fluctuate, but you will almost always have the opportunity to buy something (or see something or go somewhere) again.

TEN WAYS TO AVOID THE TRIPLE THREAT: SCARCITY, URGENCY, AND FLATTERY

1. **Check your emotions.** If you are approached with a pitch to win a large amount of money or become part of a limited-time-only investment opportunity or send money to someone you haven't met, pay attention to *your* reaction. Is your heart racing? Are you excited? Do you start dreaming of all the things you could do with the money? These kinds of reactions are signs that you may be under the ether. Don't make a decision in this emotional state.

2. **Give it twenty-four hours.** Make it a nonnegotiable personal rule to give yourself one full day to think about any financial decision. This will diminish the emotion attached to the pitch and give you time to think without any pressure from anyone else.

siblings were inclined to believe him. They might have been less inclined to trust him if the call looked like it was coming from out of state or from a more generic 800 number. As Kevin talked to Nancy, he was able to discern her eagerness to find a buyer and close the deal quickly. He was able to create excitement in Nancy about the offer from the Canadian couple (so tired of those harsh northern winters!) and made her feel comfortable about eagerly accepting that offer and paying for a fake escrow account and title search.

It's easy to find yourself under the ether when someone who seems like a friend offers you an easy solution to a problem. Here's how to avoid getting scammed by a "need filler."

- Don't get swept up in desperation or quick fixes. Look for alternatives. Before you make a decision about something, even if the answer seems promising in terms of fulfilling a need, think about alternatives. Is there something better?
- Question up-front fees. Legitimate fees, especially for real estate transactions, are typically paid after the sale is concluded or are deducted from the sale price at closing.
- Never send untraceable money. Don't pay any fees through cash or a wire transfer, money order, gift card, or certified bank or cashier's check. These payment methods are difficult to recover.
- Check your credit card company's dispute policy. Many bank cards prohibit complaints after a limited number of days. Call your card company within that time if you feel there are problems with a transaction.
- Research before acting. It doesn't matter how nice a website a company has, or what number it's calling from—find

out more. Check with local and state consumer protection agencies to see if the company contacting you has any complaints against it. Look up consumer reviews and beware of negative opinions.

- Demand everything in writing. Don't agree to anything without paperwork. Once you get the paperwork, show it to someone with expertise before making a transaction. For a timeshare, for example, call the resort where you own and ask about the deal. A lawyer or real estate agent can also be helpful in reviewing documents.

SEDUCING YOU WITH THE BIG WIN

Another tool in the con artist kit is promising a big win. Who wouldn't get excited about learning they will double their investment or have won a sweepstakes or lottery? It's human nature to be happy about an unexpected windfall—we could all use extra cash. Con artists understand this and play on it by using a claim of a big win to stir up excitement and put you in the right frame of mind to accept a scam that will part you from your money.

Phantom riches are something you want but can't have. The con artist will dangle that phantom in front of you to amp up your emotions so you will make an impulsive decision. Researchers say this is the number-one tactic found in undercover audiotapes of con pitches.

Jeremy Shipman worked in numerous gold-coin-scam boiler rooms over a five-year period and describes the use of the phantom-riches or big-win strategy this way: "We would tell people that gold would absolutely double in value in the next one to two years and that the prospect would be able to rely on it making them far more money than any other investment vehicle," he said. Of course, there's no way anyone can guarantee the future price of gold or the price of anything. Big-win scams rely on outlandish claims presented in legitimate-sounding ways to get you under the ether.

Phony state lottery setups are another major way the big-win strategy can be used against you. No matter what state the scammers claim to be representing, they all use the same techniques. The con artist will call or send a letter or email congratulating you on winning the lottery and promising a large cash payout. This will be accompanied by instructions to contact a "claims agent" who will facilitate the collection of your winnings. The con's letters and emails look especially convincing because they often use the state seal and lottery logo (which have simply been cut and pasted off of the legitimate websites). I've seen many letters written by cons that list the correct address of a state's lottery commission, complete with an embossed seal and authentic-looking signatures in ink.

If you do call, the "claims agent," who often has a toll-free number connected to a location outside the United States, will go through a series of prompts that ask you to verify your identity by revealing sensitive information like your Social Security number or bank account and routing numbers. In my experience, the supposed agent on the other end will then tell you that you need to pay certain processing fees or taxes before you can collect your winnings. He will sound confident and professional and be effusively congratulatory and quick to instruct you not to waste time, lest you lose the opportunity to collect your winnings. The agent may even convince you to stay on the line until the money for the phony processing fees has been wired or transferred, so he can confirm receipt.

Don't blame yourself if you are tempted to get swept up by cons peddling big-win scams. When that feeling comes, turn the tables by following these simple tips.

- If you are approached with a pitch to win large amounts of money, notice how you feel. Is your heart racing? Do you start imagining all the things you could do with the winnings? These are signs of being under the ether. Never agree to anything in an excited state.

- Beware of guarantees that an investment will earn a certain amount over any period of time. If someone tries to use the big-win strategy when discussing an investment strategy, it's a scam. Likewise, legitimate lotteries never guarantee a win; they only provide your odds of winning.

- If you didn't buy a ticket, you didn't win. Even if you get a notice that you've won, if you did not buy a ticket from an authorized vendor, there is no way you could have won the lottery.

- Go to them. Legitimate lotteries won't contact you with news of a win. It is the responsibility of the winning ticket holder to reach out to the lottery commission.

- Pay no fees. There are no up-front fees to pay for an authentic lottery win. You may have to pay taxes on your winnings, but that comes after you collect. Virtually all lotteries, prizes, and sweepstakes offers that require payment to win are scams.

- Check and verify. Always check winning numbers with a lottery website. If you are skeptical about a winning lottery notification (and you should be), go to the website of the nonprofit Fraud Aid to check its list of known phony lottery games.

Report all suspicious winning notifications to your state lottery office and attorney general.

USING AGGRESSION AND THREATS

If the con artist tries all his tricks and you're still not biting, he'll typically escalate to more aggressive means to reach his goals: fear and intimidation. It is not uncommon for con artists to call a potential victim fifty to sixty times a day to get them to invest, buy something, or send money for a lottery. In one case, after a victim stopped answering the litany of abusive calls from one scammer, she received nasty voicemails. "Why don't you want to pick up the [expletive] phone?" he said on one message. "Pick up the [expletive] phone when I am calling you and stop playing games with me. Want me to come over there and set your home on fire?"

Getting victims under the ether has absolutely nothing to do with how smart or educated they are. In fact, those with college degrees are twice as likely to become victims of a scam than those without. As a young man, I convinced very smart people that I was an airline pilot, and I conned savvy bankers into believing that I had large, legitimate accounts at their banks. The overarching principle that scam artists rely on is not a target's lack of intelligence but how easy it is to manipulate a target's emotional state to a place where trust is established. If they struggle with getting you to trust them, they'll try to scare you with threats. Con artists are very good at finding and pushing emotional hot buttons—and we all have them, including me. It's important to identify what yours are so you can be prepared in case someone tries to con you. My hot buttons are my children and my wife—I know that if someone in my family was threatened, I'd have to work very hard to keep my thoughts and actions calm and collected and my decision-making logical. But as long as you follow the steps above and don't let potential scammers manipulate you, you can protect yourself from getting under the ether.

Hall of Shame: Michael Romano

Between 1997 and 2008, Michael Romano ran three lucrative coin companies—Wall Street Rare Coins, Atlantic Coin Company, and Northeast Gold and Silver—out of boiler rooms in Massapequa and Lindenhurst, New York. Targeting older Americans, Romano and his cohorts racked up millions of dollars in profits. The money—more than $40 million—was used to underwrite a lavish lifestyle that included multiple homes and rare vintage cars. Romano and his gang would lie to victims, telling them that the coins they were selling were highly collectible and would grow in value.

Describing the tactics used in an interview with CNBC, one victim said, "I got a phone call telling me that they knew I was interested in a particular type of coin, the Franklin half dollars, and that they had some good deals." After he purchased a roll of coins over the phone, he was bombarded by numerous high-pressure pitches from Romano's colleagues, who badgered him to buy more coins, "telling all these great stories" about the coins to lure him in.

More high-pressure tactics followed, where Romano's team would try to convince buyers that their coins would be more valuable if they purchased complete sets. The crooks also claimed to know of investors to whom coins could be sold for a profit, but obviously those investors never materialized.

"Romano took advantage of the trusting nature of hundreds of senior citizens across the United States by promising to sell them rare collectible coins, when in fact he was selling them near worthless change," said then–U.S. Attorney Loretta Lynch. "Many of the victims purchased the coins in order to leave a legacy for their children and grandchildren."

In February 2014, Romano was sentenced to twenty years in prison, followed by five years of supervised release. As part of the sentence, he was ordered to pay more than $9 million in restitution to victims and forfeit more than $32 million of his ill-gotten gains.

TEN SIGNS YOU'RE ABOUT TO BE SCAMMED

Here is my at-a-glance how-to guide for identifying scam tactics.

1. **Request for action.** If a salesperson asks you to "write down what I'm about to tell you; it's important," or words to that effect, it's a sign of a scam. Once con artists get you to do something, they have taken control of the conversation and put you in a more vulnerable position.

2. **Demand for fees.** If a lottery, prize, or sweepstakes requires a payment to collect winnings, step back. Virtually all prize offers that require a payment to win are scams.

3. **Guarantees.** Cons love to claim reliable and often astonishing guarantees, like the one where you're guaranteed to double your money in six months. Guarantees like that often signal a scam.

4. **Act now or lose.** Be skeptical of anything that demands urgency. "You must decide today" or "I need an answer in the next eight hours" is the lead-up to a scam.

5. **Request for personal information.** If a con asks a lot of personal questions or requires you to reveal personal information like your bank account or Social Security number, passwords, health background, or information about your mortgage or outstanding loans, it's likely a scam.

6. **Grammatical errors.** Email scams are often perpetrated by people in foreign countries who may be unfamiliar with all the precise rules of the English language or are using an online translation service. Look for errors in spelling and language usage in communications— these are often a giveaway that you're dealing with a scammer.

7. **No address.** If an offer comes from a company that has no street address or physical location you can verify, it could be a scammer sitting in a coffee shop thousands of miles away. This is especially true of e-commerce offers— if a website doesn't have detailed contact information, such as a phone number, email address, and street location, it may be a scam.

8. **Request for untraceable payment.** If an offer requires you to send a payment from Western Union, a gift card, or another untraceable source, beware. Legitimate businesses have legitimate banking details that can be verified.

9. **Computer access required.** Don't let people get remote access to your computer unless you have requested it and verified them. The technician who claims to be able to fix your computer problems "for free" just by getting access to your desktop in all likelihood just wants to steal your personal information.

10. **Unsecured web addresses.** A secure website is often indicated by "https" at the beginning of a URL, as

opposed to "http." That is important. Secure websites encrypt sensitive data such as payment information. Never submit personal or financial data to unsecured sites. Web browsers can also help you identify a legitimate e-commerce site: Look for a small closed lock symbol at the left end of the address bar. An open lock means the site is not secure.

CON ARTISTS NEAR AND FAR

The number of con artists has increased in the past fifty years. Technology actually makes it easier for larger numbers of people to scam more people from the comfort of their homes. As Robert Cialdini writes in *Influence: Science and Practice,* in a technologically advanced world where we are bombarded by information, we often fall back on a decision-making approach based on generalizations that allow us to act with a limited amount of thought and time. In everyday life, this usually works out okay for us, but this psychology can also be exploited by cons.

Today's scammers also have the ability to find out a great deal about their targets—even without the strategies outlined here. The scammer's playbook now includes social media research and data theft. Even people who do not have social media accounts, who limit their contact with these websites, or who are very private individuals can be vulnerable to profile building. That's because cons also steal, buy, and trade information about likely targets. They get this info from other scammers, fraudulent data brokers, and even legitimate sources, which is the case when employees steal information about customers and patrons for their own personal gain. For example, after Nancy was scammed the first time, I learned that she was conned a second time by someone pretending to want to rent her unit. She lost money in that scam, too. Based on my experience, I'd say it's very likely that her name ended up on a list of targets that was sold or traded by scammers.

Once scammers build a profile of you, they can use that information to scam you or others. This kind of activity is so insidious, I want to share with you just how it happens. That's next, in our first and second rules: Protect Your Identity and Secure Your Finances.

RULE #1

Protect Your Identity

2

How Identity Thieves Work

I n this chapter, I talk about identity theft and how to avoid or drastically reduce it. Getting your identity stolen can affect far more than your bank account or credit card. And it's not just inconvenient—it can cause serious problems for the rest of your life. Read on for what to watch for and how to protect yourself.

In 2017, I gave a Talk at Google (similar to a TED Talk) about my life. During the question-and-answer period that followed, a young man posed a question that I'm often asked: Given all the advances in computing and technology, isn't it harder for today's criminals to steal your identity than it was back in the 1960s? My answer was the same as what I'll tell you now: No, and in fact, as I always say, it's about four thousand times easier today than it was when I was sixteen. Identity thieves love technology. It makes their lives so much easier, because it gives them a convenient pathway to the details of your life. Just think about all that is available to you with just a few taps on your keyboard—credit reports, account numbers, personal and family details. It's all out there if you know how to look for it. And con artists are very good at seeking and finding information.

Identity theft, which happens every two seconds, is the deliberate use of someone else's identity (name, address, Social Security number, bank accounts, and so on) to get money and credit, obtain employment, steal property, falsify educational and other credentials, access healthcare, and more. Although there have long been impostors—people pretending to be someone else— the first use of the term "identity thief" I can find is in a 1966 newspaper headline for a story about a young man killed in Vietnam. Apparently, William Joyce had been in some trouble with the law back home, so he enlisted in the Marine Corps under the name Richard Preskenis, a boy from a nearby town. In those days, even the armed services didn't go to great lengths to verify identity.

Victims of identity theft can suffer undesirable and even ruinous consequences, including theft of money and benefits, a bad credit rating, psychological anguish, and loss of dignity and credibility—especially if they are held responsible for the thief's actions. The worst-case scenario is when an identity thief drains your bank accounts, takes your property, ruins your reputation, and sells or trades your sensitive information. On top of that, proving that your identity was actually stolen can be difficult and financially and emotionally draining. Recovering from identity theft can take many years for some people—and others never get their money back or their reputation restored. Helen, from chapter 1, is still reeling from having her identity stolen by Alice. She's lucky Alice was caught; only a minute percentage of identity theft cases are successfully prosecuted.

TECHNOLOGY IS THE IDENTITY THIEF'S BEST TOOL

With today's technology, it doesn't take much effort at all to duplicate a check. In Helen's case, Alice stole her identity and had checks printed with her name at banks where Helen had accounts. Some of Alice's thievery was done manually, but much of the information she obtained came from online sources like social media and credit-reporting agencies. All a thief has to do is go online, give a check-printing service your name and account number, have the checks sent to a post office box, and voilà— there go the contents of your checking account.

With today's technology, a criminal can do what I did decades ago—make up phony checks—right from a home computer. In the 1960s, when I wrote fake checks under a business's or individual's name and account number—in essence, stealing their identity—I needed a four-color printing press, typesetting equipment, and the technical know-how to run those machines. Now all I would need to do is go to a corporate website to grab its logo, and then to a banking website to download its logo. Next, I'd have to make a phone call to the accounts receivable department of the company whose identity I plan to steal and ask for wiring instructions so that I could ostensibly wire funds I owe them. Just like that, I would know which bank the company uses and its account number at that bank. Then I'd go online to access the company's annual report. Lo and behold, now I have a copy of the chairperson's or CEO's signature from the letter at the beginning of the report, which I can put on the checks I've created through the miracle of technology. All of it totally authentic to the last detail—except that the money's not mine, and the check is a fake.

One of the first tips I give for avoiding identity theft: Keep your check writing to a minimum and be vigilant about examining your bank statement *frequently*. And don't use debit cards. I don't own one. I never have and I never will. I don't recommend them to anyone—not my family, not my friends, not you. Why? It's simple. Every time you use a debit card, you put your money and your bank account at risk. Instead, use a credit card. I use a credit card for practically all of my purchases, even when I'm traveling abroad. Why? Because with credit cards, federal law limits my liability if there is an unauthorized use of my card. For this reason, I strongly urge you to use credit cards for your purchases.

If there is a large data breach (and you know that there will be) and your information is stolen, the worst that can happen is that your credit card company will cancel your card and send you a new one in a couple of days. You won't be responsible for any purchases made on your card. If the same thing happens and the criminals get your debit card information, you could lose the money in your bank account and have a difficult and lengthy time recovering it. When we use credit cards, we're using the credit card company's money, not ours.

THE DARK WEB

Technology isn't used just to create fake checks and steal people's identities by breaking into accounts and taking them over. The so-called dark web is a place where scammers and other criminals buy, sell, and trade personal information about potential victims, and it is a major factor in identity theft. The dark web is a place where individuals can operate undetected and anonymously.

Think of the Internet as the ocean. The surface is the web that you and I are familiar with and use every day—it's where we access Amazon, CNN, Facebook, Google, Yahoo, newspapers, our banks, and thousands of other public websites. This is where the vast majority of us spend our Internet time. It's all public and searchable, and most of it is friendly. These websites are indexed, so they can be found using search engines.

Dive a little deeper and you hit the "deep web"—a place that requires logins for the databases and websites found there. Most activity that takes place in this part of the web is legal; it's just not as easy for everyday folk like us to see. NASA, the National Oceanic and Atmospheric Administration, the U.S. Patent and Trademark Office, and private databases like LexisNexis and Westlaw use this part of the Internet. Since these pages aren't indexed, traditional search engines can't find them. You need to know exactly where you're going and have an authorized password to see them. Some of the pages, like NASA's, cannot be accessed by regular citizens, but others, like LexisNexis, require payment for access or at least usernames and passwords to access.

Go deeper still and you find the dark web, also called the "darknet," which is accessible only to those who use software called Tor (originally known as "The Onion Router"). Tor software was developed by the U.S. Navy in the 1990s so that intelligence agents operating overseas could communicate anonymously with colleagues in the United States. It was released to the public in 2003 as open software, free and available to anyone to download onto his or her computer. It's perfect for preserving anonymity for political dissidents, journalists, and spies—and also, it turns out, criminals. The dark web allows scammers to buy and sell illicit goods and information without being detected. The Tor browser hides users' IP addresses, and transactions are usually conducted in a cryptocurrency like bitcoin to make them untraceable.

PROTECT YOUR PAPERWORK

Old-fashioned hands-on thievery is, unfortunately, still a fact of life when it comes to identity theft. Fortunately, you can minimize the vulnerability of your paperwork.

- **Go paperless.** Don't keep papers with valuable information in your car—not even your insurance and registration cards. Identity thieves have been known to break into cars to steal information, especially in large mall parking lots, beach parking lots, and long-term lots. The National Insurance Crime Bureau recommends taking a picture of your insurance and registration cards on your cell phone and keeping photocopies of them in your wallet. If you get pulled over, most law enforcement will accept this and can verify the information on their computers.
- **Keep personal items within sight.** Never leave your wallet, handbag, or other personal belongings unattended.

When you are out and about, keep them on your person and in your sight. When you are in a crowded place, make sure you know where your belongings are at all times.

- **Stay close by.** Don't leave workers or other strangers unattended in areas of your home where they could access and steal sensitive information.

- **Keep cards at home.** Keep your Medicare card—after your first visit to a provider—and your Social Security card at home. (We'll talk about that further in chapter 4.)

- **Shred it.** Buy a shredder and use it faithfully—on *everything*, not just financial and medical information. Even the most innocuous-looking piece of junk mail—a fashion catalog—is a tool for an identity thief if it contains your name. Shred anything that has your name and other identifying information about you: labels on your empty prescription bottles, sales receipts with digits from your credit card number, solicitations from charities. You must shred everything. Yes, this takes time, but considering the potential consequences, it's time well spent. There are several kinds of shredders out there, and they all cost about the same, so you won't have to spend more to get the one that will thwart the thieves. I don't recommend buying ribbon shredders, which turn out long, thin strips of paper that are easy to reassemble. I know, because we've done that in the FBI labs, and it's not rocket science. Same with crosscut shredders, which create small rectangles that can be put back together with the aid of software called ePuzzler. The best shredders have "high-security

which means the shredder turns your mail
...nfetti. This makes it virtually impossible for scammers to reassemble the shredded paper.

- **Use a locking mailbox.** Sometimes, even if you shred,
  you are locking the barn door after an identity thief has
  already stolen your horse by simply rifling through your
  mailbox for those catalogs, pre-approved credit card
  offers, or any other piece of mail that looks promising.
  You can drastically cut the risk of this kind of theft happening to you if you invest in a mailbox that locks—so
  that the mail placed there by the mail carrier goes in and
  stays there until you, and you alone, remove it.

- **Say no to offers.** Opt out of receiving pre-screened offers
  of credit and junk mail in general. Call 888-5-OPT-OUT or
  visit www.optoutprescreen.com. This service is legitimate,
  since it is run by the credit-reporting companies.

- **Go paperless for bills and bank statements.** Many
  Americans still receive their bills in the mail. Yes, paperless statements can also be breached, but with the right
  security measures, online bill payment and banking is far
  safer than paying paper bills.

OLD-SCHOOL TECHNOLOGY: HOW COMMON THIEVES STEAL YOUR IDENTITY

To an identity thief, a recycling bin, a mailbox, a parked car, or a lonely purse sitting on a church pew are like all-you-can-steal buffets. You can fill up your plate and then go back for more. That's what Alice Lipski did with Helen Anderson's mail. In a victim's home, Alice would use her cell phone to snap a photo of the mail and then put it back where she found it, with the homeowner none the wiser. Or she and her criminal friends would break into cars in large mall parking lots, long-term lots near train stations, or gym or beach parking lots, where people often leave not only their vehicle registration but also their briefcases, bags, and wallets for extended periods of time. Even items considered detritus by most people—gas station and ATM receipts— have scraps of usable information, such as the last four digits of your credit card, debit card, or bank account, which can be used to reconstruct the entire number. Names, addresses, and ID numbers are right there for the taking—and believe me: They do get taken.

Carole Crane, considered one of the most prolific identity thieves in the Portland, Oregon, area, is known for rifling through handbags in churches, preschools, and doctors' offices, places where people often let down their guard. She took the information she found and created fake credit cards, driver's licenses, and bank accounts for herself and her associates. Crane's gang victimized more than fifty people and fifteen banks and stole $200,000, according to an FBI press release.

You can also be a victim during an innocuous visit to your

favorite café. Angela was having lunch with her friend Suzanne at a local sandwich shop. It was a little crowded and noisy, but they'd managed to snag a good table and were enjoying the chance to catch up. When it was time to pay the bill, Angela reached for her purse, which she'd carefully (or so she thought) corralled near her feet, only to find that it was a few inches from where she'd left it. Her wallet was missing. Suzanne picked up the tab while Angela frantically searched for it, but it was nowhere to be found. Angela told the shop's manager, hoping that someone would turn in her wallet. After that, she didn't know where to begin. Her driver's license, credit and debit cards, insurance card, AAA card, spare blank checks, and work ID were all in her wallet. Now what should Angela do?

Before we answer that question, let's take a step back and think about mitigation—the steps we can take to avoid some of the hassles that ensue after such a theft.

WHAT TO DO *BEFORE* YOUR WALLET IS STOLEN

Your wallet should not contain your life. Don't carry what you don't need. Here's my recommendation for what to carry:

- your driver's license
- a copy of your health insurance card
- a copy of your automobile insurance card
- a copy of your car registration
- a copy of your Medicare card with all but the last four digits blacked out

- one or two credit cards
- your identification card for work
- a small amount of cash for incidentals

Beyond these essentials, what else do you really need? Blank checks in your wallet are a really bad idea—they give the thief easy access to your bank account.

Carrying around a wallet full of store credit cards also doesn't make a lot of sense for most of us. If you do have many store credit cards, it's a good idea to take only the ones that you are planning to use when you leave the house. While store credit cards can help you establish credit and may give you a discount or benefits, you probably don't use them all that often, so you may forget what exactly you've been lugging around. Moreover, many store credit cards are really Visas or Mastercards. Having multiple major credit cards can be a good strategy if you want to separate purchases into categories and save some money, but only if you pay the cards off on time. Another downside of having too many cards is that you may be tempted to use them and not pay them off, which can ruin your credit score and get you into debt.

Before Your Wallet Leaves the House with You, Do the Following

- **Reduce the number of credit and debit cards you carry in your wallet.** After her purse was stolen in the café, Angela vowed to carry only those cards she used daily: one debit card for taking cash out of the bank ATM and one credit card for purchases. The fewer cards you have with you, the fewer you will have to freeze or cancel should your wallet disappear. She stashed the others in a safe place at home, where she could easily find them if she was going to a particular store. Angela also canceled store cards she had not used in more than a year, disabling the magnetic strip by cutting it lengthwise (she also could have run a magnet along it), then cutting the card into small pieces to make her information unreadable. And, for maximum protection, she discarded different pieces on successive trash pickup days.

- **Use credit whenever possible.** When I use a credit card, I am spending the credit card's money every day until I pay my bill at the end of the month. Meanwhile, *my* money is earning interest in a bank account. If a criminal does somehow get my credit card number and charges $1 million on it, I am protected. If someone uses your debit card fraudulently, they are taking your money directly. It can take up to three months for your bank to investigate and give you your money back.

- **Leave your checks at home.** If you know you have to write a check for some reason, take one, and only one, with you. Check fraud is just too easy to pull off, so I don't write many checks. If I do have to write a check, I use an inexpensive gel pen, because that ink cannot be washed off. Look for gel pens with specially formulated ink that becomes trapped in paper, which helps prevent criminal check washing and other document alterations.

- **Only write checks that go directly to the addressee.** For example, it's usually safe to write a check to your insurance company. But if I write a check to Walgreens, I know that more than one person will see it before it gets deposited. I have to give the clerk at the register my check, which contains all kinds of information she or someone else could use to take money from me. It has my account and routing numbers, along with my name and address, and she may ask me to write my driver's license number on the check along with my date of birth. My signature is on the check, too. Anyone from the clerk to other workers or managers and even couriers could see the face of the check and potentially gain access to my bank account. It's too simple to do.

- **Leave your bank deposit slips at home.** These slips contain exactly the same information as your checks and are a key that unlocks your bankbook.

- **Do not carry your Social Security or Medicare or insurance card in your wallet on a regular basis.** You'll need your Medicare or insurance card only the first time you visit a provider. Other than that, keep these cards at home in a secure place.

- **Have a list of the information you carry in your wallet in a safe, accessible place at home.** Write down your driver's license number, car and medical insurance numbers, credit card numbers, and work ID and keep them with the telephone numbers of the places you need to call should the cards go missing.

What to Do After Your Wallet Is Stolen

If your wallet is stolen, don't panic. The theft of your wallet is unnerving, to say the least, but it has happened to many of us and will happen again. Instead:

- **Act promptly.** Notify the institutions and agencies affected by your loss. Time really *is* money here—*your* money.
- **Notify the police.** In all likelihood, the police won't do anything to recover your wallet, but you want a record of the theft. Have the police write up a report, and keep a copy; it provides you with a record for insurance and other purposes.
- **Notify the bank.** If you were carrying checks or deposit slips or any other paper with your banking information, including your debit card, notify the bank immediately. The bank will issue you a new account number and a new debit card. Do not delay in making this call. The bank's liability is typically limited to thirty days, and you may be held accountable for only $50.
- **Call your credit card companies.** Notify the credit card company for each card that is stolen. To verify your identity, the card company may ask you what your last purchase was or read back to you a number of recent purchases and ask if you recognize them. Within a few days you will receive a new card with a new account number and your liability will be zero.
- **Notify your state's department of motor vehicles.** Make arrangements for a replacement driver's license or identity card. Request a new number so that if an identity thief attempts to use your old number, it will no longer be listed as yours.
- **Call your health insurance carrier.** If your medical insurance card (including Medicare) is stolen, the personal costs can be staggering. Do not forget or delay making this important call.

- **Sign up for a fraud alert.** This is a free service. I would do this in addition to a freeze, especially if you've been a victim of ID theft. An initial fraud alert can make it harder for an identity thief to open more accounts in your name. When you have an alert on your report, a business must verify your identity before it issues you credit, so it may try to contact you for this purpose. Fraud alerts are temporary; they're usually good for three months but can be renewed. There are also extended fraud alerts that last up to seven years; for these, you'll need to complete paperwork and provide documentation showing that you have been a victim of identity theft. To set up a fraud alert, visit one of the credit bureaus (Experian, Equifax, or TransUnion). You need set up only one alert; that agency will notify the others.
- **Notify the Social Security Administration.** If your Social Security card was stolen from your wallet, the SSA won't issue you a new number, but it will note your report, and you will have a record should a future attempt be made to use your number.

Hall of Shame: Gerald Barnbaum, aka Gerald C. Barnes, aka Donald Barnes

Gerald Barnbaum was born in Chicago in 1934 and was trained as a pharmacist, but he became a longtime medical impostor and identity thief instead. After his pharmacy license was revoked in 1976 for Medicaid fraud, local media reported, he made his way to California and legally changed his last name to Barnes. There, he stole the identity of an actual licensed medical doctor in Stockton named Gerald Barnes. He managed to work as a medical doctor, practicing in Los Angeles and elsewhere in Southern California.

In 1979, John McKenzie, a twenty-nine-year-old undiagnosed Type 1 diabetic, sought out Barnes's help. His symptoms were classic for the disease and would have been immediately recognizable by a trained physician: chronic increased thirst and hunger, dizziness, and rapid weight loss. Barnes had his physician's assistant draw blood, which was sent to a lab for testing. In the meantime, he prescribed McKenzie a drug for vertigo and sent him on his way. When the results of the blood test arrived, Barnes's PA was alarmed: McKenzie's blood glucose was 1,200 milligrams per deciliter, a sign of acute hyperglycemia. The PA knew the patient could be in trouble, so he called the police, who went to McKenzie's apartment, where they found the young man dead.

The PA expressed his concerns to authorities about Barnes's legitimacy as a doctor, and an investigation followed, which confirmed the PA's suspicions. In 1981, Barnes pleaded guilty to involuntary manslaughter and was sent to jail for three years, according to news reports. He served a year and a half and was paroled.

But none of this stopped Barnes from practicing medicine after his release. He then served as a referral doctor, again assuming the identity of Dr. Gerald Barnes, but he was caught in 1984 and convicted of grand theft and writing fraudulent prescriptions. For this, the con man was sentenced to three years and four months in jail. The state medical board had never flagged the real Dr. Barnes's file, which could have warned future employers about an impostor.

After his second stint in jail, Barnes was convicted again, in 1989, for stealing the identity of a San Francisco pharmacist named Donald Barnes. He was discovered after he applied for a job at a Los Angeles pharmacy using a phony license. He served another brief jail sentence and was arrested again in 1991 for parole violations. But after he was released from jail again, his ID theft continued: For four and a half years, Barnes worked as a medical professional in numerous healthcare facilities around Los Angeles, again as Dr. Gerald Barnes.

In 1995, he was hired as a staff physician at Executive Health Group, a Los Angeles clinic, where he handled physical checkups of agents and senior officials with the FBI and other government and private entities. But eventually his fraud was revealed when the state's medical board hired a new investigator to look into the Barnes case and questioned him. A fraud in every way imaginable, Barnes pretended to commit suicide during questioning, and when that didn't work, he faked a heart attack.

Since Barnes had now defrauded federal employees, federal law enforcement joined the investigation. This meant the possibility of spending the rest of his life in a federal prison, which Barnes didn't want to do. As a result, he pleaded guilty to mail fraud, unlawful dispensing of controlled substances, and fraudulent use of a controlled substances registration. He was sentenced to twelve and a half years in prison.

When he was being transferred to another prison in 2000, Barnes escaped. He was captured four weeks later by federal marshals, but in that short span of time, he had managed to get a job working in a medical clinic. He was taken back to prison, where he died on June 15, 2018, at the age of eighty-four. The real Dr. Barnes spent many years repairing his credit and his reputation as the result of his identity theft.

The story of Barnes's ID thievery has a deeply disturbing psychological component to it. He obviously was not doing it purely for financial gain—estimates put the money he earned as a fake doctor over twenty years at $400,000, which isn't all that much. Maybe there was something in him that desperately wanted to be a doctor, even though he didn't succeed through the normal channels. He hurt the real Dr. Barnes, and he hurt actual people, killing at least one of them. His story demonstrates that ID theft can be not only financially ruinous but also deadly. This is an unusual story, and one I would characterize as extremely rare. Still, I think it's useful to understand the lengths to which some identity thieves will go to achieve their aims.

SOCIAL MEDIA: THE IDENTITY THIEF'S BOUNDLESS BUFFET

When it comes to identity thieves, social media is a treasure trove. Even the least hip among us use Facebook to keep in touch with far-flung friends, relatives, and high school chums. Lots of

us use Instagram to post pictures of ourselves having fun or din-
ing out with friends and family. We use LinkedIn to connect pro-
fessionally. Let's face it: Social media is easy and fun to use and
provides us with a way to stay in touch with people in our lives.
These are good reasons to use it. Sadly, though, it's also prime
territory for criminals to conduct their activities.

John and Ed are colleagues at a midsize company. They're golf-
ing buddies, and they get together with their wives for dinner and
socializing every few weeks. They're also Facebook friends, and
they've both posted pictures of their victories in charity golf tour-
naments, photos of civic functions they've attended as representa-
tives of their company, and group shots of themselves with their
spouses. John was about to head out of town for a long weekend
with his wife when he opened an email from Ed, asking him to
make sure before noon that day that he wired a generous contribution to an organization that helps the homeless. The email also
wished John and his wife bon voyage for the weekend and thanked
him again for picking up the tab for the after-work drinks they'd
shared the night before. Before John asked his assistant to make
the transfer, he dropped by Ed's office to return a book he'd borrowed and asked in passing about the deadline for the wire transfer that Ed had mentioned in the email. "What transfer?" Ed
asked. "What email?" It was another case of identity theft.

On the face of it, it looked like any other email he would
receive on a daily basis. And the personal details about John's
and Ed's lives—the drinks, the upcoming trip—were all correct.
The identity thief knew them all.

The source? John's Facebook page, where he'd "checked in"
the night before at the watering hole where he and Ed had
stopped for drinks and commented about the inn where he and

his wife would be staying that weekend. There were also posts about his concern for the homeless and his related fund-raising efforts. The first lesson John and Ed learned was one that has broad application: Be careful what you share on social media. It can be used in nefarious ways.

It doesn't take much effort at all to research a potential victim of identity theft on social media. Personal information about where you are, where you will be, and who your friends are is money in the bank for identity thieves. So be smart about what you put out there. Names, cover photos, and profile pictures are all public on Facebook, and when we add details such as a birthday, pet's name, or mother's maiden name, a competent thief is on his way to stealing our identity, as these are often used as passwords and security answers. When you "check in" or post your exact location, you're also letting would-be thieves know when you're not home (a good time to break in or rifle through your trash). More sophisticated criminals, such as the one who targeted John and Ed, will scour your account for personal information about your spouse, kids, friends, and other relationships and put it all to good use. It doesn't take much, either, to create an email account that looks like the real thing but maybe varies by one letter or number that you might not notice in the course of a busy day.

By all means, enjoy those pictures of your family on Facebook, and catch up with colleagues and friends, but keep your personal, identifying details out of your profile. Don't post your birthday; don't make purchases through Facebook; don't mention where you work; and don't give away your physical location, whether you're at home, at the mall, or on vacation.

Think about the last time you uploaded a photo to Facebook and it asked you if you wanted to tag yourself and others in the picture. Did you do it? Did you think, *Gee, this is really great—I don't have to label my photos anymore. Facebook will do it for me?* Facial recognition software is everywhere now. Facebook uses it. Banks and corporations use it. Governments use it. It can be a powerful tool for verifying your identity, because it works by measuring your features to a high degree of accuracy—then associating the result with you and you alone. Sounds great, except that once those unique measurements are written into a computer code, they are vulnerable to a data breach, and what once seemed like it might be a foolproof way of safeguarding your identity becomes just another source of information for criminals to steal and use to impersonate you online.

You also should think carefully about the kinds of pictures you post of yourself on Facebook. To prevent criminals from using facial recognition software to steal your image, avoid posting full-face photos, like passport photos, which make it easy to take the precise measurements that recognition software depends on. Instead, stick to group shots and angled poses so that it's difficult to get those measurements.

MORE ON MINIMIZING YOUR RISK OF IDENTITY THEFT

1. **Stop and verify.** Put your guard up the minute someone tells you that you must share personal or financial information *right now*. Don't do it. If someone calls you and claims to be from your credit card company and asks

for your PIN, hang up. Then call the 800 customer service number printed on the back of your credit card and ask the representative if the company requires the information the caller requested. The representative will tell you no, and through your caution you will have prevented unauthorized access to your account. If, as in the case of John and Ed, someone emails you to make a contribution, stop and verify. It takes a little time but can save you from falling prey to any number of attempts to steal your identity or scam you out of a lot of money.

2. **Freeze them out**. If you have reason to believe you are a victim of identity theft or may become one due to suspicious activity on an account or the loss or theft of a credit card or other identification, consider putting a freeze on your credit. A credit freeze (or security freeze) prevents a would-be identity thief from opening new credit cards in your name. It works by denying access to your credit reports, so that when the bank or credit card company where the thief is attempting to open an account in your name goes to check your credit, the request will be denied, and so, in turn, will the thief's application for credit in your name. You can "unfreeze" your credit reports if you need to have a bank, employer, or other entity check your credit, and then afterwards reinstate the freeze. Personally, I think it's a good idea for everyone to freeze their credit for extra security. And it's now very easy to do, because in September 2018, credit freezes became free in the United States. Now you can place

and lift freezes for free at all credit agencies
agencies must comply with your request within one day
of your online or phone notification or within three days
of receiving a mailed request. To set up a credit freeze
online, go to the freeze page at each of the three agencies
websites (see the Resources section for contact information). They will provide you with a PIN that you can use
to lift or reinstate the freeze in the future.

3. **Be cautious with social media.** Keep your profile
   bare-bones: no birthday, no place of employment, no
   home address, and no real-time clues to your whereabouts. Allow only friends to see your profile.

4. **Use caution with public Wi-Fi.** Hackers have multiple ways of intercepting information you send using a
   public Wi-Fi network. When you are in a public Wi-Fi
   space, keep in mind that this means that everyone
   has the potential to see and read what you are doing
   online. In fact, most Wi-Fi hot spots don't encrypt information sent over the Internet. If the network you logged
   on to didn't require a WPA or WPA2 password, it is very
   likely unsecured, which means that other users on the
   network can see what you see, write, and send. They can
   set up fake hot spots that look legit or tap into the legitimate hot spot you are using and capture the emails you
   send, the log-in credentials you use, and the credit card
   information you share. New, easily available, and free
   online hacking tools make hijacking your sessions easy,
   even for users with little technical know-how. All your

personal information, documents, contacts, photos, and login and password info is vulnerable in these situations—making identity theft a breeze! Hackers can use your usernames and passwords to gain access to websites that store your financial information. The best way to protect yourself is to avoid using public Wi-Fi altogether and, to ensure you won't slip up, set your devices to airplane mode so they're essentially turned off when you're out and about. If you *must* use insecure or public networks, use them only to access sites that do not require you to enter a username, password, or any other identifying information.

No one likes to think about identity theft, but it is a fact of life now, and it will be in the future. The best we can do is be as careful and proactive as we can. As we continue with our journey through scams and scammers in this book, you will note that many types of scams contain aspects of identity theft, so, unfortunately, you'll learn more about this subject throughout the book.

3

Tax Fraud and IRS Scams

Remember that old adage that nothing is certain but death and taxes? Today's sophisticated scammers have added uncertainty to the mix by perpetrating crimes to steal taxpayers' identities and their tax refunds. Criminals use every kind of technology available to pull a fast one on Uncle Sam. Every year, the IRS sees new variations on tax scams, and nobody—not even tax professionals themselves—is immune to being scammed. It can happen to anyone. This chapter looks at how criminals work to perpetrate the most common tax frauds and the specific steps you can take to protect yourself from getting your taxes and tax refund hijacked.

"It was in early 2016, and I had just sent my tax information to my accountant," said Jamie, a healthcare worker. Not long after, she got a call from her accountant. He told her someone had already filed her tax return—and gotten her refund. "What does that even mean?" she asked him. "How does that even happen?" Then, a couple of weeks later, all her credit cards got hit. "Within twenty minutes or so, I saw seven charges made all around the world, at the same time," she said. "I had not gotten my tax refund, either. I wasn't responsible for those charges."

Jamie worked with her accountant and the IRS to file her true return so she would receive the refund owed to her. Now she has fraud protection and each year needs to obtain a unique PIN (personal identification number) from the government to file her return and receive her refund—and she'll have to do this for the rest of her taxpaying years.

Every day, scammers find new ways to swindle not only private citizens—you, me—but also the government. They do it by filing tax returns in your name or through predatory phone calls and emails. Scammers also come in the form of criminal tax preparers. All of them compromise your money—and your identity.

WHERE'S MY REFUND?

At one time, filing a phony return was the most common tax scam, but in recent years there have been fewer of these crimes as the IRS has become better at identifying them. In 2017, the agency reported that an estimated 597,000 tax returns were filed fraudulently, down from 883,000 in 2016 and 1.4 million in 2015. Still, the IRS estimates that in 2016, between $1.68 billion and $2.31 billion was paid out in refunds that may have been based on fraudulent filings and identity theft.

If someone fraudulently files a return and gets a refund under your name, there are steps you can and should take to remedy the situation. And, yes, once the IRS is satisfied that you and the tax return you filed are legitimate, you *will* get your refund, even if the thief already cashed the first check. It may take a while, as it did for Jamie, and the burden is on you to prove you are who you say you are.

Happily, the IRS is often able to detect tax-related identity theft before it reaches the point where your refund is redirected to a scammer. The agency uses hundreds of processing filters to flag suspicious returns. If one is spotted, the IRS will review the return and send you a letter asking you to verify your identity through an online tool or in person at a Taxpayer Assistance Center. But if you believe you may be a victim of tax-related identity theft—if, for example, you are unable to file electronically because the online filing system indicates that a tax return with your Social Security number already has been filed—you should immediately contact the IRS. It's a fairly streamlined process. You submit Form 14039, Identity Theft Affidavit, and refile your taxes. The IRS says the process to correct your tax situation usually takes four months, although in some circumstances it can take longer.

FOUR WAYS TO PROTECT YOUR SOCIAL SECURITY NUMBER

Your Social Security number can unlock many doors that a thief can pass through to victimize you, including IRS scams. Be vigilant about protecting it.

1. Never carry your Social Security card with you.
2. Provide your Social Security number only when it's

absolutely required. If someone asks you for it—in a doctor's office, for example—ask if it's necessary.

3. Go to www.ssa.gov/myaccount and establish online access to information about your Social Security benefits, review your earnings history, on which your benefits are based, and request replacement documents when necessary. The IRS uses a new identity verification process to protect your privacy and Social Security statement. To verify your identity, it asks you for personal information, including answers to questions that only you should be able to answer. You need two forms of identification to sign in: your username and password along with a security code provided via text message or email. This is an important means of protecting your Social Security number and your benefits—scam artists have been known to establish this access to unknowing victims' accounts and steal their benefits.

4. If you discover that your Social Security number has been compromised, notify the Federal Trade Commission (FTC). See Resources, page 321.

IRS CALLING? PROBABLY NOT!

The IRS relies on the U.S. Postal Service to deliver its good or bad news. If you owe money, the IRS mails you a notice telling you that you owe money. What happens if it doesn't get paid?

With the private debt collection program that began in 2015, the IRS inadvertently gave fraudsters an advantage. Now scammers can pretend to be from a government-approved collection agency. If you receive a phone call or email from someone purporting to be from the IRS but did not receive a letter from the IRS beforehand telling you your debt has been transferred to a debt collection agency, do not respond. The IRS, as a rule, assigns older, overdue accounts to private collection agencies. It is rare, but not out of the question, that you could receive a legitimate call from a private agency representing the IRS after it tries to contact you by mail. That collection agency will follow up with a second letter confirming this transfer. The key is that neither the IRS nor any collection agency should be contacting you before you receive written notice in the mail.

At the time of this writing, four agencies work with the IRS: CBE, ConServe, Performant, and Pioneer. Any other agency claiming to work for the IRS should be verified before you respond to any phone calls or emails. Even the four agencies that work with the IRS will welcome your request to confirm their legitimacy, so don't be afraid to ask. Additionally, the outside debt collectors working on behalf of the IRS will never ask that back taxes be sent to them. Back taxes (or any other taxes owed) should be paid to the U.S. Treasury and sent only to the IRS.

You should ignore all other communication. If it's a call, hang up. If it's an email, trash it. Do not, under any circumstances, open a link. As with other email scams, links are the mechanisms criminals use to hijack the contents of your computer or to plant malware to steal your passwords, credit card numbers, and other stored information.

In March 2018, Megan Murfield got a call from a woman and

a man who claimed to work for the government. The woman said, "We have never gotten a response from you, so it has been considered an intentional fraud, and a lawsuit has been filed under your name by the United States government." Then a man told her, "The arrest warrant is released in your name."

Murfield did what the scammers told her to do. "They said I owed $2,085 in back taxes, and if I didn't put 50 percent down, I was going to go to jail," she told reporters. "I was scared." Because she didn't drive, she walked to a nearby Walgreens and bought gift cards as instructed. She scratched off the strip revealing the numbers on the back and read them to the scammers over the phone. "He kept telling me that they were going to freeze my bank account if I don't get everything out of my account. The man would tell me I had to go back into the store and buy more cards, then go outside and scratch the numbers off to tell them what they were," she said, the emotions still raw almost a year later. "I kept telling him how cold it was outside, and he'd just say, 'That's okay, ma'am, just keep scratching off and reading the numbers to me.'" The man kept her on the phone the whole time, warning her not to tell anyone why she was buying so many cards with cash. In all, she bought $650 worth of gift cards—not half as originally demanded, but enough to appease the crooks. After that scam, the con artists called her three or four times and left voicemails asking for more money.

Murfield was so frightened that she called one of her coworkers to tell her she might not make it to work the following Friday because she was going to be arrested for tax evasion. After hearing the story, the coworker said she was worried her friend was being scammed. Murfield then realized what had happened to her. But it was too late: $650 was gone for good. She filed a police

prepaid debit card sold in drugstores and supermarkets), or use Apple Pay. Again, remember that the IRS does not ask for these forms of payment.

Hall of Shame: Sahil Patel

In 2015, Sahil Patel was sentenced to more than fourteen years in prison by a judge who said he wanted to send a message to others considering similar crimes. That's because Patel and his ring of thieves, posing as IRS officials, threatened U.S. taxpayers into sending him millions of dollars by accusing them of owing back taxes. He was arrested for aggravated identity theft, conspiring to extort money and impersonate government officials, and committing wire fraud. He was forced to forfeit $1 million for crimes he committed between 2011 and his 2013 arrest.

Court papers said that Patel's ring worked from call centers in India, impersonating law enforcement officials and often threatening victims with financial penalties and arrest. Internet-based technology that the gang used made it look as if the calls were coming from U.S. law enforcement agencies. Timothy Camus, deputy inspector general for investigations, who probed crimes for the Internal Revenue Service, told the *Los Angeles Times*, "The caller is so aggressive it scares people. And then using the IRS as the foil—you know, 'Hey, this is the IRS. You owe this money. If you don't pay it immediately you're going to go to jail. I'm going to have you arrested tomorrow'—makes it even more terrifying."

The judge who oversaw Patel's case, Alvin Hellerstein, said, "This crime robbed people of their identities and their money in a way that causes people to feel they have been almost destroyed." In court, Assistant U.S. Attorney Andrew Adams told the judge that the fraud was "perfectly designed" to manipulate financially distressed people who would fear arrest threats, according to reports.

Prosecutors said Patel exploited "desperate" co-conspirators, especially women and people he thought were "dumb" and would act at his direction for a fraction of the money he generated. "In particular, Patel held the grossly misogynistic view that women, above all other recruits, were pliable, easily manipulated, greedy and easy to control," they wrote. "Perhaps most disturbingly, Patel applied that view to his own sister."

EGREGIOUS EMAILS

I've mentioned emails before, but here I want to drive the point home, because so much of our daily business is conducted via email and it's all too easy to let our guard down. Scammers continue to use "phishing" techniques with authentic-looking logos and disclaimers to lure you into reading emails and following their links. Each tax season, the scams change slightly, and each year the scammers get a little better at what they do, so the best defense against them is to doubt authenticity from the get-go. Assume emails you receive from "the IRS" are fraudulent.

The name of the email sender is often "IRS Refund" or something similar. That's a giveaway that plays on people's excitement about receiving their tax refunds. It's fake, even though the rest of the message seems to be totally legit. If you click on the request to "confirm your security," you will be asked to divulge your Social Security number and other personal details. If you respond, the thief who sent this email has just gotten his hands on your identity.

There are also scammers who think even bigger. Rather than target one taxpayer at a time, these criminals, posing as IRS officials, send fake emails to try to get professional tax preparers, certified public accountants (CPAs), and human resources officers to divulge personal data about their clients or employees. Once the scammers have this data, they use it to file hundreds of phony returns to get their hands on the refunds. I know I'm delivering the same message over and over, but I cannot stress this enough: Whether you are a private citizen or a tax professional, the IRS will never get in touch with you using email, text messages, or social media as the first means of contact. They will send you a letter. They will not call without telling you in writing that they plan to do so. If you take nothing else away from this chapter, remember this!

BEWARE SHAM TAX PREPARERS

Although the IRS does not publish numbers on these types of scams, tax preparer fraud is bad enough that for several years in a row, it has made the IRS's Dirty Dozen list—its watch list of common tax scams.

Tax preparers have been known to steal identities and file fraudulent tax returns on behalf of nonexistent clients. In 2013, a federal jury found Bernando O. Davis guilty of filing false federal income tax returns that claimed millions of dollars in bogus refunds. From 2010 to 2013, Davis operated "Davis Tax Service," a tax preparation business in Clayton County, Georgia. He led thousands of victims to believe they could apply for "government stimulus payments" or "free government money" by providing their names and Social Security numbers.

The U.S. Department of Justice reported that Davis used toll-free telephone numbers, websites, flyers, and radio spots to advertise the "stimulus payments" and collect victims' personal information. He recruited "runners" who promoted the scheme by word of mouth and collected victims' personal information. Davis also acquired names from other sources such as prisons and homeless shelters. Many victims testified that they had never heard about the "stimulus payments," but their identities were nonetheless used by Davis and his co-conspirators to file bogus tax returns. In reality, no stimulus payment ever existed, and Davis simply used victims' information to file phony tax returns, collect refunds, and enrich himself—a total of over $19 million.

Fraudulent tax preparers have also claimed more refunds than clients are entitled to, defrauding the government (and compromising their clients' identities as well). Noemi Pender, a tax preparer in Rosenhayn, New Jersey, was sentenced to a year in prison for filing false federal income tax returns for five years, between 2007 and 2011. She and a co-conspirator defrauded the Treasury out of more than $340,000 by getting their clients refunds greater than they were legally entitled to receive, according to the Department of Justice.

A federal judge in Orlando, Florida, ordered Jason Stinson, a businessman from central Florida, to pay a civil penalty of nearly

$950,000 for preparing false returns. Stinson owned Nation Tax Services, a business operating out of Florida, Alabama, Georgia, and North Carolina. Like Pender, he was charged with getting inflated refunds for clients by fabricating dependents, business expenses, and charitable contributions. The court found that Stinson's stores targeted "underprivileged, undereducated poor people," charging them as much as $999 to prepare a single return. Sometimes those fees would be taken out of the customer's refund, so the customer never knew about it.

HERE'S HOW TO PROTECT YOURSELF FROM A FAKE TAX PREPARER

- Be cautious about using a preparer whose work space is temporary. Often, but not always, scammers rent temporary office space—once they're gone, they're gone, and good luck finding them.
- Be on your guard right away if the preparer promises you a giant refund. Even if the return is based on false numbers, you *will* be responsible to the IRS for the amount you actually owe.
- Be skeptical if a tax preparer says you can get a "stimulus payment" in exchange for your Social Security number and other personal information.
- Don't trust a tax preparer's IRS endorsement; there is no such thing. The IRS never endorses a tax preparer or accountant. If the person you are considering tells you he's been endorsed by the IRS or shows you an IRS letter of endorsement, run in the opposite direction. The letter is fake and he's a fraud.

- If a tax preparer pegs his fee to the amount of your refund, walk the other way. Accountants don't work on percentages. They work either on an hourly basis or for a flat fee. If someone you are about to work with proposes this kind of arrangement, terminate the conversation right then and there.

- Never do business with an accountant who suggests your refund be sent to him or his bank account. This is a giveaway of criminal intent.

- Don't work with a tax preparer who says she knows how to fix your filing to inflate your return. Of course she should know the law and understand how to legitimately obtain all the deductions you legally can claim.

- Examine your return before signing it to make sure that all income and deductions are truthful.

- Determine a tax preparer's legitimacy by asking to see his IRS ID number, and check it with the IRS.

- Make sure your tax preparer signs your tax return. By law, both of you must sign it. If you have gotten to that point in your tax preparation when it is time to sign off on the return and your preparer refuses to do so, it may be late in the game but it's time to find another tax preparer. A person who refuses to sign is known as a "ghost"—according to the IRS, a ghost prepares the taxes but refuses to sign off on it—a way dishonest tax preparers who want to make quick money by charging fees based on a percentage of a promised return scam taxpayers. Refusal to sign is a red flag.

What to Do If You Are a Victim of Tax-Related Identity Theft

The IRS is getting better at screening for false returns. Should the IRS suspect that a return is fraudulent, it will send you a Letter 4883C. This letter alerts you that the IRS believes your return is suspicious. You will have thirty days to respond, and then you must produce specific documents either to prove that the suspicious return is indeed yours or that, no, you did not file the return. To respond to Letter 4883C, you'll need:

- The Letter 4883C you received, which contains a toll-free number you'll be asked to call.
- A copy of your tax return from the prior year.
- The tax return for the year the notice is for.
- Any supporting documents for both years' returns, such as W-2 or 1099 forms and Schedule C or F.

Based on this information, a representative from the IRS's Taxpayer Protection Program will be able to determine whether the suspicious return is actually yours. If you did in fact submit this return, the IRS will continue to process it, and if you're entitled to a refund, you will receive it as usual. If, on the other hand, the filing turns out to be phony, you will be told to file a paper return, and the fraudulent one will be removed from your IRS record.

There's no question that dealing with fraud can be a nerve-racking process, but the IRS really is trying to help and protect you. At the end of the process, if you have been victimized, the IRS will note that in your records. If the risk of being victimized a second time is high, the IRS will issue you an IP (identity protection) PIN, which is good for one year and must be renewed each year you are flagged as high risk. You'll use this when you file returns as a means of establishing your identity.

If the IRS rejects the return you filed electronically and you suspect it's because a false return has been filed in your name, the IRS has very clear steps to follow spelled out on its website (see Resources, page 321). You'll fill out a Form 14039, Identity Theft Affidavit, discussed earlier in this chapter, and file a paper return. After the IRS receives your return and Form 14039, it will send you an acknowledgment and investigate your claim through its Identity Theft Victim Assistance organization. The investigation is comprehensive and will take time. The IRS will look to see, for example, if you have been victimized in the past, if you are part of a larger scam involving other victimized taxpayers, and if you need the additional protection of a PIN. Your returns will be flagged with an "identify theft indicator" to afford you additional future security. Remember: The IRS will always work with you to protect you from tax scams.

I know paying taxes to the IRS isn't our favorite thing to do, but remember that our taxes pay for critical services. And when you need to work your way out of the tangled mess an identity thief can make of your tax return and refunds, the agency really is there to help and to prevent future attempts at fraud. It works diligently to identify fraud, combat it, and help you avoid it.

4

Sick: Medical Identity Theft

Personal data—containing everything a crook needs to commit financial identity theft, including your Social Security and financial account numbers—sells for about $25 on the black market, said Jon Ramsey, chief technology officer of SecureWorks. But stolen health insurance and medical records can fetch far more: about $2,000 per person. That's because scammers use your information to submit fraudulent claims in your name to Medicare and other health insurers. The greater potential yield of medical identity theft—a $20,000 surgery, say—justifies the higher price. In this chapter we look at ways medical identity thieves can rack up bills, steal your identity, and disrupt and even harm your medical care. And, of course, I show you how to prevent that from happening.

In May 2018, Louisiana resident Heather Karpinsky and her family went on vacation. When they returned, Heather checked the mail and noticed something unusual: the large amount of mail addressed to her five-year-old-son, Gavin. "I wondered why there were so many advertisements addressed to him, but I ripped them up and tossed them and didn't think much about it," recalled Heather. But the next day, Gavin received two more ads in the mail. She checked with her neighbor to see if her young children were also getting ads in the mail, but the neighbor said no. Then, two days later, Gavin received a collection notice in the mail. Inside was a bill for $200 for health and nutrition products bought through a television infomercial. Gavin didn't watch a lot of TV, and, being only five, he wasn't yet adept at ordering products over the telephone. And he certainly didn't have a credit card, though these orders had been placed with one.

Heather immediately called the credit card company, which determined that the bill was indeed fraudulent. Four days after she received that collection notice, her son's medical provider called to tell Heather its computer had been hacked, compromising the names, dates of birth, Social Security numbers, and insurance company information of fourteen minor patients of the office, including Gavin and his brother. His brother's information had not yet been used, but Gavin's information had been used to buy many over-the-counter health and nutrition products.

The only way for Heather to combat this scheme was to get Gavin fraud protection, which he will need for the rest of his life. "I was told his information will continue to be sold on the black market, and his medical identity can continue to be used," said Heather. Credit cards opened in Gavin's name also generated credit reports from the big three credit bureaus. "He's five—he shouldn't really have a credit report or a credit rating." But since he does, he also has credit monitoring. Heather will have to monitor Gavin's credit until he is an adult, and then he will need to monitor it.

"Since Gavin's information was leaked, his insurance company, Blue Cross Blue Shield, has a new policy in place," explained Heather. "His account has been flagged as compromised, and if we receive any fraudulent charges for medical care, he is not liable for them. The bill goes back to the provider." When Gavin visits a new provider, Heather must present a photo ID. For now, it's Heather's driver's license, but when Gavin gets older, he will have to provide his own photo ID.

Heather did contact the police, who found that the doctor's office was not liable. The office had paid for a security system to handle its data, and that was where the breakdown had occurred. "Protecting your medical identity is a burden that falls on the victim," said Heather. She wonders how hard it will be for her son when he grows up and wants to use a credit card or needs to prove his medical identity to new doctors. For now, his credit is frozen—but his personal information and medical records are out there forever.

"I did not realize that this information was so valuable," said Gavin's mom. "I thought I was so careful. I never even wish a happy birthday to my boys on social media because I don't want to put that personal information into the public. Now I know that you're still vulnerable, even if you take precautions." Heather thought she was protecting her family, but she was powerless to stop her son's information from being stolen. We can't prevent data breaches, but we can take steps to protect ourselves.

MEDICAL IDENTITY THEFT HURTS

You want to protect yourself against medical identity theft because crooks can use your medical insurance or personal medical information to get treatment or medication, or to submit false billings in your name. Medical identity thieves can steal more than your insurance ID number—they can also rob you of your health. If someone gains access to your medical files or insurance card and uses them to get services, you might receive improper care because the thief's medical information can become mixed up with yours—and you could end up fighting a long battle with your provider for the bills an impostor racks up for prescriptions and health services, including expensive surgeries. The thief can also use this information to engage in nonmedical fraudulent activities.

Unlucky victims have been arrested and charged with drug crimes after an identity thief used their information to buy thousands of dollars' worth of opioids or other drugs with street value. One day, Deborah Ford, a retired postal worker from Houston, received an unsettling phone call, according to *Consumer Reports*. A bail bondsman told her she was going to be arrested for procuring more than 1,700 prescription opioid painkillers from a variety of local pharmacies. That call was *not* a scam, and she *was* arrested on drug charges. "I had my mug shot taken, my fingerprints taken," Ford told a reporter. She suffers from psoriasis, and the stress from being arrested led to a severe breakout. "The policemen looked at my hands and said, 'That's what drug users' hands look like.' They just assumed I was guilty."

What ultimately saved Deborah from being prosecuted and

convicted was a police report she had filed a couple of years earlier, after her purse was stolen from her car while she was inside a gas station. Ford did all the right things as soon as she discovered the theft: She filed a police report, canceled all her credit cards, obtained a new driver's license, and applied for and received a replacement health insurance card. After making sure none of her bank accounts had been compromised, she forgot about the incident. Life went on. Until that call from the bail bondsman.

The thief had altered Ford's driver's license, swapping out the photo but leaving her name and other identifying information. Then the thief used the license and her health insurance card to go to doctors to request prescription painkillers. One local pharmacist became suspicious about multiple prescriptions for a controlled substance and called the police, which led to Ford's eventual arrest. Even though the arrest was a mistake, it took seven years, from 2008 to 2015, for Deborah to clear her name.

SMART WAYS TO MINIMIZE THE RISK OF MEDICAL IDENTITY THEFT

You can't prevent data breaches or employee theft. But you can use these steps to spot problems and protect yourself.

- Monitor your bank and credit card accounts to check for medical costs you did not incur, especially if you've been notified of a breach of your medical information. Act promptly to correct the record. Report scams to your insurer and the three major credit-reporting firms— Equifax, Experian, and TransUnion.

- Read your "explanation of benefits" statements and your Medicare Summary Notices (received quarterly) thoroughly and carefully. This is the paperwork your health insurance company provides that shows the doctor visits, tests, and services the company has paid out for you. If you see a payment for a service you don't recognize, follow up on it immediately and persistently, until it is corrected or resolved. It could simply be a billing error, but it could also be an indication of attempted medical identity theft. This is often the only clue you get until the thief has made off with thousands—or hundreds of thousands—of dollars in medical services using your name. Read every letter from medical insurers and healthcare providers, including those that say "This is not a bill." If you see a doctor's name or treatment date that looks unfamiliar, speak up. And don't hesitate to ask someone you trust to look over this paperwork with you. Sometimes a second set of eyes will catch a suspicious charge you might have missed.

- Bring your Medicare or insurance card to the initial visit with a provider. After that, carry only a copy of the card, with all but the last four digits blacked out.

- Keep your medical bills, records, and any information with your insurance, Medicare, or account numbers in a safe place. If you do not need the information contained in these papers, use a micro-cut shredder to dispose of them—and that includes prescription drug labels and receipts.

- Unless you've placed the call, do not give out personal information over the phone about your healthcare or health insurance. Do not respond to emails that ask you to give this information by return email.

- Be extremely skeptical of offers of "free" medical services. Be wary of giving your medical information to anyone promising you something for nothing.

- Avoid posting on social media about any surgery, medical procedure, or visit to a specialist. Medical identity thieves can appropriate the information to augment a false identity they assume with your credentials.

- Ask all your doctors to give you a copy of everything in your file (you may have to pay for copies) so you'll have a paper trail if needed.

- Avoid getting screenings (free or otherwise) at unfamiliar health fairs or storefronts that require your insurance information.

- Hang up on phone calls from people promising free supplies or asking for information about your health, healthcare, or health insurance.

- If you have a caregiver or housekeeper coming into your home, make sure to keep medication bottles locked up. With everyone carrying smartphones with cameras included, it's easy to snap a photo of the medication label to get a refill.

Hall of Shame: Yennier Capote Gonzalez

In August 2010, the Department of Health and Human Services got a tip that a man in Miami, Florida, had attempted to wire $17,000 from a newly opened Tennessee account to a Florida bank. That account had also recently received $38,000 from Medicare, according to a Department of Justice press release. Transactions of large sums of money often raise suspicions at banks, and in this case, the suspicions were justified. Yennier Capote Gonzalez had opened the account for his recently incorporated business, Gainesboro Ultimate Med Service, in a rural area of Gainesboro, Tennessee. But when law enforcement officials visited the property, it was pretty clear it wasn't a medical services company: The only structures on the property were an old barn and an uncompleted house.

The investigation that followed showed that Gainesboro Ultimate Med Service was a fake company and that, through it, Gonzalez had stolen the identity of a Knoxville, Tennessee, physician and used it to obtain a Medicare provider number. He then submitted claims under the guise of the phony company using the names of several Medicare beneficiaries who lived in South Florida—people who had also been victims of medical identity theft. These patients were billed for services purportedly rendered at Gainesboro Ultimate Med Service, even though they had never been to Tennessee.

In 2010, the U.S. government caught up with Gonzalez after he attempted another wire transfer. He was tried, sentenced to 67 months in federal prison, and ordered to pay restitution of $19,296 for his role in the fraudulent scheme.

MEDICAL RECORDS THEFT: WHAT HAS THE EXPERTS WORRIED

In November 2017, police in East Brunswick, New Jersey, got a call about a break-in at a storage facility. The burglars had methodically removed some thirteen boxes full of papers. This seemed like a peculiar heist. If thieves went to the trouble of breaking into a storage facility, wouldn't you think it would be to steal the jewelry, silver, or other valuables stored there? Did the criminals break into the wrong storage unit by mistake?

It turns out this was no run-of-the-mill theft. Inside the boxes were patient records from a medical practice, Otolaryngology Associates of Central Jersey, and those boxes full of paperwork were a bonanza for identity thieves. The records contained patients' names, addresses, phone numbers, dates of birth, medical histories, insurance and Medicare information, Social Security numbers, driver's licenses, and details of military service.

The street value for peddling this information meant a sweet payday for the crooks and endless headaches for the medical practice, which had to notify a thousand patients that their information had been compromised. After an intense investigation that involved not only the police but also the U.S. Department of Homeland Security and the Middlesex County Prosecutor's Office, arrests were made and the records were recovered before the majority of them were sold. One of the thieves was caught when he tried to sell an identity to someone who alerted authorities.

What makes this story unusual is, first, that it was an old-fashioned burglary of actual paper files and, second, that justice was swift and the perpetrators caught. Identity theft from large medical organizations is usually done by hackers who steal digital files. These thieves are rarely identified or caught, because they do not leave a "digital fingerprint," or they are overseas and beyond the reach of domestic law enforcement. In fact, one of the major factors behind the increase in medical breaches and theft is that medical records today are predominantly digitized. "Digitized records are much easier to steal than paper ones," Deborah Peel, a physician and founder of Patient Privacy Rights, a nonprofit advocacy group in Austin, Texas, told MarketWatch. Digital medical records are also often stored in millions of databases, which makes correcting them after they've been altered by thieves incredibly difficult, said Peel.

Data breaches cost the healthcare industry more than $6 *billion* annually, according to the Ponemon Institute. Often officials who oversee hacking thefts have a hard time determining whether anyone's information was actually used. Some twenty-seven million individual medical records are stolen each year. In 2017 alone, 477 healthcare data breaches were reported to the U.S. Department of Health and Human Services or the media, which affected about 5.6 million patient records, according to Protenus, a company that tracks healthcare industry breaches. Some experts even predict that by 2024, all people living in the United States will have been part of a health records data breach!

Most data breaches in the healthcare industry are actually inside jobs. As I warn my corporate clients time and again, *data breaches don't happen by themselves*. A crooked or disgruntled employee can pilfer information from a single file or files, or simply remove an entire filing system. But employees don't have to be angry or greedy to cause a data breach. They can simply be careless.

The major reasons for data breaches in medicine are different from those in other industries, according to a 2018 study by Verizon, "Protected Health Information Data Breach Report." According to the report, 35 percent of digital breaches are caused by human error, including misdelivery of information, disposal mistakes, and loss. More than 16 percent of breaches are caused by internal theft of information. Not securing a password, leaving a device where it can be stolen, or failing to update software with a security patch can lead to data breach. Security procedures are only as good as the people who implement, maintain, and monitor them. A slip-up at any point in that process leaves an opening for a data thief to take advantage of.

And take advantage they will. Even if they don't have an unwitting "accomplice" like a careless employee making it easy for them to get into a company's records, data criminals have other means of stealing medical information. Malware, denial-of-service (DoS) attacks, and ransomware are all ways to obtain information illegally. In some instances, companies whose data has been snatched by these methods don't even know it.

MEDICARE RECIPIENTS ARE ESPECIALLY VULNERABLE

Many of us acknowledge turning sixty-five with mixed feelings. I know I did. But I was (and am!) thrilled to reap one reward of that milestone: my Medicare card. I was less than thrilled, however, when I saw my Social Security number emblazoned across the card, for any and all to see, copy down, and claim. If you have received Medicare for a while, you've probably noticed the same thing on your card.

It wasn't until 2015 that the government passed a law requiring that Medicare and Social Security numbers be different—something I lobbied hard for, as did AARP. Since April 2018, the Centers for Medicare and Medicaid Services of the Department of Health and Human Services, which administers Medicare, has been rolling out its replacement card program. New Medicare cards bearing a new identification number—*not* your Social Security number—are being sent to all Medicare recipients on a state-by-state basis. If you're on Medicare, you should have yours by now. There is no question that having two different numbers dramatically reduces the threat of identity theft from a lost or stolen Medicare card. That's the good news.

The bad news is that the longtime use of your Social Security number for Medicare has spawned more than a few organized efforts by scammers to trick Medicare recipients into giving away their Social Security number. Some scammers will call you, spoofing the caller ID so it looks as if they're calling from Medicare. They'll ask you to pay a processing fee to receive your new card. Or they'll say they need to verify your Social Security number in order to send your new one. This is fraud. The cards are free, and Medicare would not call you to verify your Social Security number—the administration already has it.

RESOURCES: MEDICARE IDENTITY THEFT

If you receive Medicare and think that you have been a victim of medical identity theft, you have dedicated resources available.

- Report suspicious calls regarding your healthcare or health insurance to 800-MEDICARE (800-633-4227).
- Each state has a Senior Medicare Patrol (SMP) that can give you reliable information and help with all your Medicare questions, including those about possible fraud or identity theft. You can locate your state's office at www .smpresource.org/content/what-smps-do.aspx. Staff here will also help you determine whether fraud or theft has occurred.
- If you have established that someone else is using your Medicare benefits, follow the same procedure as with any other kind of identity theft and begin by making a report at www.identitytheft.gov.

MEDICAL RECORDS THEFT: WHAT CAN BE DONE TO STOP IT?

We're a long way from eliminating the threat of medical identity theft through cybercrime, but I see some hopeful signs of improvements. First, the industry itself is more aware of the problem than ever before, due to the high-profile nature of breaches. For example, in 2017 a breach caused by a ransomware virus left information from more than 266,000 patients vulnerable at the Pacific Alliance Medical Center, in Los Angeles. The hospital's IT staff had to scramble to figure out how to deactivate the virus before re-encrypting the vulnerable files. We don't know if the hospital paid a ransom to the criminals. We do know that it notified the patients affected and offered to pay for two years of credit monitoring for them. Two years is not long enough, in my experience. Criminals are patient and have been known to wait five years or more to use stolen information, so credit monitoring and ID protection need to be done long-term. Any credit-monitoring service you use should look at the big three credit bureaus (Equifax, Experian, and TransUnion) and give you real-time notifications of any breaches.

Businesses that work with medical records should take action to heighten the security of those files. As a consumer of the services these businesses provide, I check to see if they have certain policies and procedures in place. I recommend you ask these questions as well; they should become part of how you advocate for yourself with your providers. After all, the accuracy and safety of your medical information is crucial for receiving the best and most appropriate care. I ask:

- Are employees trained in the correct procedures for safe-guarding data? Training should be frequent and updated as new threats appear and new solutions are identified. Proper data security should be an integral requirement of every job that requires employee access to data, and employees should be evaluated on these criteria.

- Is employees' access to secure data limited through the use of passwords as well as the devices that can connect to the information? Portable devices such as tablets, smartphones, and laptops are easily lost or stolen—and can be left in a place where an unauthorized user can help himself to information.
- Does the business have a recovery plan in place, one that is reviewed and updated frequently, spelling out the actions to take in the event of a data breach, including a plan to help patients recover and correct their medical records?
- In the event of a data breach, does the business offer affected patients a minimum of three years or, ideally, at least five years of identity theft protection?
- Is the business insured against data breaches? If one happens, are there funds available to investigate the crime, fix the vulnerability in the system, and assist victims with the damage done to their lives and reputations?

MEDICAL RECORDS THEFT: WHERE DO WE GO FROM HERE?

Awareness is the best place to start, and businesses are paying more attention by looking for vulnerabilities in their computer systems, running mock scenarios, and holding employees to higher standards of accountability. The government has taken a major step by changing Medicare numbers so they're different from our Social Security numbers. We may want to see if legislation recently enacted by the European Union, called the General Data Protection Regulation, is effective in limiting data theft of personal information. It's a complex law, but one of its key provisions, called pseudonymization, replaces identifying information about you with random codes or "pseudonyms." That means that anyone working with the information—employees or thieves—would not be able to identify the individual it belongs to. It can be used in conjunction with encryption for an extra layer of protection. A special digital key is required to match the code with the information. It's a start, but as of this writing, pseudonymization is not widely used in the United States. So for now we must remain vigilant when it comes to the valuable commodity that is our medical identities.

RULE #2

Secure Your Finances

5

Protect Yourself Against These Bad Investments

My overarching message in this chapter on investments is this: *Walk away from big promises.* Here I cover everything from Ponzi schemes to affinity fraud, email investment shams, churning, and gold coin scams. Along with reviewing the most common investment frauds, I give you some ways to avoid getting seduced by financial scammers. If someone tells you she always beats the market or guarantees a certain level of return or outlandish returns (say, 500 percent in six months), decline the offer. While there is always risk involved with any investment, no truly qualified, honest financial planner can guarantee investment results.

Consider this seemingly low-risk and straightforward investment: (1) Purchase consumer debts owed to banks and credit card issuers, student loan lenders, and car and truck financers that have gone into default for pennies on the dollar—these are called "consumer debt portfolios." (2) Either collect the debts for less than the original owed but more than the debt cost to buy *or* sell the portfolios to third-party debt buyers for a profit (a practice called flipping). That's what Kevin Merrill, Jay Ledford, and Cameron Jezierski are accused of doing. Debt portfolio investment is legitimate and *can* be profitable. Merrill and his colleagues' investment offer was allegedly so popular that more than four hundred people—including numerous small business owners, restaurateurs, building contractors, lawyers, doctors, accountants, talent agents, bankers, professional athletes, and even financial advisers—wanted in on it.

The problem, according to the government, was that the men were running what's called a pyramid or Ponzi scheme, in which fraudsters use money collected from new victims to pay the high rates of return promised to earlier investors. The payouts give the appearance of a legitimate profit-making enterprise. But in reality, the only source of funding is the investors themselves. That's how this debt portfolio scheme allegedly worked, with the men defrauding investors of more than $364 million and using the money to buy high-end homes, luxury cars, diamond jewelry, boats, and even a share in a jet airplane. They also used some of the money—$25 million—for casino gambling.

Financial frauds like this one abound. In 2017 alone, the FBI says investment scams cost consumers nearly $97 million. That calculation is based on the scams that law enforcement knows about. Other investment crimes go unreported, because victims may be embarrassed to admit they were defrauded or because investors chalk up losses (including those based on fraud) to the risks inherent in investing.

The truth is, investment schemes can and often do sound plausible, well thought out, and *very* tempting. They work because fraudsters use the strategies we discussed in chapter 2 to make their schemes seem credible and legitimate. They set a trap with smooth communication skills, enthusiasm, talk of scarcity and urgency, flattery, and the idea of a big payoff to get you under the ether. The investment scammer's portfolio can include glossy brochures, letterhead with impressive-looking embossing, fake degrees and accreditations, phony track records of success, and claims of association with prominent brands or successful companies or individuals.

PONZI SCHEMES

Almost a hundred years ago, one fraudster pulled off a scam so monumental, for the time, anyway, that thereafter it bore his name. Unfortunately, Charles Ponzi led the way for many unscrupulous cons to follow.

Ponzi bilked investors by convincing them to invest in a deal involving postage stamps and postal reply coupons that started out legitimate but quickly became a pyramid scheme that used money from new investors to pay dividends to old investors. Ultimately, none of the investors' money was invested in anything—the only source of funding was the investors themselves. Eventually the scheme fell apart. Ponzi was arrested in August 1920 and served fourteen years in prison.

Bernie Madoff is a contemporary example of how devastating a Ponzi scheme can be. The former stockbroker, investment adviser, and financier fleeced some of the most intelligent and sophisticated investors to the tune of $20 billion—that's "billion" with a *b*—in what is likely the biggest Ponzi scheme ever carried out. More than 2,200 people had invested with Madoff, including longtime investors and financial industry professionals. Others were famous celebrities, including the nonprofit Wunderkinder Foundation of movie director Steven Spielberg (who produced and directed *Catch Me If You Can*), real estate magnate Mortimer Zuckerman, actor Kevin Bacon, and Hall of Fame pitcher Sandy Koufax. But ordinary people were victims, too, including Michael De Vita of Bucks County, Pennsylvania. He entrusted to Madoff the $5 million retirement account he and his mother had saved, money that might have allowed him to retire early and given his mother lifelong security as well.

One victim was a hedge fund marketer who understood the risks of investing firsthand. "I lost $50,000 with Bernie Madoff, and I should have known better," Arianna said. "So many of my colleagues and friends were making money with Bernie, I thought, *How could it not be legit?* That's despite the fact that even I didn't quite understand how he was making such huge profits."

In another recent example, in December 2017, the SEC charged Woodbridge Group of Companies LLC and Robert H. Shapiro with operating a $1.2 billion Ponzi scheme. This scheme allegedly made money by giving other companies short-term loans at high rates of interest. Problem is, most of Woodbridge's "loans" were phony transactions to companies Shapiro owned. The early investors who made money were—you guessed it— reaping their profits from the investment dollars of the investors who followed them. But by end of the 2017, Woodbridge had declared bankruptcy.

What is remarkable about this scam, in addition to its illegality and its size—some 8,400 people invested in it—is how brazen it was. Hundreds of agents were involved in sales of the product, and Woodbridge had advertisements all across mass media—TV, radio, newspapers, and the web. There were seminars and other presentations—complete with free meals—and glowing social media testimonials. This was no petty backroom operation. The SEC has frozen Shapiro's and Woodbridge's assets and is seeking to recover investors' money. In 2018, Woodbridge reached a deal with the government to appoint a new board and to pay for legal representation for its victims. In January 2019, Woodbridge and its former owner were ordered to pay $1 billion.

HOW TO RECOGNIZE A PONZI SCHEME

- **The promise of low or no risk and high returns:** All investment involves risk, but promises of low risk with high returns is a huge red flag. High returns are generally associated with high risk (such as gambling), while low-risk investments are usually associated with low returns (think government bonds).
- **The promise of consistent returns:** The stock market has historically gone up and down, sometimes week to week, often month to month, and certainly year to year. Any investment tied to markets is likely to offer variable returns. Paperwork that indicates no variation in returns is another huge red flag.
- **Unregistered investments:** Ponzi schemes often involve investments that have not been registered with the SEC or with state regulators. Registration provides investors

with access to key information about the company's management, products, services, and finances.

- **Unlicensed or unregistered sellers:** Federal and state securities laws require investment professionals and their firms to be licensed or registered. Most Ponzi schemes involve unlicensed individuals or unregistered firms, although that's not always the case—Bernie Madoff was registered with the SEC, and his filings look conventional and legitimate.

- **Complex and secret strategies:** It's common to hear that amazing investment results are a result of secret and complex strategies. You may also be given an explanation that's ambiguous or filled with jargon, rendering it incomprehensible. That's because it doesn't make sense and isn't real. Still, not all Ponzi strategies are cryptic. The debt collection scheme I started the chapter with was fairly straightforward and presented in simple terms—it seems the people who ran it were good liars.

- **Paperwork problems:** Legitimate investment companies have reporting systems and statements that are relatively straightforward to read and understand. If you don't receive statements on time or if you spot errors or anything confusing in them, ask questions.

- **Difficulty receiving payments:** Be suspicious if you do not receive a payment or have a hard time cashing out your investment. Ponzi scheme promoters routinely encourage participants to "roll over" investments and sometimes promise even higher returns on the amount rolled over.

AS SEEN ON TV OR HEARD ON THE RADIO

Just because something is advertised on television or radio or any other media platform does not guarantee its legitimacy. Companies generally run ads through a review-and-approval process. Some ads are highly regulated: ads for cigarettes, cigars, and chewing tobacco are effectively banned on TV and radio. While there are rules governing financial advertisements, they are easy enough for fraudsters to get around. Never assume that advertisements bestow honesty on a company. Be skeptical.

EMAIL INVESTMENT FRAUD

The Internet is a great tool for investors. It makes researching investments easy. We can find stocks, trade online, and read an almost limitless amount of material about investing and investments, companies, and trends that could become viable investment opportunities. We can follow almost any lead and check up on the claims we hear. It's all at our fingertips. That's why when I received an email like this, I could quickly do my research, discover it was a con, and delete it:

June 28, 2018
TO: Frank
SUBJECT: Limited Time—Guaranteed Investment Opportunity

Hi Frank,

I usually don't send emails like this, but I can't keep this amazing investment opportunity to myself. I've recently learned about what I think is the ULTIMATE TRADING PLATFORM. Its developers have determined how to pick the next Apple or the next Amazon, and avoid the next Sears and Toys R Us failures. I've been using the platform for less than a year and I've already seen a 1500% return on my investment. It really works! I know you're a smart investor, so there's no way you would not want to get involved.

It's such a SURE THING and so EASY TO USE I got my mom into it, and she's already seen huge returns in just a couple of months! The developers guarantee that you will not lose your initial investment. There is absolutely NO RISK with this investment!

The problem is, if you want in on the platform, you have to send me just $399—but you have to do it today, or the opportunity will be gone forever. Only then can you start using what I think is the most incredible investment tool on the Internet. There are only a limited number of people who can sign on to the program at this time, and too many who want in.

DON'T LET THIS OPPORTUNITY PASS YOU BY!

Cheers,
Mike P.

I have no idea who "Mike P." is, or any of the other scammers who send out emails like this one, but the friendly and personal tone and language are instructive. It seems like he knows me—he wants me to think that maybe I've already met him. Not only that, but this guy says he put his own mother into the system—how could it not be legit? Who would scam his own mother?

Notice how this scammer uses many techniques described in chapter 2 to get me under the ether. The email urges me to take advantage of an opportunity *right away* that will be available for only a short time (urgency and scarcity) to a small group of preselected investors (flattery: I'm special), carefully chosen for their investment savvy (flattery again) so they can benefit from this extraordinary opportunity if they act right away (another reminder of urgency). The email also "guarantees" a return on investment (that big win) and assures me that there's "no risk" involved.

This email (and others just like it) sent me to a website where the investment opportunity was described in vague terms and provided multiple references to impressive-sounding regulations, laws, and agencies. Of course, it told me that my returns would be far in excess of what I might expect from an ordinary investment. Bogus companies like this often have social media accounts where lots of so-called insiders say great things about the opportunity. There are often links to investment bulletin boards where I or anyone can find "objective" commenters hyping the phony company. If somebody tweets it, it must be true, right?

A talented fraudster can set up such a website in no time and plant comments on social media sites that direct you back to the phony website. The "small group" referred to in the email consists of the hundreds of thousands of recipients of the scammers' carefully worded electronic missive, sent in bulk. The website is phony, and all those happy investors chattering away on their social media accounts are in reality fakes, probably "bots"— digital fakers programmed to post in social media settings.

Email investment scams come in many forms, including all those mentioned in this chapter and others: real estate investment scams, film investment scams, stock tips—you name it.

RECOGNIZE AND AVOID INTERNET INVESTMENT SCAMS

- **Unsolicited emails:** Some investment professionals still go door-to-door pitching their products—and some also make cold calls via telephone. However, unsolicited *emails* are rarely legitimate, and at any rate, no decision on any financial investment should be made without researching it first.

- **Act now or else:** If the offer is based on your immediately writing a check, forget it. Never invest your money without taking the time to do your due diligence—that means researching the person making the offer and the product you will be investing in.

- **You're special:** It's true: You *are* special. But not to a scammer out to collect your money. Be wary of offers that single you out as a member of a special group. This is simply an attempt to manipulate you with flattery and should rightly set off alarm bells.

- **Overwhelming number of online accolades:** There are numerous investment "bulletin boards" online where anyone can post and comment on investments—and it's next to impossible to separate the truth from the lies.

Online bulletin boards come in various forms, including newsgroups, web-based boards, and social media platforms. Some large online bulletin boards, like those found on the websites Raging Bull and Silicon Investor, can receive thousands of messages every hour! While they can be interesting to read, who is to say which comments are reliable and which ones aren't? In fact, a large number of tips on these sites are bogus. Fraudsters use sites like these to hype fraudulent or poor investments. That's because online bulletin boards and most social media platforms are anonymous or make it easy for people to pose as someone they're not. One poster could be operating under several aliases.

AFFINITY FRAUD

So-called affinity fraud is a technique for luring in investors, not money. Affinity fraudsters typically target an established group—such as members of a house of worship or a specific religion, a racial or ethnic group, alumni groups, professional associations, charitable groups, or even a civic society—any group where there are preexisting relationships of trust and respect. From that starting point, the criminal begins offering his fantastic—in more ways than one!—investment opportunity, tailored just to members of the group. As more and more people sign up, the investment seems to take on an air of authenticity, because if your friend has put her money in, it must be a great deal, right? Wrong.

Ephren W. Taylor II was an inspiring figure. A minister's son, he wanted to make his mark in the world by doing good. Taylor called himself "the Social Capitalist" and wrote three books about how to be a successful entrepreneur and make money. He was a rising star who appeared on the Montel Williams and Donny Deutsch TV shows as a young self-made millionaire. He created an investment company, City Capital, that would use investors' money to support small businesses in underserved neighborhoods and communities.

This sounds like a pretty terrific idea, and Taylor advertised on radio and television and offered webinars that described how investors could choose the kinds of businesses they wanted to invest in by letting City Capital manage their IRAs, or by purchasing promissory notes. In return, investors would earn big interest and have the satisfaction of knowing how much good their money was doing. He had other investment opportunities, including a chance to buy into "sweepstakes machines" that, he claimed, would give you back 300 percent of your investment!

Some, but not much, of the millions Taylor raised through these schemes was invested in businesses owned by underserved people in often neglected communities. Unfortunately, most of it went to Taylor and his cronies or funded Taylor's promotion of his books and his wife's career in show business. Before the SEC stepped in and charged him for his crimes, he had swindled millions from some four hundred investors, mostly churchgoers across the United States—a prime target of Taylor's investment pitch. These people were often in the very communities Taylor allegedly sought to help. After pleading guilty, he was sentenced to nineteen years in prison and ordered to make restitution of the money he stole.

HOW TO RECOGNIZE AFFINITY FRAUD

- **Group offers:** Be cautious about an investment opportunity that is offered to you as a member of a religious, alumni, or other group or organization. Scammers love the captive audience an established group represents, and they *will* target members for fraudulent deals.
- **People you trust:** Be wary even if you are approached by another member of the group—someone you already know well, like, and trust. One way fraudsters gain the trust of group members is to persuade one person, perhaps in a leadership position, to buy into the investment. That person unwittingly becomes a walking advertisement for the con.

CHURNING: A NAUSEATING FINANCIAL SCAM

Churning is excessive and unnecessary trading activity. Typically, brokers make money when clients or trades generate commissions. When trades are done for the benefit of the broker and not the client, that is called excessive trading, or churning. It's not only unethical but illegal. Under the law, even *one* unnecessary trade can be considered churning. That's one reason it might be best to select a financial adviser who works on a flat-fee or percentage basis rather than on commission.

The SEC spells out how to recognize whether or not a client's account has been churned. If your broker is making trades on your behalf every month, and your fees are increasing but your portfolio is not, there's a good chance that churning is occurring. Say you have $100 in securities and your broker trades $1,000 of securities on your behalf over a twelve-month period. That would mean that the turnover in your account is 10 ($1,000 ÷ $100 = 10). The SEC says that a turnover ratio of 3.3 could be excessive for some investors, so a ratio of 10 would absolutely be an indication that your account is being churned for commissions.

HOW TO RECOGNIZE CHURNING—AND WHAT TO DO ABOUT IT

- **Watch for an unusual increase in transactions.** If you see activity on your account but no increase in the value of your portfolio, this could be a red flag for churning—especially if you also see an increase in fees.
- **Check your risk designation.** Make sure your account is designated at a risk factor you feel comfortable with. One of the ways unscrupulous brokers try to mask churning as legitimate trading is to mark accounts "speculative" or "aggressive." By convincing you to choose that route, brokers can make large numbers of trades look more legitimate.
- **Follow the "six times turnover" rule.** The rule of thumb used to measure for churning is the "six times turnover" rule. If an account's equity has been turned over six times in the course of a year, with the financial adviser making all or most of the transactions, the account likely has been churned. For instance, if an account is worth $100,000 over the course of the year,

and $600,000 in trades was made on that $100,000 net equity (not counting margin), then the account turnover rate would be 6 ($600,000 ÷ $100,000). That's churning.

Prevent churning by opening mail from your financial adviser and carefully reviewing monthly statements for signs of trades you did not approve. If you believe that churning has occurred on your account, ask your broker for an explanation of the trades and how your account is designated. If you're not satisfied with the response and suspect churning, find a new broker and send a complaint to the SEC using its online complaint form, at www .sec.gov/tcr. You may also have to gather critical documents (reports and statements) and possibly contact a lawyer who specializes in such matters—but always file a complaint with the SEC first.

If churning has occurred, there is a method for calculating the damages you may be able to collect. A landmark opinion, *Miley v. Oppenheimer & Co.*, created a framework for computing damages in a churning case, and lets the victim recover both commissions and the amount lost in the value of the portfolio, plus interest. The following statistical measures of annual account costs and turnover are thresholds considered to represent three levels of evidence for a "churning" claim.

Cost Ratio	Turnover Rate	Level of Evidence
4 percent	2 times	Suggestion of churning
8 percent	4 times	Assumption of churning
12 percent	6 times	Conclusively churning

A REMINDER: COMMON INVESTMENT RED FLAGS

- If it sounds too good to be true . . . it is.
- A promise of "guaranteed returns" (they don't exist).
- Use of flattery, urgency, and scarcity.
- The "halo effect" of the charm offensive, a communication technique that makes con artists seem likable or trustworthy.
- "Everyone is buying it" pitches.
- Pressure to send money right now.
- Small favors (free lunch or workshop).

ALL THAT GLITTERS IS *NOT* GOLD: RARE COIN SCAMS

Certain collectibles are more vulnerable to scams and scammers than others. History shows that rare coins and bullion made from gold, silver, and platinum have been good investments, protecting you from inflation and the ups and downs of the dollar. And that's exactly why these commodities are especially vulnerable to fraud. While rare coins and precious metals can be a viable investment *if* you are knowledgeable about what you are buying, you must be aware of how fraudulent salespeople operate so you can avoid them.

Rare coin fraud is especially prevalent with modern gold coins like the American Eagle, the Canadian Maple Leaf, and the South African Krugerrand, because the value of these specific coins fluctuates during recessions and inflationary periods. Novice coin investors see buying and selling during market downturns and upswings as a potentially quick and easy way to profit. These newbies are often tempted to use their savings or cash reserves to buy these coins, especially if an offer from an unscrupulous dealer sounds attractive.

In some cases, companies have bilked investors out of millions of dollars' worth of money by promising that coins bought today would double or triple over a short period of time. Only later do these buyers discover that they bought coins for three or more times their actual value. That's what happened to Daphne, who bought gold coins from Merit Gold & Silver, a business that seemed legitimate. She received an invoice but never a report on her coins' value. She phoned the company to find out but was sent directly to voicemail and never received a return call. When she had the coins appraised, she realized she'd been duped: Instead of 1 percent over cost, as she was told, she'd been charged a 35 percent markup. And as the price of gold plummeted, the value of her investment kept melting away. Online, she found that several customers were suing Merit for deceptive marketing. Later she learned that a consumer protection lawsuit had been filed against the firm, alleging that it had engaged in an "aggressive, nationwide fraud scheme that has bilked consumers out of tens of millions of dollars."

HOW TO AVOID GETTING FLEECED
IN A COIN SCAM

- **Verify qualifications.** Check the credentials of any coin dealer you are considering buying from. Find out how long the company has been in business. If the dealer says he or she is a member of a professional numismatic or other related industry organization, follow up and confirm their affiliations and standing. The American Numismatic Association is one such organization, and you can check membership and contact them with a complaint against a member via their website, www.money.org. The organization also provides a great deal of information about coins. Likewise, the Industry Council for Tangible Assets is a national trade association and watchdog of coin and precious metal dealers. You can report problems with members and nonmembers to them at www.ictaonline.org. The Professional Numismatists Guild is another organization for coin dealers; it provides education and guidance.

- **Shop around.** Compare prices for comparable coins. See what is out there and available within your budget before you make a buy.

- **Handle the coins.** Always take possession of the coins so you know they are real. Scammers may try to sell you a phantom coin, telling you they'll hold it for you when it doesn't actually exist.

- **Check the return policy.** Before you buy, make sure the terms of the agreement allow you to return the coins for a full refund within a reasonable time if the coins do not appraise as promised. In other words, don't accept what a coin dealer tells you about the current or future value of coins you are considering buying. As soon as you receive your coins, get a second opinion about both grade (the actual condition of the physical coin) and value from a reputable and independent dealer.

- **Be skeptical of certification services.** These can also be run by dishonest dealers. There are some certification services that use lower standards than services accepted by reputable dealers and professional organizations, so their evaluation may be part of the scam, or simply wrong.
- **Question claims about value.** Don't always trust valuations provided by the dealer that come from the Salomon Brothers Index, which are prices based on a list of twenty extremely rare coins. Most coins sold by dishonest dealers are not rare. So it's not that the index itself is wrong; it's the way scammers use it to quote appreciations from 12 to 25 percent a year for coins you don't actually own.

FINANCIAL SERVICES YOU SHOULD AND SHOULDN'T PAY FOR

A subcategory of investment fraud is paying for investment and other financial services that are unnecessary or that can be obtained at no cost. Successful investors know which services are worth paying for, and which aren't.

DON'T PAY FOR

- **Credit reports.** Every twelve months, you are entitled to a free credit report from each of the three nationwide credit-reporting agencies: Equifax, Experian, and TransUnion. To get this free annual report from the big

three credit-reporting agencies, visit www.annualcredit
report.com. (You'll find contact information for all three
agencies in the Resources section on page 326.) Some for-
profit companies use similar-sounding names and URLs
and then charge you for the report. Other companies
offer a "free" trial that requires you to provide payment
information—a credit card or bank account—and following that period charge you $20 or more a month. If a web-
site other than the three reporting agencies tells you it will
send you your credit report for free, make sure there are no
strings attached, like having to provide a lot of personal
information (which is data these companies can then sell
to other companies). If you plan carefully, you can get
three free reports on annualcreditreport.com throughout
the year, spacing out each of the three agencies. For example, you can ask for an Experian report on January 1,
another from TransUnion on May 1, and a third free report
from Equifax around September 1.

- **Insurance advice.** A reputable insurance agent shouldn't
  charge you for advice about what insurance suits your
  needs. Of course, the emphasis here is on "reputable." A
  good sales agent with access to policies from several providers will assess your lifestyle, goals, and needs and find
  the most cost-effective and efficient insurance for your
  home, health, life, car, long-term care, and so on. If you
  decide to buy insurance products directly from insurers,
  it still pays to shop around. You can also buy a policy
  through an online brokerage like AccuQuote or Policy-
  genius, which allows you to compare quotes. The safest
  plan may be to pay a credentialed financial adviser for a

couple of hours of work to put together an insurance program that is right for you, especially when it comes to life, long-term care, and disability insurance.

Q&A TIME: WHAT TO ASK YOUR POTENTIAL FINANCIAL ADVISER

I use trusted professionals to guide me in many financial decisions. I would not trust my financial legacy to just anyone—nor would I try to navigate financial waters on my own.

To understand advisers' credentials, how they are compensated, and what fiduciary obligation they have to you, you should ask a series of questions that they should be more than happy to answer. If they are hesitant, act offended, brush off questions, or try to change the subject, they could be scammers. Use AARP's guide to interviewing an adviser (www.aarp.org/interviewanadvisor) and record the answers. To get better educated about investing, visit www.nasaa.org/investor-education. And use my quick guide below to get started asking questions.

- **What are your credentials?** Misrepresentation of credentials can be a way for scammers to convince you they are qualified to handle your money, especially if you don't understand what the various financial certifications mean and who is qualified to do what kind of financial work. Numerous professional designations can qualify someone to help with your money, and if you are not aware of what they are, you could be getting advice from a person with no special education or expertise. In some states, it's more difficult to hang a shingle and start cutting hair than it is to hang up a sign and start advising people what to do with their hard-earned money. A scammer who does this can close up shop quickly, taking your cash with him and leaving you with nothing but phony products. Here are some credentials to look for:

- **Certified Financial Planner:** CFPs are licensed and regulated by the state they work in. CFPs have to stay up to date by taking mandatory classes on various aspects of financial planning as well as changes in financial planning regulations.

- **Certified Public Accountant:** CPAs are licensed by the state after meeting education and experience requirements. They can offer financial planning as well as a variety of accounting services such as tax preparation.

- **Chartered Financial Analyst:** CFAs have to pass three challenging exams and have three years of qualifying work experience, among other requirements.

- **Registered Investment Adviser:** An RIA is an adviser registered either with the SEC or state securities authorities. RIAs have a fiduciary duty to their clients, which means they have an obligation to always offer advice in the client's best interests.

- **How am I paying for this service, and what am I getting?** Some financial planners earn money based on commission; some charge a flat fee; others are paid an hourly rate. A commission-based planner may have an incentive to sell you certain products that are not necessarily in your best financial interests. Most commission-based planners are legit, but this form of payment does open the door wider for less scrupulous advisers who may sell you products you don't need just so they can collect commissions. Flat-fee planners may charge a one-time fee for a financial plan or, if they are managing your money, they may take a small percentage (usually of the amount invested) by way of an annual fee, or be paid an hourly rate.

- **Are you a fiduciary?** When a planner is a fiduciary, it means he or she has an obligation to operate with your best interests in mind. In contrast, financial professionals who are not fiduciaries are not held to this same high standard, and they can sell you anything "suitable." But suitability does not necessarily mean it is in your best interests. If you just want someone to execute trades for you, you may not need a fiduciary. But if you want someone to manage your money with the highest standard of care, you may want to consider one.

- **What certifications do you have?** Once you get the answers, a simple background check at BrokerCheck (brokercheck.org) or the Certified Financial Planner Board (www.cfp.net) can tell you if your planner has been disciplined in the past and if credentials are up to date. Go to www.finra.org and www.sec.gov to see whether any regulatory actions have been taken against your planner and to find out whether he or she is registered with your state securities department and has any history of complaints. If the planner sells insurance products, including annuities, check your state's division of insurance.

DO YOUR RESEARCH

Aside from reading about potential investments in reliable news sources like Bloomberg, Crain's, Morningstar, *The New York Times*, and *The Wall Street Journal*, you can learn about investing from financial oversight resources. The Securities and Exchange Commission (SEC) is a great place to start your in-depth education about investing. At www.investor.gov, you can get more tips on how to invest wisely, review the red flags that will alert you to scams old and new, and keep up to date on the most recent ways scammers are trying to steal your money. If you are an investor or would like to be, I strongly advise you to bookmark this site and refer to it often.

In addition to www.investor.gov, the SEC has websites that will help you determine whether an investment opportunity is legitimate. The Financial Industry Regulatory Authority (FINRA) is an independent organization that upholds standards for broker-dealers. On www.finra.org, there are many resources for investors, including a way to file a complaint against a broker-dealer. The North American Securities Administrators Association (NASAA) also has a website with helpful resources at www.nasaa.org.

If you believe you have been scammed, contact the FTC online at www.ftc.gov or call 877-FTC-HELP.

There are so many financial products and investments, and it is impossible to cover all of the scams involving them here. What I have given you is an overview of prevalent scams, how to protect yourself against them, and some ways to educate yourself about investing. In the finance-scam chapters that follow this one, I talk about how scammers can target your small business— an unfortunately all too common way to get money from hardworking people—and how impostors can try to ruin your finances and capitalize on them at the same time.

6.

Small Business Shakedowns

Compared with individual consumers, small businesses are at increased risk for fraud. That's because fraudsters deploy the same strategies that have worked against consumers *plus* approaches specifically designed to compromise the data and financial accounts of small businesses. In the end, a typical small business fraud amounts to four times more than a typical consumer fraud—on average, more than $4,000 per harmed business, as opposed to $1,038 per individual fraud case, with the total coming to $7 billion. Here's how business owners can spot scams targeting you specifically—and prevent them.

Karen had just moved to the small Gulf Coast city of Venice, Florida, from New York, where she had worked in the publishing industry for nearly forty years. At sixty, she didn't want to play golf all day, like so many others she knew in Venice. She wanted to continue to work in her profession. Setting up a simple corporation in this beach town outside Sarasota seemed pretty straightforward.

She first registered with Sunbiz, the state's business filing department. Karen paid the $75 fee for registering her business and decided not to pay extra for the optional paper business certificate. A week after registering, Karen received an official-looking letter in the mail, complete with the Florida state seal on the return address, saying she had to purchase a paper certificate for her business for a whopping $67.25. She wisely looked closer and found some extremely fine print that read, "This is not a government agency." A for-profit, private company called FL Certificate Services was simply trying to fool her into thinking she needed to buy a certificate—a worthless eight-by-ten piece of paper. Two days later, she received a similar solicitation from a different company, also official-looking. This one wanted her to send $78 for the same certificate.

Karen also received what looked like an invoice for $35 for a labor poster detailing wages and other employment laws, with a warning that employers could be arrested for not displaying the poster on a wall visible to workers. The trouble is, sole proprietors and people working from home with no employees don't need to hang such a poster in their offices—and even if she did need one, Karen could print one off the Internet for free. She wasn't fooled, because she knew about these signs, but many small business owners fall prey to this scam, and others like it, each year.

BOGUS BILLS

Federal law prohibits a mailing that looks like "a bill, invoice, or statement of account due" but is, in fact, "a solicitation for the order by the addressee of goods or services," unless the mailing includes a notice such as this, printed in "conspicuous and legible type":

> This is a solicitation for the order of goods or services, or both, and not a bill, invoice, or statement of account due. You are under no obligation to make any payments on account of this offer unless you accept this offer.

Most states also have their own consumer protection laws that prohibit sending fake bills through the mail. Minnesota law, for instance, says that people are prohibited from soliciting payment of money "by any statement or invoice, or any writing that could reasonably be interpreted as a statement or invoice," for unordered merchandise, unordered services, or unperformed services.

But scammers don't care about the law. They understand that small business owners multitask and often deal with multiple vendors and service providers. To take advantage of these people, who are often being pulled in many directions, fraudsters will mail an invoice for a service or product the businessperson never ordered, didn't receive, and doesn't want. Some are so brazen that they call business owners asking for money for a service or product never received, under threat of a collection agency coming after them—completely fake but scary nonetheless!

Another way scammers try to collect money is by sending you an item that you did not order and then demanding payment for it. This is illegal, too. You don't owe anyone anything for a product that was sent unsolicited. You're not even required to return it. You can refuse delivery of unsolicited goods, or you can accept delivery and keep or dispose of the item in any way you see fit. The law defines such items as unconditional gifts. If an invoice is included in the delivery, it's illegal—unless you actually ordered the item. In that case, you have to either return the item or pay the bill.

HOW TO AVOID PAYING PHONY BILLS

- Set up a system, either digital or manual, to compare all incoming invoices to actual work completed or goods received *before* making a payment. A ledger or accounting program that helps you keep track of payments made will greatly reduce your chances of paying a phony bill or paying a bill twice.
- Take note of invoice account numbers on bills that look like they are from vendors you do business with. If the account number on the bill you receive doesn't match the account number you have with a vendor, it could be fake.
- Don't trust solicitations that attempt to collect money for products or services outside the normal scope of your business.
- Review invoices that don't have a telephone number or other contact information on the bill. Scammers often don't put this information on their paperwork because they don't want anyone to call and question them.

Sometimes, however, a legitimate company won't include a phone number, either.
- If you have people working for you, make sure orders are confirmed with the person who placed the order.

NO CHECKS, PLEASE!

Another related scam involves "rebate" or refund checks that come in the mail unexpectedly. Don't cash one of these checks unless you can verify without a doubt that it is a refund for a product you returned or a rebate you actually applied for. There's no guarantee the check is good! If it bounces, you could be responsible for fees. Do not spend money from any check, including a cashier's check or money order, until the bank confirms it has cleared, which could take several weeks. If the check turns out to be fake, you will be responsible for money you withdraw against it. Read all the fine print on any mail that comes with an unexpected check. If you have further doubts about its legitimacy, you can ask your banker to take a look at it.

PHONY DIRECTORY LISTINGS

Small business owners often receive solicitations from companies that want to sell a spot in an industry or consumer directory.

Karen said that when she applied for incorporation, she was inundated with calls asking her to pay to be listed in directories of writers and editors, professional consultants, and business leaders. Despite the sales pitch promising that the directory would raise her business profile and help potential clients find her, few people would likely look at or use these directories.

These scam companies often want to lock you into an ongoing contract that can last twelve to twenty-four months. They frequently require full payment up front or recurring payments set up via your bank account or credit card. Sometimes these contracts ask for substantial amounts of money, perhaps $1,000 or more per year. They set deadlines for a response and payment, and if they do not hear from you within, say, a five- or seven-day period, the scammer will start calling you to demand payment. These scams often claim that you can cancel within three months, but the cancellation instructions are so difficult, often requiring written notification and mailing addresses in overseas locations, that they are nearly impossible to comply with. When you refuse to pay, scammers can be very aggressive, threatening legal action. If this happens, hold your ground. What they are doing is illegal.

The government takes these directory scams seriously, but since there are so many, it's hard for authorities to shut them down before they do harm. Here's one example.

In 2013, the U.S. Federal Trade Commission (FTC) sued a Slovakian company called Construct Data Publishers (doing business as Fair Guide), Wolfgang Valvoda, and Susanne Anhorn for bilking U.S. businesses of millions of dollars to be listed in an online directory, despite the International Association of Exhibitions and Events' repeated warnings to the group.

In 2008, Construct Data had moved from Austria to Slovakia after Austrian authorities sued the company for deceptive practices. As a result, Construct Data agreed to stop soliciting businesses in the European Union. Then they moved on to the United States. The FTC's suit alleged that Fair Guide and its cohorts had sent mailings to retailers, local associations, and home-based and other businesses that attended trade shows, saying that they were obligated to confirm the accuracy of information about their companies in a free "exhibitors' directory." The form implied that the targeted businesses had dealt with Fair Guide in the past and was simply requesting routine information about listing accuracy.

Those who signed the form that "confirmed" the listing info had unknowingly signed a contract that stipulated that they had to pay Fair Guide $1,717 per year. Businesses that refused to pay this fee then received regular demands for money to be sent to a Slovakian bank account. If they refused to pay, phony bills would keep coming, with late fees or fines attached. Some businesses said they had paid simply to stop the harassing phone calls and letters.

In September 2016, responding to the FTC's action, a federal court banned Fair Guide and two of its executives from the business directory business, ending the scam. But it wasn't until March 2017 that the FTC was able to get some restitution for victims—mailing out 974 checks totaling more than $535,000 to businesses and nonprofit organizations that had lost money in the scam. That might sound like a lot of money, but these firms recouped only about 24 percent of their loss, or an average of $549.

HOW TO PROTECT YOURSELF FROM
A DIRECTORY SCAM

- Be skeptical of all unsolicited directory offers.
- Read the agreement carefully and understand it fully before signing.
- Before doing business with any directory service, research the company online and check with organizations that deal with complaints against businesses to see if there have been any issues with the company in the past.
- If you cannot find much about the business, search online for the phrases or terminology used in the letter, as this is often a good way to identify scams.
- If the offer includes an actual invoice, make sure it's for something you signed up for before you make a payment.
- Never give or clarify any information about your business unless you absolutely know that the request is legitimate.
- Don't let anyone pressure you into making payments for services you did not authorize or request. If you are being harassed, contact local law enforcement or state or federal consumer protection agencies.
- If you *do* want to list your business details in a legitimate online or print directory, hunt around for the best options, check reviews and feedback, and research the companies to ensure they are legit.

OFFICE SUPPLY SCAMS

Office supply scams have been around for a long time. That's because the person ordering supplies and the person paying for them very often are two different people in two different departments. This is what makes the scam so appealing to fraudsters.

There are several variations on the scam, but they often involve a phone call from someone who claims to be your regular supplier or an authorized dealer calling on the vendor's behalf. The caller asks for information about the kinds of products you use, including toner for printers, paper, small office machinery, coffee, and so on, along with the name of the company's buyer. Once the scammer has gathered this information, he ships the company unwanted supplies that are generally defective or of poor quality—along with an astronomical bill.

In 2016, the FTC charged two office supply operations with tricking nonprofit organizations and small businesses into paying for overpriced office and cleaning supplies they never ordered. The two states involved, Maryland and California, froze the assets of the two fraudulent companies, and in 2017 the FTC shut both businesses down. "The defendants lied to small businesses, charities, and churches to get them to pay for overpriced supplies they didn't order," said Jessica Rich, then director of the FTC's Bureau of Consumer Protection. "That's not only shameful; it's also illegal."

According to the FTC, the companies threatened to send consumers to collections when they challenged or questioned bills. Consumers who paid under a mistaken belief that they had to do so—some paid thousands of dollars more than they were legally obligated to pay—often received more unordered merchandise and bills.

According to the FTC's complaint, these telemarketers falsely claimed that they had done business previously with the buyers and were now offering a free sample or catalog. They never disclosed that they were actually making a sales call. The scam worked because the person who processed the invoices was not the same person who received the orders, and the company did not have a verification process.

PROTECT YOURSELF FROM OFFICE SUPPLY SCAMS

- **Create an information policy.** Tell all employees who answer phones to never give anyone information regarding office supplies or equipment. Don't provide the name of the purchasing agent at your company to any caller. Instead take a message—getting the caller's name, number, and company. Let the caller know you will pass along the information, and end the call.

- **Don't complete phone surveys.** A common tactic scammers use is to call and say they are doing an "office supply survey." If you get a call asking you to take part in a phone survey for office equipment and supplies, hang up.

- **Don't pay for merchandise you didn't order.** Scammers often ship you merchandise you didn't order and then send an invoice a couple of weeks later. It's a way of making companies feel obligated to pay—because they may have already stored the items in the supply closet.

They may have even used the merchandise, thinking it was a legitimate order. You are not under any legal obligation to pay for unordered items. You don't have to pay for them or even return them.

- **Stand strong.** Don't give in to bullying, threats, and harassment. Once you pay, the scammers won't stop.
- **Complain to authorities.** File a complaint with the FTC. You can do that by going to www.ftc.gov/complaint.

HIRE RIGHT

Having pretended to be an employee of a large company when I was younger, I know firsthand that not everyone is who he or she appears to be. Small business owners can find securing quality employees challenging enough without having to worry that they might hire someone who intends to rip them off.

One common safeguard is running a background check. Background checks are especially important for employees who handle cash transactions, have access to account information and purchasing duties, or work with sensitive customer or client information and financial data. Background checks cost money, so checking every employee can get expensive. Employees who don't work with sensitive information or have access to money can likely be hired safely by checking with references and past employers.

When conducting a background check, you have to comply with certain laws. Employers are required to get applicants' written consent before running a background check. Applicants also have the right to look at the report and dispute any negative findings. The best background check firms offer a compliance system so you do not run afoul of the law.

There are several kinds of background checks, which range from criminal background, credit, employment history, driving, drug testing, and academic verification. Some companies offer searches on social media, although this can be a slippery slope, since social media checks often reveal information about an applicant that is against the law to ask about, including race, sexual orientation, political views, and family structure.

Once you've hired the right people, take the time to train them to be aware of common fraud schemes I've described in this chapter and how to avoid them. The prevention tips in this chapter will help you develop procedures that will help employees avoid getting scammed.

BUSINESS LOAN SCAMS

Sometimes small business owners are in need of extra capital to start a business, buy equipment, or put money down on an office or retail location. While small business lending has loosened up in the past few years as interest rates have risen, making it more profitable for banks to loan money, and while there are several legitimate sources of funding, acquiring a decent loan can still be challenging and expensive. That's why business loan scams are still problematic.

BUSINESS LOAN RED FLAGS

- **Asks for money up front.** A legitimate lender or loan broker will never ask for money up front to receive a loan. If the application process requires you to pay a fee of any kind, move on.
- **Has no street address.** Legitimate lenders should have a physical street address and not just a post office box or email address. If a lender or broker cannot provide a street address, move on. This is an indication of scammers operating on foreign soil.
- **Offers cash advances.** Never work with so-called lenders who offer cash up front and fast. Loans requiring no credit check into your history—sometimes called "startup loans"—often come with usurious interest rates and terms that are nearly impossible to comply with. It's almost like taking a loan from an organized crime syndicate. But be aware that there are exceptions to this rule. A merchant cash advance is a legitimate way to get a quick loan. That's when a legitimate finance company advances you some capital in exchange for a percentage of your daily credit card sales plus a fee. As a consequence, the rates for these kinds of legitimate loans can be higher than those of conventional business loans, but they could be appropriate for businesses that are highly seasonal or have less than stellar credit. Make sure the lender is legit by checking with the Small Business Administration, understand the terms of the agreement, and make sure you can meet your obligations.

- **Guarantees loan approval.** An honest and reputable lender won't advertise guaranteed approval of a loan before you apply. Never deal with a company that makes such promises.

TECH SUPPORT SCAMS

In these scams, criminals pose as tech support, calling your company and claiming there's a problem with your computer and they need remote access to fix it. In the most common scenario, the scammer tells you that emails are being sent from your account because it's been hacked and the content of the emails is illegal. If you don't let the scammer fix your problem, he claims, you could face serious fines and even jail time. You've heard me say this before: Any pitch that demands immediate action on your part is likely a scam. Once scammers get remote access to your computer, they can use it to steal personal data, financial information, and other sensitive material.

Pop-up windows claiming you have a virus are also scams—never click on a pop-up asserting any information about your computer, viruses, or tech support! Never respond to pop-ups that say you need to download software. Do not even click the X button on the pop-up to close these windows, because that is another way scammers can infect your computer with a virus. Just close the window on your computer.

HOW TO FIGHT TECH SUPPORT SCAMS

- Make sure your employees know that they should be skeptical of all unsolicited phone calls or pop-up messages on their devices.

- Don't let employees give control of their computers or other devices to any third party unless you've confirmed that it is from a legitimate computer support team with whom you are already a customer. Tell your employees to hang up when someone calls claiming to be a tech support person from your service provider or computer manufacturer and says there is an issue with their computer. Companies like Apple and Microsoft won't call individuals or companies unsolicited about technical problems. Any communication they have with you must be initiated by you.

FOUR WAYS TO PROTECT YOUR SMALL BUSINESS DATA

Your information is crucial to your success as a small business owner. Protecting it is paramount.

1. Automated backup systems

Use an automated backup system to preserve your company data. You can use a local or external hard drive to back up information on your computer or server; these cost less than $100 in the electronics department of any large big-box or tech store, or online. But consider adding an extra layer to that backup system with a third-party or off-site service. That way, if your data is destroyed, you can retrieve it from another location. Cloud backup services are another option. Companies like Dropbox and Carbonite will replicate, back up, and store your data in the cloud.

2. Server virtualization

With server virtualization, you can run several virtual server environments (for example, your email, database, and web servers) on one physical server machine. Essentially, one server performs the work of many. Along with cost benefits, virtualization also simplifies recovery in the event of a disaster.

3. Appliance-based firewalls

Computer viruses, malware, ransomware, and virtual break-ins are potential threats to your computer data. Hardware firewalls can protect your software, but by the time they're installed and activated, the threat could already be inside your network. Be sure to install a secure appliance-based firewall between the Internet and your business data to block intruders and threats before they can enter your network.

4. Filters

Antivirus software and spam filters offer another layer of protection for incoming and outgoing data. Content filters protect local computers from malware threats by blocking entry to potentially harmful websites.

W-2 PHISHING SCAMS

It was a Thursday afternoon, and Betsy was finishing her payroll work, eating lunch at her desk, thinking about the coming weekend, and worrying about her daughter's upcoming SAT test. In other words, she was having a typical workday. Since she was multitasking and had a lot on her mind, she didn't blink when her boss emailed her asking for the file containing all the company's employee W-2 forms. It was March, and tax season was on the horizon. Betsy emailed the file and didn't think anything of it. A couple of hours later, he asked her to wire some money into his bank account, providing the routing and account numbers. She wanted to get home, so she did it quickly, again without thinking too much about it.

When she showed up for work the next morning, her boss and his partner were waiting for her. A nightly check of the business accounts had revealed the theft. You probably know the end of this story: Betsy had answered a fraudulent email that was disguised to look like it came from her boss, when it was really from a cybercriminal. Now criminals had gained access to the names, Social Security numbers, addresses, and salary information of the company's 150 employees—all the information the scammers needed to submit phony tax returns or to sell on the dark web (read more about the dark web in chapter 2). Not only that, but she had wired money into a criminal's account. By morning, the money was gone—the bank might be able to provide some recompense for the theft, but the loss of employee information was irreversible.

According to the IRS, W-2 email phishing scams are one of the most dangerous tax scams. Cybercriminals first identify chief operating officers or chief financial officers, school administrators, or hospital or charity executives, which is not hard to do, as much of that information is widely available online. Next they use a strategy known as business email compromise (BEC) or business email spoofing (BES) to send messages to key employees, such as payroll workers, requesting copies of W-2s. Since the emails look legit, staffers often comply without questioning the request or checking in with their supervisors.

In 2016 (the most recent reporting year as of this writing), more than two hundred employers were victimized—hundreds of thousands of employees had their identities compromised at businesses large and small, academic institutions, hospitals, and charities. If you have a business of any size, even one with just a few employees, educate them about this phishing scam and have a procedure in place to follow up on email requests for sensitive information or money. After the scam at Betsy's company, they immediately put into place a system whereby any request for sensitive employee information had to be delivered in person and in writing, never in an email.

If your business or organization receives a suspect email requesting W-2 data, report it immediately to the IRS. Send the full email to phishing@irs.gov and use "W2 Scam" in the subject line. If your business *has* been victimized by one of these W-2 phishing scams, notify the IRS as soon as you discover the breach.

RANSOMWARE SCAMS

Many businesses have become victims of ransomware scams, in which a virus infects their computer systems, encrypting all their files and making them inaccessible and useless. The scammer then sends a message claiming that you accessed illegal content on the Internet and demands a payment, with a link attached. Sometimes the message will say something like "You only have 72 hours to submit payment. If no payment is received within the time period, all your files will be permanently encrypted and become unrecoverable." If you click on the link, there's a great chance you will be infected with more viruses. Retail operations, hospitals, and service providers have all had to deal with the horror of ransomware screwing up their systems.

The U.S. Department of Justice recommends taking these steps to combat ransomware fraud.

- **Educate employees.** Make sure everyone who works for you understands the threat of ransomware and how it works. Make sure they know not to click on any links unless they absolutely know they are legitimate. Do not open any emails that look suspicious or like junk mail. Delete them immediately.
- **Use strong spam filters.** These can prevent phishing emails from ever reaching the email inboxes of those who use your computer system. The DOJ says that technologies like Sender Policy Framework (SPF), Domain-based Message Authentication, Reporting, and Conformance

(DMARC), and DomainKeys Identified Mail (DKIM) can help to prevent email spoofing.

- **Use firewalls effectively.** Configure firewalls to block access to known malicious IP addresses.
- **Keep your software up to date.** Regular updates will provide "patches" for operating systems, software, and firmware to prevent malicious viruses from entering your computer via email or other avenues.
- **Use antivirus protection.** Antivirus and anti-malware programs should be programmed to conduct regular scans automatically and eliminate threats immediately.

CREDIT CARD AND BANK ACCOUNT FRAUD

Credit card and banking fraud is a serious issue for businesses, as it is for individuals. Here are my tips on keeping your business cards and accounts safe.

- **Keep them apart.** Always separate your personal banking from your business banking, by using separate accounts, credit and debit cards, and checks. This helps prevent scammers from taking all your money. It also helps you keep better track of what you are spending in your business. It makes doing your taxes easier, too.
- **Be card selfish.** Never give employees access to your business or personal credit cards. Likewise, don't give your card numbers to vendors unless you know they are

legitimate and you have ongoing business relationships with them.

- **Use one-stop pay options.** Instead of writing checks, I recommend using bill-pay features via your vendors or bank or going paperless. If you need paper bills, store them securely. Paying bills directly through your bank account allows you to track payments and organize them in one place, making bookkeeping and tracking of funds much easier and less vulnerable to fraudsters.
- **Set up alerts.** You may be able to set up alerts for any transaction over, say, $1.
- **Check it.** Monitor your accounts daily to spot any suspicious or unfamiliar activity.

Scams that target businesses make the already tough job of being an entrepreneur or small business owner even tougher. Fraud is a problem for large companies, too, not just costing money and causing financial damage but resulting in lost productivity, reputational damage, and diminished customer trust. What about scams that are operated by people who pretend to be officials in some capacity, governmental or otherwise? Those scams can also affect our finances. We deal with those next.

7

I'm (Not Actually) from the Government: Social Security, Government Grants, and Other "Official" Scams

Frauds that involve claims of association with authority of some kind, whether government, law enforcement, or some other institution or entity, are insidious, because we are taught to follow laws and trust authorities in general. Scammers play on these beliefs. In this chapter, I describe the common official-sounding scams, how they go down, what to watch out for, and what to do if you think you might have become a target.

DISORDER IN THE COURT: JURY SCAMS

Martha's children were grown and out of the house, which left the Florida resident with time to do charity work in South America. She had recently returned to the States from one of her trips abroad. A message was waiting for her on her answering machine. The caller said he was a sergeant at her local police precinct and had something important to discuss with her. "I didn't think much about it. I returned the call," said Martha. She asked to speak to the sergeant and was transferred to his answering machine. The voice on the machine sounded the same as the man who had called her, so she left a message, with her cell phone number.

The sergeant called back a short time later and told her she had received a summons for jury duty but had not shown up. "He said my full name, my address, and my birthdate. It seemed authentic to me," Martha said. She told him she'd never received the notice and asked when the county had started issuing arrest warrants for missing jury duty. He told her this was the new law in Florida.

Many states are cracking down on no-show jurors. In 2003 alone, Massachusetts fined nearly 48,000 people $2,000 each for missing jury duty. In 2012, one Florida judge sent notices to thirty-five people who failed to show up for contempt-of-court hearings. In 2018, thirty Arizonians were fined as much as $500 for not showing up for jury duty.

If there was a warrant involved, Martha told him, she would need to speak to her lawyer about it. "He said, 'Oh, no. It will cost you more to get a lawyer involved than it will to pay the fine,'" she recalled. The fine for missing jury duty was $1,000, he said, and she could pay either at the police station or over the phone. He warned her that going to the police station could put her at risk of being arrested.

"He did not sound threatening," she said, "and in retrospect, remembering other times when I have spoken to actual sergeants at the real police station, they never sounded as nice as this man did. He was very friendly." That's typical of jury duty scams—a friendly person puts targets at ease and tends to keep them on the line longer. A belligerent caller will set off warning bells in a target's mind.

The "sergeant" told Martha to go to the Winn-Dixie grocery store and buy two $500 gift cards. "Keep your phone on," he told Martha. Once she had purchased the cards, he asked her for the numbers on the back. Again she complied.

He then told Martha to go to the police station, giving her the address of the real police station in her Florida community. At the police station, he told her, she would hand the money cards to his boss. But while she was driving there, she recalled, "he told me not to go to the station because his boss had to leave because of an emergency. He said it would be best to mail the cards." Of course, the scammer never had intended to let Martha go to the police station. Telling her to do so was part of the ruse, to make the setup seem authentic. Instead the phony sergeant had her mail the cards to an address he supplied. She did, but the $1,000 was already gone. Remember: Martha had given the scammer the numbers on the back of the cards.

After the call ended, the ether began to lift and Martha got to thinking about how things had played out: "I felt violated and angry. I felt fear. This person invaded my life. He had my name and address and date of birth, which he probably got online. That's when I made a call to the sheriff's office."

The sheriff's office confirmed that Martha had gotten trapped in a scam. The court never calls people who do not show up for jury duty, and it does not require them to buy money cards at supermarkets to pay fines. City municipalities simply don't work like that. But she had been put under the ether with his refined technique.

Jury scams have been around for years. While published statistics on how many people are caught up in these scams are hard to come by, there has been an uptick in the number of reports in recent years, according to the FBI. This scam's bold simplicity may be what makes it so effective. Facing the unexpected threat of arrest, victims are caught off guard and may be quick to part with information to defuse the situation.

Scammers use the "failure to appear" jury ruse not just to steal your money. Sometimes they are after your identity. In this scenario, the scammer, claiming to be from the court, tells you that you missed jury duty and there is now a warrant out for your arrest. The scammer asks for information to verify your identity: Social Security number, birthdate, and sometimes mother's maiden name and banking information—in short, all the information needed to steal your identity and your money.

But like I said, the court, as a rule, will not call you if you missed jury duty, and neither will it call asking for personal information. Instead, courts generally send notifications through the mail. Since more states are cracking down on no-show jurors, you could be served with court papers for not appearing. This is done by mail, by courier, or, in rare instances, in person by a process server. If you do get a notice in the mail concerning fines for not appearing, always call the courthouse or county clerk directly to confirm that the letter is legitimate.

FAKE MONEY: GOVERNMENT GRANT SCAMS

Sid Kirchheimer was amused when he got a call from someone who told him he was eligible for a $3,200 grant from the government because he always filed his IRS taxes on time. Sid was skeptical; he knew it was a scam. The call came in at 7 p.m., long after normal working hours for federal agencies, and he knew that the government doesn't reward people for paying their taxes on time. In these scams, the caller will claim to be from the Treasury Department or even a phony agency—the "Federal Government Grants Department," for example, or the "Government Grant Association."

But grant scams don't start with a phone call. Scammers also use social media to entice people to apply for a chance to win large government checks. One emblematic government grant scam is supposedly from the IFC (International Finance Corporation) Fund. While the IFC is a real organization, there is no such IFC Fund, and it's all a scam.

Here's how it works. You, the target, typically receive a message on a social media platform like Facebook that tells you that the IFC Fund exists "specifically for those who need assistance in paying bills, buying a home, starting their own business, going to school, or even helping raise their children with old and retired individuals." Often scammers, posing as a Facebook friend, will say they have received large sums—as much as $15,000—after applying for an IFC grant. They explain how this amazing new opportunity could help you obtain a government grant, too, and they encourage you to apply. You'll probably be told to contact an

IFC government agent who will facilitate the grant application. Of course, this "agent" is part of the scam, too.

In the second part of the scam, you're asked to fill out a form sent by instant message. It asks for your name, email address, phone number, address, occupation, employer information, Social Security number, monthly and yearly earnings, how much grant money is needed, and the reason for applying (or how you plan to use the grant money). The form looks authentic, complete with what looks like a government seal.

Once you've filled in the form and sent it back to the phony agent, you're sent more information about the grant, including claim and serial numbers—both bogus—and other details that give it an air of authenticity. After a day, or sometimes sooner, the agent tells you that the information has been verified and you now qualify to receive the grant. But to receive the money, you first have to send the agent money—for a "government process-ing fee." The fee depends entirely on the amount of the grant—the higher the grant, the higher the fee. These phony fees can range anywhere from hundreds to thousands of dollars.

If you try to question the agent about when you will receive the money, that person might become abusive and threatening or send a message that says something like "Because you are not ready to receive the funds, we have reserved the right to offer the grant to the next individual. Thank you for applying, and congratulations for qualifying, even though you were unable to claim the grant." Or, more likely, you'll never hear from the scammer again.

If you receive Facebook messages about government grants, you should immediately report the scam to Facebook and the

FBI's Internet Crime Complaint Center (IC3), at www.ic3.gov. If the message came from a Facebook friend, let that person know that his or her Facebook account has been hacked.

How can you protect yourself? Know that the government does not solicit grant applications via Facebook or other social media messaging and never asks for fees to release grant money. You cannot receive public assistance for food, rent, or utilities through social media.

Other grant scams involve people posing as government officials who solicit targets by phone, email, or mail, informing them that they've been approved for money they never applied for. Generally, these impostors follow a script and use a common language and expressions—telltale signs they are attempting to fool you. Be on alert if you hear any of these terms.

- "You've been selected out of thousands of applicants." If you don't remember applying, it's probably because you didn't!
- "You've been selected for a government grant because you pay your taxes on time and have no criminal record." Unfortunately, the government does not reward you with money for being a good citizen!
- "The information about this government grant isn't available anywhere else." That's because it doesn't exist.
- "All you need to do is provide a credit card number to secure this grant." And the scammer will go on a shopping spree.

FIVE IMPORTANT RULES ABOUT REAL
GOVERNMENT GRANTS

1. All government grant applications and information about them are free and available online at www.grants.gov. In fact, this is the only *official* clearinghouse for information about government-based grants.
2. The names of other local and national nonprofit, nongovernment organizations, agencies, and foundations that award grants are available for free at any public library or on the Internet.
3. The government never charges fees to apply for government grants.
4. All government grants are for projects with a purpose that benefits the public and are never intended for personal use, to pay off bills or purchase personal items.
5. The government will never contact you to solicit a grant application or to ask for payment for processing a grant. No fees are associated with government grants.

SCHOOL YOURSELF ON GOVERNMENT
COLLEGE SCHOLARSHIP SCAMS

In college scholarship scams, targets are tricked into thinking that government financing will provide them with money for school—but that the information about the scholarship is proprietary and can be accessed only for a price.

Some of these scams require applicants to attend a "free seminar," which is really a sales pitch for expensive access to scholarship information readily available for free online or at the public library. Other scams, often Internet-based subscription services, require a monthly "membership fee" if you want to be added to a list of potential scholarship recipients. But the promised refund fees are often elusive or nonexistent.

The *only* government application that determines eligibility for financial aid is the Free Application of Federal Student Aid (FAFSA), at https://fafsa.ed.gov. As the name of the application clearly states, it doesn't cost a dime.

If you attend a free seminar on financial aid and scholarships, follow these basic precautionary steps.

- **Don't write a check at the seminar.** Educational seminars practice high-pressure sales tactics to get you to pay for a service that is usually unnecessary—and often available for free via an Internet search. Keep your cool and don't let anyone talk you into spending money on information you can find yourself.

- **Verify whom you're dealing with.** Before signing up for services you may not need, ask your guidance counselor or the college financial aid adviser about solicitations you receive. Check out scholarship seminar companies on the web, look them up on consumer sites that register complaints, and read consumer reviews (not testimonials).

- **Don't believe testimonials.** Testimonials on a company's website can be fairy tales told by paid shills. Verify a success story with an actual person. Consumer reviews, while not foolproof, can be a better indication of a company's reputation.

- **Ask questions and expect answers.** Before you sign
  up for any scholarship services, understand what you're
  getting. Ask how much the service costs, how long it lasts,
  and what you get for it. If the rep is unable to give you
  detailed and precise answers in writing, say "No thanks"
  and move on.

UNREAL WINNINGS: STATE GOVERNMENT LOTTERY AND SWEEPSTAKES SCAMS

State lottery scams are a perennial problem from coast to coast.
One investigation revealed that half of the twenty most frequent
lottery ticket winners in New Jersey were licensed lottery dealers
or retailers, or family members of store owners. That means they
were beating incredible odds, cheating customers out of winning
tickets, or cashing in tickets for winners in exchange for a cut of
the prize.

In Michigan, thirty-seven store owners had turned in winning
tickets worth nearly $3.6 million over a two-year period. One
retailer collected 107 prizes worth $346,312 in just one year. Also
within a single year, six store owners failed to report their lottery
winnings—more than $500,000—on their tax returns. This is a
scam that rips off taxpayers, too, since both the price of the lottery tickets and the taxes paid on winnings go toward education
and other beneficial programs.

Some recent stories involve targets receiving a letter about the
Mega Millions jackpot that alleges to be from the FBI and the
Federal Deposit Insurance Corporation (FDIC). These convinc-
ing letters advise recipients that they've won the lottery but that

to receive the winnings, they must wire a processing fee into an account. This is an advance fee, and it's a scam. The letters often look real, printed on quality paper stock and emblazoned with the official seals of the FBI and the FDIC. But here's what you need to remember: Neither the FBI nor the FDIC will ever send a letter to a lottery winner—and no fee is ever required to collect winnings from a lottery.

Another version of this scam involves a phone call from someone who introduces himself as a government official saying you've won a government-sponsored sweepstakes. Sometimes the scammers say they are from the "National Consumer Protection Agency" or the "National Sweepstakes Bureau," both of which are fake organizations. Sometimes they say they are calling from the Federal Trade Commission, which is a real entity—but the calls are fake. No government agency will do any such thing. If you buy a lottery ticket, it's up to you to come forward to claim your prize.

These sweepstakes scammers often say that you:

- Must pay taxes or service charges before you can collect any winnings. Not so. Applicable taxes on winnings don't kick in until after you've collected your money.
- Must wire money to an agent of Lloyds of London or some other well-known insurance company so that delivery of your money is "secure." Again, no. Even mega checks from big government lottery windfalls don't require you to pay an insurer to access or "protect" the money.

Another type of state-run lottery scam takes advantage of people who have actually bought a winning lottery ticket. In one such ticket scam, retailers who sell the tickets, often convenience stores and gas stations, shortchange unsuspecting customers who have returned to the store to scan their tickets. These dishonest clerks will tell their customers that they have won far less money than they really have, keeping the rest for themselves, or tell winners that they haven't won at all, simply keeping the ticket and claiming the prize for themselves. In one such reported scam, a Raleigh, North Carolina, store clerk was arrested for bilking a customer out of a winning lottery ticket by scanning the ticket behind the counter and telling the customer that the ticket was a loser. The clerk then pocketed the $1,000 winnings. But the customer was actually an undercover agent, and the clerk was arrested and ultimately given twenty-four months' probation.

There have also been cases where clerks ripped winning scratch tickets out of the owner's hands and refused to give them back. In one New York City convenience store, a worker refused to hand back an elderly man's $14 million winning Lotto ticket. Eventually the man received his winnings, but not without several visits to the store and complaints to law enforcement.

To help reduce these crimes, lottery officials in some states have installed scanners in many stores, which allow customers to read their own tickets. If you think you may have a winning ticket or just want to check whether you do:

- Always sign the back of a lottery ticket as soon as you buy it, to demonstrate ownership.
- If possible, bring a trusted relative or friend with you to check tickets and collect your winnings if they are less than the amount a state guarantees a retailer will give you

(this amount can vary state to state). For larger wins, it makes sense to contact lottery officials to collect.

- If you bought a winning scratch ticket, do not hand it to the clerk until he or she has visually acknowledged that the ticket is a winner.
- If you can, scan the ticket yourself or check winning numbers online with your state's lottery commission.

One thing you *do* have to pay if you win a lottery: taxes. But not until the following April 15, *after* you collect your winnings.

SIX SAVVY STRATEGIES FOR BEATING A GOVERNMENT IMPOSTOR SCAM

1. **Never wire money.** Scammers often try to bully people into wiring money to a bank account or putting money on a prepaid debit card and sending it to them. Don't do this.
2. **Don't pay a fee to get a grant or sweepstakes winnings.** If you have to pay to collect a grant or sweepstakes money, it's a scam.
3. **Don't give unknown callers financial information.** Never give out or confirm personal information, account numbers, or other identifying material to unknown callers.
4. **Verify all communications asking for money or telling you that you've won or received money.** Con artists use official-sounding names, phone numbers,

letterhead, logos, and paperwork to try to convince you they are legit.

5. **Verify ID.** If someone claims to be from the government, a local agency, or a utility, ask for identification in person or an ID number over the phone. Then verify the information by calling the agency he or she claims to be from—and also confirm with that agency that this person should be contacting you.

6. **Report the scam.** If you think you have received a fraudulent government phone call or letter, file a complaint at www.ftc.gov/complaint. Be sure to include:

- Date and time of the call.
- Scanned copy of the letter if applicable.
- Name of the government agency the impostor used.
- What the caller said, including the amount of money you supposedly owe or won, as well as the payment method requested.
- Phone number of the caller. Even though scammers use spoofing to simulate real numbers, or create fake ones, law enforcement agents can still potentially track a number to identify the caller.
- Any other details from the call.

It's easy to be fooled by these scams. After all, we trust the government to have our best interests in mind. That's why it's so important to know the signs of an official-sounding scam so you can protect yourself and others.

RULE #3

Preserve Your Digital Presence

8

Fend Off Cyberattacks

In the past twelve months, pieces of your personal information have likely been stolen, leaving you vulnerable to identity theft, which we talked about in chapter 3. How? Cyberattacks, a growing problem that leaves us vulnerable to identity thieves and other scammers. There were 918 data breaches that compromised 1.9 billion data records in the first six months of 2017, according to Gemalto, a digital security firm. That was an increase of 164 percent over the last six months of 2016. Of the 918 breaches, twenty-two of the largest data breaches compromised more than 1 million records. Credit agency Equifax acknowledged that the information of 143 million Americans was compromised in a single 2017 data attack. Let's walk through how cyberattacks work and how to fend them off.

In 2010, FBI Special Agent Robert Cameron, a computer expert, was waiting for a nongovernmental computer training class to begin when he used his instructor-provided computer to check the local news. The computer became sluggish and began to function improperly. Numerous pop-ups demanded money for "anti-virus" software. The next day, one of the local news organizations apologized to readers, explaining that an advertisement it thought was legitimate had installed a virus on the computers of users who had visited its site. "You didn't have to interact with the website at all or click anything. There's nothing the user could have done to prevent it," Cameron said. "The pop-ups would keep coming to the point that you couldn't do anything on the computer. You'd have to click the link and buy the software." Cameron and other FBI agents investigated the hacking crime and found that a Latvian hacker was behind what turned out to be a sophisticated attack.

Peteris Sahurovs and some of his associates had created a fake advertising company called RevolTech Marketing earlier that year. They contacted the local news site to purchase advertising for a "client," a brand-name American hotel chain that, it turned out, had no knowledge of the scam. RevolTech then created an ad for the hotel that directed people to what appeared to be a legitimate site. The hackers waited until they believed the ad had been adequately tested and then swapped in an ad that would direct computers to a malware-infected website.

Even if users did not click on the ad, the malware installed on their computer. Once the computer was infected, the only way to get rid of the malware was by purchasing fake antivirus software for about $50. The FBI and the Latvian State Police, working together, eventually tracked down and arrested Sahurovs, who fled before his extradition hearing. Five years later, in February 2018, he pleaded guilty to conspiracy to commit wire fraud and was sentenced to thirty-three months in prison.

By the time you read this, we may well have surpassed the $6 trillion cost that cybercrime is predicted to reach by 2021. Today, hacking is about stealing money, but the malevolent uses of technology will get more aggressive and dangerous as time goes on. I predict that technology will be used as a tool by terrorists who want to do physical harm to people. Today we can shut off someone's pacemaker or commandeer a car from thirty-five feet away. In the not too distant future, we'll be able to do those things from five hundred or five thousand miles away. Someday, more and more people will come to realize that social media websites are not necessarily good things: If you can control the psychology of two billion people, the risk of real harm becomes insidious. We give away far too much information on social media. This sounds scary, but it's important that we know this, because it encourages us to use caution.

Because at the end of the day, hackers do not cause breaches by themselves. Crooks look for open doors to enter so they can take advantage of what is inside. Most hacking happens because companies and individuals open digital doors or fail to close them. But we can *all* fight malevolent uses of technology with technology. I believe each of us can do better at reducing and preventing security breaches right now. As an individual— whether you're using a smartphone, tablet, desktop, or laptop— you have to practice what I call defensive computing. You also have to have a plan in place in case you *are* hacked.

MALWARE: ADVANCED PERSISTENT THREAT

If "advanced persistent threat" sounds like something out of an action-adventure film, you're not all that off base. What I'm talking about is a broad range of software that is programmed with evil intent and, as you read this, is running on tens of millions of computers around the world. Otherwise known as malware, it has been around for more than forty years and is growing more powerful every day. That's what Cameron and his fellow FBI agents ran into.

Simson Garfinkel, a computer scientist and expert in digital forensics, says that defenses like so-called strong passwords (which I discuss at length in the next chapter) are rendered impotent under sophisticated hacking conditions like the one I just described. And hacking could get more complex. "We are going to see more AI-assisted hacking, in which AI [artificial intelligence] agents appear to be humans and convince people to do unreasonable things," the scientist predicts.

The most common defense against malware is to install antivirus software on your digital devices. But, said Garfinkel, "antivirus software only works against threats that are well known. Today, targeted threats increasingly involve new, unpublicized threats." Also, he said, people will override antivirus software if they want to run a program that is being blocked by it, defeating the purpose of running antivirus protection in the first place.

Hackers can also write sophisticated programs for malware that remain undetected for days, weeks, and even months, according to Garfinkel. Because antivirus software is often unable to match the power of malicious programs and unable to fight these programs, you often have to take other, more old-fashioned or manual precautions, including not clicking on unknown links and not opening files you receive by email unless you know that the email and the attachment are legitimate.

The news is mixed for your phone, depending on what you use. If you have an Android phone, he advises you not to download apps from any website other than Google Play. And don't open attachments on your device—it is far safer to put them on Google Drive and convert them into Google Docs, which you can view on the Google interface.

Malware can attack an iPhone, but it's very rare. Garkinfel has found that Apple devices are safer from malware than Windows XP is. "For most people, the easiest way to have a secure computing environment is to exclusively use an Apple iPad or a Google Chromebook," he said. "Both of these are managed by Apple and Google, respectively. They do a better job than you can" of protecting you against malicious hacking and software.

There are several ways a hacker can wreak havoc on your computer with malware. While some software, like spyware, can have innocuous uses (like keeping track of your child's movements on the Internet), the following, in the wrong hands, can all be used for destructive and fraudulent purposes. Many versions of malicious software can be removed manually by opening up your browser settings and resetting it to the default setting. Other times, you may have to use antivirus software to locate hidden malware on your computer and have the protection system remove it for you. What follows is a lexicon of malware you need to know.

Malware's Dirty Dozen

1. **Malicious browser helper objects (BHOs):** BHOs gain entry through downloads, sometimes unwittingly on your part. It works like this: When you open a browser, a BHO begins running in the background. Unfortunately, a BHO can succeed in capturing information about where you're going on the web, or in enticing you to click on ads for unwanted products and services. This may not always be malicious, but it can expose you to spam, unwanted toolbar add-ons, extension programs, and pop-up advertisements.

2. **Browser hijackers:** This malware modifies your web browser settings, often by using software downloaded unknowingly from phony security websites without your permission, and redirects you to websites you had no intention of visiting. You know those pop-up windows warning you that your device is in "danger"? It's in danger from that link in the pop-up window. If you click on it, your device could be hijacked. A browser hijacker can also change the default browser search engine or home page. So, for example, instead of Google or Bing, it might reset it to a malicious search engine that slows down your movement on the Internet, or it might generate numerous pop-up ads. The aim of a browser hijacker is to help criminals earn fraudulent advertising revenue.

3. **Ransomware:** Ransomware is malicious software that enters the victim's computer system through a downloaded file or network vulnerability and covertly encrypts files on the victim's computer. Without knowing the key

to decrypt the information, the victim can't access files. Of course, the cybercriminals will happily provide the decryption key—for a price. That is called extortion, and it's illegal, of course. It doesn't matter to them whether it's your personal computer or one belonging to a business, hospital, school, or even law enforcement agency.

4. **Keyloggers:** Keyloggers, also known as keystroke loggers, can record the real-time activity of computer users, including the keys they press. Keyloggers do have legitimate uses. For instance, information technology workers use them to troubleshoot technical problems with computers and business networks. Parents can use them to monitor their children's usage. But cybercriminals can also use them to steal sensitive information. The programs are downloaded unwittingly through a malicious URL or download that looks legitimate. Once a keylogger has access to a computer, it can capture passwords, take screenshots, record URLs you visit, steal instant messaging (IM) conversations, and copy emails. It then automatically sends this information to bad actors in remote locations. Finding malicious keyloggers can be difficult, because they often reside in invisible or hidden folders or directories. Anti-keylogging programs have been developed to thwart keylogging systems, and these are often effective when used properly.

5. **Backdoors:** If you've ever had a problem with your computer, you may have allowed a technician to access it remotely. This is done through an Internet portal called a backdoor. Hackers, too, can use secret portals to gain illicit access to a computer system. In these scenarios,

cybercriminals install a backdoor system on a computer, which allows them to come and go freely and remotely. In 2013, Reuters reported that up to 200,000 National Security Agency (NSA) documents had been leaked to the media by Edward Snowden, which in turn revealed a decades-long effort by the agency to pressure makers of encryption systems and other companies into installing backdoors into their products so they could be hacked by government spies.

6. **Rootkits:** This is a collection of malicious and clandestine computer software that gives unauthorized users or criminals access to a computer and areas of its software system. It's often installed by piggybacking on software you trust and install. The rootkit plants itself in a hidden location on the device. There have been cases where the rootkit was installed by the computer manufacturer, to be used for remote diagnosis and troubleshooting, but vulnerabilities in the rootkit opened it to malicious users. Hackers can use the rootkit to control the device without its owner knowing it.

7. **Trojan horse:** This term comes from mythology, which tells the story of Greeks who built a large wooden horse that the people of Troy pulled into the city, thinking it was a gift. Hidden inside the horse were soldiers, who emerged after dark and opened the city's gates to let their fellow soldiers in, thus overrunning the city. In computers, a Trojan horse makes its way onto your device in the same way as the rootkit does. Once the Trojan horse is installed, a hacker can take control of your computer.

8. **Internet worms:** This malware duplicates itself to spread to uninfected computers. Before the use of networks, worms infected computers via storage systems like discs and USB drives. Your computer could be infected if you work for a company that encourages you to use your own device—when you bring a laptop or tablet into the office and sign on to the company network, you could be vulnerable.

9. **Trojan dialer:** A dialer is a software system that allows numbers to be dialed automatically. Malicious dialers can self-install onto a computer, often without your knowledge after you've visited a website, especially gaming, pornography, and file-sharing sites. They can also be unwittingly installed if someone illegally downloads music, which can be a concern for those of you with younger children who may not always understand that they are downloading a song illegally. These malicious dialers can drop your normal Internet connection in favor of another number, such as a 900 premium-rate or International Direct Dialing (IDD) number. This can lead to exorbitant per-minute charges for Internet phone calls.

10. **Adware:** You've probably seen adware, because it's so obvious. Usually, these ads show up in annoying pop-up windows that can be difficult to control and eliminate. Adware can track where you go on the Internet and attempt to figure out what kinds of ads might appeal to you. It can also make your device sluggish. You'll notice that pages take a long time to load, and other functions of your computer slow down.

11. **Spyware:** Spyware is often, though not always, malicious. As I've mentioned, parents can install legitimate spyware on children's computers to track their movements online. Employers can install spyware as well, to make sure that employees are not goofing off at work and looking at websites that they shouldn't be looking at during office hours. Illegitimate spyware, however, is used to track a computer owner's movements online in an effort to gain and steal personal information. Like a lot of malicious software, spyware will slow down your computer.

12. **Botnet:** A botnet is a kind of robot that works over a network. In this context, it's a malicious robot. For cybercriminals who spend their time writing and operating malware, a botnet allows them to manage a number of infected systems simultaneously. Since even the cleverest cybercriminals can't manually log on to every single computer they've infected, they depend on botnets to do that work for them automatically.

HOW TO AVOID BEING A VICTIM OF MALWARE

- **Keep away from kiosk computers.** Avoid using public computers at hotels, airports, libraries, and business centers to access webmail accounts, because there is no way to tell whether these computers are infected with malware or not. If they are, your email account could be compromised.

- **Close out open Wi-Fi.** Those public wireless access points that don't require an encryption key to access them may seem easy to use, but keep in mind that they don't protect your data as it transits through the air. "This means that your username and password can be 'sniffed' by anyone else using the access point as well," Garfinkel wrote in an article published in MIT's *Technology Review.* "The only way to protect yourself is to be sure that the websites and e-mail servers you use employ SSL ('https:') for everything, not just for logging in." The same open Wi-Fi access points that can sniff out your password use what are called "man-in-the-middle" attacks. That's what happens when your computer sends information to the wrong website, which takes what it wants and then passes it to the correct one—so that the communication channel seems fine. "Man-in-the-middle attacks are especially easy over Wi-Fi, but they can take place anywhere on the Internet," wrote Garfinkel. Be sure that the certificate of the SSL-enabled website is legitimate, he advises. (A forged certificate will tell your browser that it's connecting to the right site using SSL.) Most people also ignore certificate mismatch errors.

- **Think different.** Many websites, like those for newspapers and magazines and online shopping outlets, require that you set up an account with an email address and a password to access content. Don't use the same password you use to access that email account. Otherwise the website's owners and anyone who happens to hack into the website will be able to take over your email account.

- **Authenticate.** Some websites have systems that let you strengthen your security by using a cell phone or even a handheld security token that can be used in conjunction with or instead of a password, sort of like an electronic key card that opens a hotel door. Sometimes these devices generate a number like a PIN to the owner to access a device. The security token can also be called a Universal Serial Bus (USB) token, cryptographic token, hardware token, hard token, authentication token, or key fob. These systems offer a layer of security that is stronger than a password alone, though unfortunately they can still be defeated by sophisticated hackers.

- **Don't go it alone.** Maintaining multiple accounts with email providers gives you some backup in case your email is hacked.

- **Go old school.** Your data should never be kept only on the cloud or only on your laptop or other device. Print out important information and keep it in a home lockbox. Make a backup copy on an external hard drive. That way, if you lose your online access for any reason, you have a copy of important information in another form. Routinely back up computer files and store them offline to minimize information lost, should a ransomware attack occur.

- **Stay up to date.** Keep software up to date to protect against known vulnerabilities.

- **Stay secure.** Use security software or antivirus protection to help prevent computer invasions. Read user and technology reviews of the latest systems to stay up to date on antivirus software advances and pros and cons. Look for systems that offer on-demand malware scans, ratings showing low risk and high risk for malware and blocking of malicious URLs.

- **Beware of stranger danger.** Download only trustworthy software, and do not click on unknown email attachments or links.

Hall of Shame: Anonymous

Anonymous first came on the scene in 2003. It is not an individual, but a decentralized group of hackers without a known hierarchy or even official membership. Despite this amorphous persona, Anonymous may be the best-known "hacker" of all time—and the most inscrutable. Members often wear a grinning Guy Fawkes mask, which they use as identification during public protests and other events. (Guy Fawkes was a British soldier and a participant in what is known as the Gunpowder Plot of 1605, which sought to blow up the palace at Westminster during the official opening of Parliament, to protest increasing oppression of Roman Catholics in England.)

Anonymous has been credited with attacking several substantial global targets, including Amazon, PayPal, and Sony; parts of the so-called dark web; the governments of Australia, India, Syria, and the United States; Donald Trump; ISIS's website; and dozens of other victims. On a Sunday afternoon in 2011, Anonymous attacked San Francisco's Bay Area Rapid Transit website www.bart.gov, in response to BART's blocking cell phone service to try and stop a protest after an unarmed man named Oscar Grant was shot by BART police at an Oakland train station. In 2012, after the FBI shut down Megaupload, a now defunct Hong Kong–based company providing online file storage and viewing services, over copyright laws, Anonymous retaliated by shutting down the websites of the Recording Industry Association of America and the Motion Picture Association of America.

YOU DON'T HAVE MAIL: EMAIL HACKING

At presentations across the country, many people tell me how hackers took over their email accounts and used those accounts to send phony messages to people in their address book. Oftentimes, someone receives an email claiming that a person they know has been robbed, so they need to wire money. Sometimes the incident happens "overseas" and coincides with the fact that the person whose email was stolen is in fact abroad. This makes the scam very effective. Sometimes people tell me the email hack was later used to send out spam. I think we've all received those emails that say, "Hey, I tried this great vitamin (or disinfectant, or any number of other products). Check it out!" with a short link that will take you to a malicious URL that can infect your computer. Or it may just take you to a site that is trying to sell you something you don't want. I get emails like these at least twice a month.

How to avoid email hacks

Email can get hacked in a variety of ways—either via a hack of your provider, a hack of a system where you use your email address and password, malware, or a con artist who has sniffed you out while you were using public Wi-Fi. If your email account has been hacked, here's how you can reclaim it.

- **Diagnose and detect.** The Federal Trade Commission recommends updating or installing reputable security software or antivirus protection and running a scan. As I mentioned earlier, look for antivirus software that can detect and delete (or quarantine) known malware.

- **Change your password.** If you're lucky, the hacker merely logged in to your account to send mass messages, under your identity, to those in your address book, without locking you out with a password change. So change your password immediately, and if you use similar passwords on other accounts, change them, too. If you're locked out of your account, first try using the "Forgot Your Password" link and answering security questions. If you can't regain access, contact your Internet service company by phone or from another email account, or in an online chat.

- **Enable two-factor authentication.** Amazon, Apple, Facebook, Google, Microsoft, and Twitter have an option to enable two-factor authentications. Many banks and other institutions do, too. In addition to a password, two-factor authentication requires a second form of authentication, such as a cell phone number, once enabled. After logging into an online account, you'll receive a code, usually four to seven digits, in a text to your phone or an email. Only after entering that code, typically for initial logins from a new or unrecognized device, can you access your account.

- **Divide and conquer.** If you haven't already done so, establish a separate email account, such as a free Gmail, Hotmail, or Yahoo account, to use solely for online purchases, online banking, and bill paying.

- **Be a copycat.** Make a hard copy of your email address book contacts and file it in a safe place so you're protected, should future hacking occur.

TOSS YOUR COOKIES

If a store or organization tells you there has been a data breach and your information might have been compromised, don't ignore it. If your information was hacked, you are four times more likely to have your identity stolen the year *after* the breach than the general public is. That's why privacy advocates and security experts are concerned about the vast amount of personal data that companies are collecting about us. Congress is considering "Do Not Track" legislation, which would allow web users to opt out of data collecting. Until then, it's up to you to keep your activity private, including on the Internet. To limit tracking, enable your browser's privacy setting, which prevents websites from installing cookies that can monitor your movements. (See the browser's "Help" menu for details.)

CAR HACKING

Charlie Miller and Chris Valasek are what you could call professional car hackers. In 2015, they made headlines when they hacked into a Jeep that *Wired* writer Andy Greenberg was driving. He knew the guys were going to hack the car—he was willingly being hacked so he could write about it later—he just didn't know when or how. In his firsthand account of the episode, he described a series of unexpected events: "Though I hadn't touched the dashboard, the vents in the Jeep Cherokee started blasting cold air at the maximum setting. . . . Next the radio switched to the local hip hop station and began blaring Skee-lo at full volume. I spun the control knob left and hit the power button, to no avail. Then the windshield wipers turned on, and wiper fluid blurred the glass."

Car hacking is, at the moment, merely a way of pranking drivers. It's still fairly rare, but as cars become more and more autonomous and connected to networks, I predict that it will become more of a problem. Your digital life now extends to your car, and it can be hacked. For about twenty years, vehicles have contained computers that control a variety of functions, including the engine, brakes, and steering. Newer cars have diagnostic and navigation systems and entertainment systems that use wireless networks to connect passengers with streaming music and videos and the Internet. These vehicle computers, or "connected devices," could be a pathway for hackers to get access to your data (about where you go and what you do when you get there) and, as Miller and Valasek demonstrated, control over your vehicle. Car hacking not only puts your data at risk, but it also could put you and your passengers in physical danger. It could put entire communities at risk, if, for instance, terrorists or other bad actors hacked fleets of vehicles to carry out violent activities.

As carmakers continue to expand autonomous features in new cars, including self-driving technology, and work with states and municipalities to connect cars to wireless transit networks, cars may become increasingly open to hacking. To try to stem the tide of car hacking, or at least to warn people of the potential danger, in March 2016 the FBI, Department of Transportation, and National Highway Traffic Safety Administration jointly released a public service announcement that warned consumers about the potential dangers of car hacking.

Automakers and legislators have taken notice of these concerns and are working to make vehicles more secure against potential cyberattacks. In the meantime, the PSA serves as a high-visibility warning to consumers about the need to protect their vehicles. The PSA recommends that consumers take the following steps to protect the cybersecurity of their vehicle:

- Keep the automotive software up to date and follow any recalls that require manual patches of the vehicle's software.
- Avoid making unauthorized changes to the vehicle's software.
- Be cautious about connecting third-party devices to the car's network.
- Be careful about giving strangers physical access to the vehicle.
- Inform the FBI of any suspected cyberattacks on a vehicle.

PARKING LOT PERILS

Your digital life can even be hacked at the local shopping center parking lot. Scammers place phony parking tickets on cars, which direct owners to an "official" website that claims to have photos of the alleged violation. The tickets look incredibly real, thanks to new handheld digital printers that can create authentic-looking tickets. In one version of the scam, when you do go to the website, you inadvertently download a nasty virus that can compromise your computer. In another scam, victims are directed to a website that gives them an option to "pay the fine"—and asks them to provide their credit card info and pay a fee. Here's how to tell if a parking ticket is fake:

- **You're legit.** You're parked in a legitimate space. Look around. Are you parked properly and in a designated space? If so, the ticket may be phony.
- **Tourist trap.** Out-of-towners can be especially vulnerable, because scammers assume they may not be familiar with local parking rules and so may be more easily convinced they've done something wrong. If you're from out of state and get a ticket on your windshield, be extra skeptical and call the county clerk's office to check on the legitimacy of the ticket.
- **It's a dot-com.** Does the website have ".gov" or ".com" at the end of it? Local, state, and federal government use ".gov," so it may be a scam if the website is a ".com" or a ".net." I would also be skeptical of a ".org."
- **It's insecure.** Government agencies do allow you to pay tickets online, so if you go to a payment portal on a website, you should see an "https"—the signal of a secure site. If it's not there, log off immediately.
- **Check, please.** Call the municipality's department of transportation to verify that the ticket is real.
- **Picture it.** Some consumers use their smartphone to take a picture of their parked car and the signage around

it if they have any doubts at all about the parking space. If there's a visible address nearby, try to include that in the photo as well. That way, if the ticket is real but you disagree with it, the photo gives some ammunition to fight it. If the ticket is phony, no worries.

WILL HACK WHILE TRAVELING

Just because you're on vacation doesn't mean hackers and scammers are also taking time off. They aren't. Living in a global world means we have a great deal of access to cultures and people—but that means scammers do, too. When I was traveling the world as a phony airline pilot, I would write bad checks to fund some of my trip expenses, and there were very few times, if any, when I took a "break" as a scammer. So while you can loosen up at the local botanical garden and let your hair down at the beach, don't let your guard down, or more than your vacation could be ruined. It's not just pickpockets and street scammers you have to watch out for; hackers are out there, too, from the boulevards of Paris to the markets of Istanbul. Here are my best practices for staying safe from hackers while on the road.

- **If you don't need it, leave it.** Are you sure you need your laptop when you go on vacation? I advise business travelers to use a dedicated travel laptop, rather than taking their everyday laptop with them. The Google Chromebook is widely considered by experts to be the most secure operating system on the market. Its automatic system updates, verified boot, and system drive encryption help to keep your information safe from attacks. Nothing is 100 percent secure, of course, and some Chrome operating systems have a bug that could allow a hacker to access encrypted data. I also recommend using an iPhone or iPad for mobile communications like email and instant messaging, instead of a laptop, because they are much more secure and resistant to hacking.

- **Shut it down.** When you're done using any device, don't just close it or put it to sleep. Log off and turn it off. This protects your data from scammers who might take advantage of open hotel room doors to do some cyber snooping on your vulnerable devices. If your hotel room does not have a safe or lockbox, ask for one and keep your devices locked inside when you're out.

- **Use privacy safeguards.** Before traveling anywhere, make sure your social media safeguards are turned on. Review the privacy settings on your Facebook and Twitter accounts to ensure that you will receive a text message or email whenever someone tries to change your password or log in to your account from an unauthorized computer. If you receive an alert when you're at home or out of town, change your password immediately.

- **Don't get skimmed.** Beware of "skimmers," malicious card readers used by thieves to steal your credit card information. These readers are often placed on ATMs or gas pumps. To be safe, especially when traveling, limit your use of ATMs to those inside banks, and pay for gas with a credit card inside the station instead of at the pump. Don't use a debit card. Unlike with a debit card, if a credit card is skimmed, the credit card company will not hold you liable, and you will not have to wait a month or more while your bank does an investigation.

- **Guilty until proven innocent.** Assume that all Wi-Fi networks outside of your home or place of work, including airports, hotels, restaurants, shopping centers, stores, and, yes, even public libraries, are out to steal your information. Don't use public Wi-Fi for anything besides web browsing, where you don't need to log on or provide sensitive information—*especially* in a foreign country.

- **Stay informed.** I always look at the "International Travel" page of the U.S. Department of State for current information on scams being perpetrated in countries I'm visiting, what to watch out for, and how to protect myself. I recommend you do the same. You can also contact the U.S. consulate to find up-to-date information and cautions.

- **Take charge when you recharge.** Don't charge your devices with anything other than your own chargers plugged directly into the wall or into your adapter. Cyber crooks can install malware on hotel and other public docking stations and get access to your computer that way. Never connect any USB drive or other removable media to your computer unless it's one that you own.

- **Avoid in-house computers.** Crooks can (and do) install malware on machines made available to the public at libraries, hotels, and other businesses. If you have to use them, do so only for tasks where no log-in or financial info is required—which means using them for basic research purposes.

- **Pack new passwords with your passport.** Before leaving on your trip, change log-in credentials and passwords for mobile device apps. Use two-factor authentication, if possible.

RISKIEST HACKING DESTINATIONS

Where are you most at risk? You might be surprised. The United States is risky: Hacking of files and data on handheld devices occurs about five million times per year, according to Keeper Security, a password manager firm. Other research done by Symantec, which makes Norton antivirus products, has found that the riskiest U.S. cities are Seattle, Boston, Washington, D.C., San Francisco, and Raleigh, North Carolina. But despite the nation's population, robust use of mobile devices, and availability of public Wi-Fi, which is ubiquitous, only about 1.5 percent of people become hacking victims—putting the nation in the middle of the pack for hacked-while-traveling risk.

In terms of per capita hacking, the United Kingdom may be the riskiest, followed by Spain, France, Poland, Canada, Italy, Portugal, the Netherlands, and Greece. Mobile threats are less likely to occur in China, India, Brazil, and Russia, because they are not as prosperous as the United States or the UK. Language barriers make Japan, Germany, and some other countries less attractive targets. These statistics can, of course, change over time.

HACKING THE FUTURE

There is some good news on the horizon—honest and committed people are working on ways to stay several steps ahead of cyberattacks. But we must remain vigilant, and in the next chapter I underscore this with an argument against passwords, a subject that is extremely important to me. I understand that it is inevitable that people will continue to use passwords at least in the short term, and that passwords will continue to evolve, expand, and change. It's best for me to tell you how to stay safe as you journey through cyberspace—but it's up to you to be proactive about your own security. So read on.

9

Passwords Are for Treehouses: Why We Need to Get Rid of Them

How many times in a typical day or week do you type in a mishmash of numbers, letters, and symbols to access a website or an online account? I can't even count how many times I log in with a username and password. We think that our passwords keep us safe, but it's a fantasy. They don't protect us from hacking or maintain the privacy of our online information, and I think they should be abolished. They are old-fashioned and useless, and the only extra layer they add is annoyance for consumers, not protection.

If you take a moment to look around at the technology that surrounds you today—iPhones, online banking and shopping, Google, and smart TVs, to name a few—none of them were invented in the 1960s. Yet the most prevalent security mechanism still used—usernames and passwords—was invented in 1963, more than half a century ago. Passwords were never intended for high-security needs. They were originally created to help secure individual time spent on computers used by multiple people; this was called time-sharing. Passwords gave us personal access to our own documents, Internet searches, and conversations, making a shared computer an essentially "private" device.

With the advent of the Internet age, passwords soon became the norm for consumers. Unfortunately, the widely adopted process of submitting a username and password to access personal information and gain private entry to websites was never meant to protect us—and it still doesn't. Widespread use quickly translated into a rampant vulnerability. The inventor of the computer password, Fernando Corbato, now ninety-two, said himself that passwords have "become kind of a nightmare with the World Wide Web." In 2016, Michael Chertoff, who served as secretary of Homeland Security from 2005 to 2009, echoed those views on CNBC, saying, "A closer examination of major breaches reveals a common theme: In every 'major headline' breach, the attack vector has been the common password. The reason is simple: The password is by far the weakest link in cybersecurity."

I agree with him, and I agree with him that the next step is to rid ourselves of passwords. "By making their replacement a national priority," Chertoff said, "the government can help rally both industry and agencies to adopt stronger solutions that make password-driven breaches a thing of the past."

WHY PASSWORDS DON'T WORK

What makes passwords so vulnerable to data breaches, and why are they an insufficient line of defense against cybercriminals? One reason is static passwords—the use of the same unchanged passwords, unchanged over time, for different service providers and accounts. When a large database is hacked, the effects of the breach are often seen across many other companies and platforms because of the one vulnerable connective thread: a single password.

Say you want to move money from your bank account. You expect the bank to move the money only when you ask, and not when a fraudster does. Thus, if you were to identify yourself with static credentials only—like passwords—how will the bank really know whether it's you or your "evil twin" online? If hackers get hold of your password via phishing, malware, or data breach, they have the proverbial keys to your financial kingdom. The same goes for your confidential health data. If you want to see your private records, you are required to identify yourself to the healthcare provider. With a static password, however, there's no guarantee that it's really you on the other end.

If you thought—as we're constantly told—that making passwords longer and more complex and changing them frequently makes them safer, well, that doesn't enhance their efficacy, either. "Length and complexity doesn't increase security but are used by organizations to signal they care about security," said digital forensics expert Simson Garfinkel. Academic research that began in 2008 showed that long passwords do not significantly increase security. Changing passwords generally involves swapping out one frequently used password for another.

Cybercriminals generally don't guess passwords; they steal them, either through mass theft of data from large organizations, public Wi-Fi monitoring and theft, phishing attacks via email and malware (see page 172), and software that helps criminals crack passwords. Typically, we're told not to use searchable information like our mother's maiden name, our pet, or our childhood street name in passwords. But even if you choose a random assortment of characters, letters, and numbers, you're not really more secure. Stealing a long or complicated password using these methods is the same as stealing a short and simple one. Not to mention that remembering long and complex passwords is difficult; writing down passwords can be a security risk; and using a digital password "manager" is a nuisance.

STUCK ON PASSWORD LEVELS

There are five levels of passwords, described here, and we are generally stuck at level 1.

Level 1: Static or "universal" (same for every website we use and rarely if ever changed over time) username and password. Where most of us are now.

Level 2: Static username and password with multi- or two-factor authentication, which requires two pieces of information instead of a single password; knowledge-based authentication, a second piece of secret personal information shared only with the website; and one-time passwords, which change every time you log on to a website or a device. Some of us have moved to this level.

Level 3: Completely dynamic and constantly changing passwords. In other words, passwords change frequently or each time you log on to a website.

Level 4: Remote identity proofing by scanning government-issued IDs. These IDs do not store any personally identifiable information. The ID-scanning machine reads a code that is instantaneously sent to a data bureau to confirm the person's identity. A selfie match to the photo on the ID can also be an option.

Level 5: In-person verification proofing (IPV) via government-issued IDs. In this process, the individual has to produce an original proof of identity (with a signature and photo) and proof of address to validate his or her identity. IPV can be done online via technology like Skype.

DATA BREACHES AND PASSWORD THEFT

The time has come to change passwords, and certainly for us to move past level 1 identification (see "Stuck on Password Levels," page 194). Unfortunately, history has shown us that the implementation of higher and better levels of digital protection by institutions, organizations, and businesses has often been too slow. The history of digital data breaches shows us just how slow we have been to react to an ever-growing problem.

Data breaches did occur before 2005—when 136 data breaches were reported—but the majority of large data breaches have been reported since then. The amount of data available to criminals has grown, and so has the number of breaches. In 2017, the number of U.S. data breach incidents hit a new record high of 1,579, affecting billions of people, according to the 2017 Annual Data Breach Year-End Review. This was a dramatic 44.7 percent increase over the already record-high figures for 2016.

It is no longer surprising to hear that yet another major company failed to protect itself and its customers against cybercriminals' concerted efforts to steal money and private information. When you conduct an informed postmortem on many of these breaches, you discover a recurring pattern: Stolen passwords and static credentials are to blame.

In late 2017, the team at 4iQ, a company dedicated to surveying the dark web for exposed identity records, discovered a file containing a staggering database of 1.4 billion unencrypted text credentials—the largest database of its kind found to date. Collected from myriad sources, including Netflix, LinkedIn, and Last.fm, the forty-one-gigabyte file hand-delivered static information on a silver platter for even unsophisticated hackers to exploit. The data, organized alphabetically, depicted how infrequently passwords changed over time and across accounts—and many of them, troublingly, were still in active use.

In terms of scope, the breach was almost twice as big as the previous largest credential exposure. Needless to say, the idea of your static credentials being freely distributed around the dark web to faceless hackers is certainly a sobering wake-up call for people who have been lackadaisical about their personal security. Regardless of who's to blame for these types of data leaks, the time has come to abolish the use of the ultimate culprit, static credentials, once and for all.

Hall of Shame: Guccifer

Romanian Marcel Lehel Lazar was a taxi driver before he became one of the world's most notorious hackers and password thieves. Lazar admitted to perpetrating a string of social media and email account takeovers while using the hacker handle Guccifer, a combination of Gucci and Lucifer. From 2012 to 2014, Lazar is believed to have hacked social media and email accounts, including Gmail, Facebook, and AOL, by stealing passwords from Romanian celebrities and officials and U.S. officials like former Secretary of State Colin Powell and President George W. Bush. After gaining unauthorized access to these email and social media accounts, Lazar publicly released his victims' private email correspondence, medical and financial information, and personal photographs. Lazar even impersonated one victim after compromising his account. The hacker first revealed Hillary Clinton's use of a private email address when she was serving as the U.S. secretary of state, and he leaked pictures of President Bush's paintings. He was sentenced by U.S. District Judge James C. Cacheris to fifty-two months in prison, followed by three years of supervised release, for unauthorized access to a protected computer and aggravated identity theft.

Is There a Successful Alternative to Static Passwords?

Initially, to combat the gaping weaknesses inherent in static credentials, the industry turned to additional authentication factors to protect employees and consumers alike. For instance, two-factor authentication, which I talked about in the previous chapter, might ask for a password and a PIN. Virtually all large online services now require some form of two-factor authentication, or "2FA." A clear example of such technology is the process of withdrawing money from an ATM, where your debit card and a four-digit passcode serve as the two factors necessary to gain access. Many companies now require your password and then generate a four- or six-digit passcode sent in a text or email.

Beyond that lies the umbrella term "multi-factor authentication" (MFA). For example, hard tokens or biometrics might be required, on top of two-factor authentication. Most of these methods still require a password within their framework, so the issue of static credentials remains.

Why Can't We Just Use Short Message Service (SMS) with One-Time Passwords?

Even with the extra level of security, accounts are still being compromised. In 2016, for example, Black Lives Matter activist DeRay Mckesson had his Twitter account hacked, and the hackers then used the account to broadcast pro–Donald Trump messaging, something Mckesson disagreed with. How did the hackers do it?

First they called Mckesson's telephone company, Verizon, claiming to be him. The hackers "verified" their faux identity with a company representative by correctly confirming static, secret questions such as the last four digits of his Social Security number—information gleaned from online research and social engineering (that is, manipulating someone into revealing personal information). Once cleared, the hackers successfully registered a different SIM card in place of Mckesson's, which redirected incoming text messages to their own phone. This allowed them to easily hijack any passcode they wanted to obtain and gain access to his private accounts—in this case, Twitter.

This growing strain of cybercrime is referred to as SIM swap. The National Institute of Standards and Technology no longer recommends the use of these one-time passwords, to avoid this very scenario. Though the practice may be more secure than using static passwords alone, it is still not enough to offer satisfactory protection.

Why Can't We Keep Using Password Managers?

The idea of password managers (also known as password vaults) is quite simple: Consolidate your passwords into one location and have a digital "gatekeeper" of sorts protecting your sensitive information. The service allows you to use a single password to gain access to a wide assortment of websites and online applications. But while the notion of keeping all your passwords in one place may be tempting from the standpoint of sheer convenience, it also creates a single point of vulnerability. In fact, some password vaults have already been compromised. In 2017, password manager OneLogin was hacked—the second breach at the firm in two years. Other major players in the password consolidation space, like LastPass, have experienced similar breaches. At the end of the day, what is protecting all your passwords from being hacked when you use a password vault? Another password. As eighteenth-century philosopher Thomas Reid once expressed, "The weakest link of the chain . . . may be the strength of the rest."

Why Can't We Just Use Biometrics?

I wish I had a dollar for every time people asked me why we can't just use biometrics. In today's technological landscape, where user experience is king, biometric security is moving swiftly toward becoming ubiquitous. People are opening mobile devices, accessing financial information, and tracking their health with the simple touch of a finger or the sound of their voice.

At its core, biometrics is the science of converting a unique physical attribute from the human body—fingerprint, voice, iris pattern, etc.—into a digital signal (also referred to as analog-to-digital, or A-to-D, conversion).

When you record a voice memo on your mobile phone out loud, for example, you use your analog voice. The phone has an A-to-D converter that transforms your sound waves into bits and bytes. Later on, when you play the recording back, you hear the digital version of your analog voice.

The same principle works with a fingerprint reader or facial recognition. The physical, analog signals are converted into their digital equivalents. So let's say that your physical fingerprint, when scanned, is converted to the following "digital signature": ABC123. This digital information is then compared to what your biometrics ought to be, and if it is correct, you are authenticated. Do you see the problem? What is the difference between me choosing a static password like "ABC123" to gain access and using the digital signature "ABC123" based on my fingerprint? None. Biometric information is, at the end of the day, a static rendition of you and can be replayed if intercepted by malware.

In other words, if you have malware "listening in" on the biometric information, it can then replay it later to gain access, even though your actual fingerprint is not involved. Without replay protection, biometric information is just like a password—but with the facade of impenetrable safety.

Yes, it is more convenient and does not require the user to remember it. Yes, it is potentially safer in that you cannot give your fingerprint to an attacker over the phone. Yet the operative issue at the heart of the security battleground remains: It is already inside your device. Thus, we must protect the data from session replays. While the appealing characteristic of biometric authentication lies in its being inexorably tied to a specific person, that fact also makes the potential risk even more costly. No password reset or quick fix can easily assuage that biometric damage.

This threat is worldwide. The Unique Identification Authority of India has undertaken a countrywide project to create a unique identifier for each citizen with Aadhaar, the world's largest biometric identification system. But, like any other server, it's prone to being hacked—and Aadhaar has been susceptible to data breaches since its inception. It has been reported that the personal data of more than a billion people from a breach of the system is available online for a nominal fee—a harrowing statistic that only reinforces the need for greater precautions. No matter the case, the core issue with biometrics remains: Once our information is stolen, there is little we can do to change our "credentials" and prevent future attacks.

Why Don't We Have a Government Database for Identities?

In the United States, we do not have a federal-level system that can authenticate and identity proof all our citizens. The closest thing we have is our passport system, but only 137 million people—about 42 percent of the population—have passports. Beyond that, each state has its own system, primarily using the department of motor vehicles to issue driver's licenses or state IDs for identifying residents. When you are pulled over for a traffic violation, a police officer will ask to see your driver's license, not a username and password. But not every state maintains the same standards of security, so we really have no uniformity. Many people and organizations, including the ACLU, believe national IDs would have damaging consequences to our privacy, so it's hard to get a consensus on their use.

In some places around the world, banks issue smart cards with card readers that connect to a computer at the bank or another location. The card and its reader are intended to transmit the secure smart card to the bank and authenticate the user. This process is expensive, requires the consumer to carry the card and reader everywhere, and still does not solve the issue of malware on the computer. If the system is not built right, the malware can "listen" to the information from the smart card and simply replay it. Because solving this problem is so difficult, online crooks have an easier time masquerading as their victims and committing identity theft without a hitch.

WHY I ADVISE TRUSONA

A few years ago, I was offered the opportunity to advise a company that aims to get rid of passwords. As you can imagine, I was eager to help. Trusona, whose name derives from the fusion of "true" and "persona," is engaged in lifting the veil of anonymity on the Internet—and allowing the rightful owner of any account to correctly identify themselves. This, I believe, is the answer to the password problem.

Trusona helps companies to wean their consumers off passwords—for good. Its technology allows those companies that have a mobile app to authenticate their users without creating, remembering, or updating a static password, ever. They do that by tying the mobile device (not the phone number) of a user to his or her account—thus allowing only the rightful owner to truly authenticate. It requires a physical "token" and a six-digit PIN to get into the software on your device, and then you have to swipe your ID, like a license. The software will recognize and reject a duplicate or fake.

Not only that, but the solution is more convenient and simple to use than a password—if you know how to snap a photo, you can use the technology. It's that simple.

Trusona pioneered the #NoPasswords revolution, and I regularly speak about its vision in my presentations. I would like to see more companies, large and small, join this revolution, as it will be a powerful force in helping curb the funding of evil. Anyone can sign up for Trusona and try its easy-to-use technology—it is available as an app for your smartphone. You can also opt in for two-factor authentication on the websites you visit regularly that offer it (for example, Facebook offers two-factor authentication). You can also follow the tips below for optimum password security.

IN THE MEANTIME...

In May 2017, the National Institute of Standards and Technology (NIST), a nonregulatory federal agency within the U.S. Department of Commerce that promotes innovation, changed its password guidelines. Although NIST guidelines are meant for federal agencies, private companies and citizens should pay attention to what it says about passwords. Here are some ways experts say you can best protect your password while we work on getting rid of the need for them.

- **Don't go changing on me.** Frequent password changes are counterproductive to good password security, as people tend to swap out one password for another frequently used one. Human nature is hard to change. Changed passwords may also be forgotten, and they can be stolen just as easily as infrequently changed passwords. However, if a device is stolen, change your password.
- **Keep it simple.** Studies that look at arbitrary password complexity requirements that call for symbols and upper- and lowercase letters repeatedly find that these kinds of password restrictions result in *less* secure passwords.
- **Screen it.** NIST says that a requirement worth having is the one in which new passwords are compared against lists of commonly used or compromised passwords. Screen them against lists of known compromised passwords.

Enzoic.com and Passwordrandom.com are two examples of websites where you can do this.

- **Don't recycle.** Don't reuse the same password across multiple sites. Recycling is especially dangerous for email, banking, and social media accounts. Don't reemploy previous passwords, even if you haven't used them in years. Stolen passwords can be used to access many different sites.

- **Don't be too familiar.** Don't use the following in passwords or answers to website security questions: loved ones' names (pets included), maiden names, hometowns, birthdates, wedding dates, or anything else that can be gleaned with some online research.

- **Don't remember.** Never save passwords or use "Remember me" options on a public computer. The next user could easily access your account.

- **Be uncommon.** Never use the most common and easily hacked choices, such as "123456," "qwerty," or "password." While most password hacks are orchestrated by criminal organizations and involve stealing passwords, not guessing them, a lone hacker set on stealing your information might use guessing as a point of entry. Why make it easy for him or her? For the same reason, try a complex password such as 70YrS@n%styll&LUVN^Lfe!? It can be memorable, too, if you base it on a phrase that you privately choose, such as "70 years and still loving life!"

- **Be smart about your phone.** Don't leave your smartphone unprotected by a password, as one in three users do. Pick a code that isn't something obvious, such as your birthdate or birth year. Also avoid common passwords like 1234, 0000, 2580 (a top-to-bottom sequence), and 5683 (which spells "love").

- **Cheat.** A password cheat sheet is fine, as long as it's not stored on your computer or smartphone; if you do that and your device is infected with malware, you're doomed. A pen-and-paper reminder, kept in a safe place, is better. Ideally it will consist of hints rather than actual passwords.

THE COST OF DOING NOTHING

As I was writing this book, I celebrated my seventieth birthday. Over the years, I've learned that change—even good change— takes time. It also takes willpower. I dread thinking about what will happen if the industry does not heed the call to move away from passwords. We have to act now—the cost of doing nothing is far too great. When cybercriminals breach a database with usernames and passwords, they are after something: the identity of the user. With the identity, and the credentials to accounts, they get something that is "fenceable" on the dark web. They can convert these identities to cash or cryptocurrencies like bitcoin. Once an identity has been sold, the money is used mostly for illicit purposes. These funds are used in additional crimes—far worse than just stealing money.

By not doing anything—and simply maintaining the status quo—we are allowing the "bad guys" to win. As the great parliamentarian Edmund Burke is believed to have said, "The only thing necessary for the triumph of evil is for good men to do nothing."

RULE #4

Safeguard Your Home
and Hearth

10

The Calls That Just Keep Coming: Robocalls and Nuisance Calls

Not a day goes by that I don't hear about another attempt to swindle consumers through convincing pitches made over the telephone. You probably get these calls, perhaps even daily, on your cell phone or landline. Millions of people do. The volume of nuisance telemarketing, bill collecting, and illegal robocalls has risen steeply in recent years. Today, *half* of all mobile calls are fraudulent, according to a report from telecommunications firm First Orion. In 2017, the Federal Trade Commission logged 4.5 million complaints about robocalls, more than double the 2.18 million complaints logged in 2013. Callers—many of them con artists—spend about $438 million per year on robocalls. In May 2019, the FTC settled with four operations responsible for billions of illegal robocalls, and its fight continues. Under the agreement, the four companies were banned from making more calls and all were fined. Those calls generate more than twenty times that amount in income, reaching almost $10 billion a year. As lucrative as they are, it's no wonder their number is skyrocketing.

In April 2018, then–New York Attorney General Eric Schneiderman alerted consumers about a scheme that targeted people with Chinese last names. The caller would say he was from the Chinese consulate and then demand money, under threat of negative consequences or arrest upon traveling to China. According to the New York Police Department, twenty-one Chinese immigrants lost a total of $2.5 million in this scam. This is just one of many phone scams that happen every day. While the scripts and targets vary, the phony pitches and demands contain common data points that you can learn to identify and respond to immediately simply by hanging up. Phone scammers pretend to be calling from the IRS, Microsoft, your local police or fire department, charities, the Chinese or any foreign consulate, or whatever may sound official to get your attention and win your trust.

While the scripts and targets vary, the phony pitches and demands all aim to grab your attention, win your trust, and get your personal data and money.

How can you be so sure they're not legit?

SPOTTING SCAMMERS

- The Internal Revenue Service will *never* call you about unpaid taxes without first attempting to reach you by mail several times. (See chapter 3 for more on this.)

- If you get an unsolicited call from Microsoft or Apple warning you that you have a virus, it's likely a scam.

- Many fund-raisers claiming to be calling on behalf of your local police or fire department are bogus. If you want to support your local cops and firefighters, call them directly to ask where to send a donation.

- Foreign consulates will not call or email you to demand that you pay fees or fines.

- The Health Insurance Marketplace (set up by the government to administer the Affordable Care Act) does not employ robocalling to sell policies. Robocalls purporting to be from the Health Insurance Marketplace are phishing scams looking for personal information. According to the FTC, "If you get a recorded sales call, but you didn't give the caller written permission to call you, the call is illegal. Don't press 1 to speak to the operator or get your name taken off the list, and don't give any personal information. If you respond, you'll probably get more calls. If you want information about health insurance in your state, visit www.healthcare.gov. If you get a call like this, please report it to the FTC."

What exposes each call as fraudulent is the request—or sometimes threatening demand—for personal or financial information. The best way to deal with such a call: Don't answer. If you don't recognize the number, don't pick up. Scammers can spoof numbers, so make sure the number belongs to someone you know and is not just *close*. If the call is important, the caller will leave you a voicemail.

If you do answer and realize it's a crank call, hang up. Don't press a number, even if the recording tells you to press 8 or some other number to supposedly to be taken off the call list. You won't get taken off the list. Answering the call launches robocall recordings or transfers to call centers, where a live operator will try to get your personal and financial information. If the call is from an unsolicited "live" caller, hang up. If you don't recognize the voice, hang up. Never, ever respond by giving your information to a caller.

Some calls from legitimate companies that you've done business with can also be illegal—if you've asked them to stop calling and they continue to do so. Anytime you feel harassed by calls from businesses you've dealt with, let them know. They are required to stop calling at that point, and if they don't, they're breaking the law.

A CASE STUDY

Some scammers will fraudulently represent themselves as legitimate companies to try to persuade you to give them information so they can steal your identity. That's what happened to Shanna Dix when she and her friend made a claim for a replacement phone through Verizon. The process included a courtesy call to assist in setting up the new phone.

"I received a call on my cell from Verizon Wireless (800-922-0204) with an automated message asking to press 1 if we needed help setting up the phone or 2 to cancel the request," Nix wrote on Facebook. "I pressed 2 because I already had the phone set up and working."

The following Monday, Shanna said she received three calls in a row from the same 800 number. She answered the third call to let Verizon know she did not need assistance setting up the call. "Instead of getting an automated recording like last time, it was a person," she wrote. "I started to explain I didn't need any assistance but he said that wasn't the purpose of his call."

The live person told her that Verizon was in the process of upgrading its 4G LTE network. He explained that he needed to send some codes to her phone to set up the replacement phone. That gave Shanna pause, because she had already set up her phone and it was working. But the text she received with the codes looked like they were coming from Verizon, originating from the same number as the previous automated text she'd received from the company.

As she received the texts, she read the numbers back to the man slowly so he could understand them, because, she said, "his English was not very good." The man continued with Shanna, explaining that even though she had an upgrade, her bill would remain the same. He also told her that she might lose service at times during the upgrade and that as a courtesy, Verizon was going to give her a 25 percent credit on her next bill. Before the call ended, the man told Shanna, "God bless you." "Although for a split second it warmed my heart and made me feel good," Shanna said, "that was the kicker to something isn't right."

Shanna immediately called Verizon and relayed the story. The authentic Verizon rep asked her if she had just purchased three devices, and she said no, she had not. The rep connected her to the fraud department, and she filed a complaint. "I was lucky enough that they didn't have enough time to process and ship," she wrote. "Had I not called, I . . . would be stuck with the bill to fight."

Let's look behind the scenes at what happened.

The scammer was able to spoof the Verizon Wireless customer

service number. (Spoofing is when the caller ID looks like something it isn't—in this case, Verizon.) The scammer knew her number *and* the fact that she had recently requested a phone replacement. The codes Shanna received on her phone were legitimately from Verizon. The scammer was requesting them from Verizon and having them sent to Shanna's phone. At that point, the scammer took over her identity by changing her password, logging into her account, and ordering three new and expensive iPhones.

Shanna asked Verizon how to avoid such ID theft scams in the future, and the company told her that Verizon never calls customers from the customer service number. Moreover, if Verizon *does* call you, the caller ID will not say "Verizon." It will say "Unknown." If you do believe you've received a call from Verizon, it's best to hang up and call the company back, using a number you find online or in your bills, and see if the call was legitimate.

THE SCOOP ON SPOOFING

Because we tend to trust numbers that look legitimate or familiar, illegal spoofing is an insidious crime that is hard for law enforcement to prevent. The caller "spoofs" the caller ID to make the number look legit. Maybe it looks like a local number, or the name of a known company or organization. Not only does the number look legit, but spoof callers can also be very convincing. They often seem to know a lot about you, including account information, home address, and workplace. And if, when you answer, it's one of those prerecorded telemarketing calls, know that those are *always* illegal unless you've given your written consent, whether you're on the Do Not Call Registry or not.

WHEN SPOOFING ISN'T AGAINST THE LAW

While the call Shanna received was illegal, not all spoofing is against the law or necessarily bad. When is spoofing legal? Intent matters. Under the Truth in Caller ID Act, Federal Communications Commission rules prohibit transmitting misleading or inaccurate caller ID information "with the intent to defraud, cause harm, or wrongly obtain anything of value." But if the intent of spoofing is to help or legitimately protect callers and those being called, then the law says it's okay.

Newspaper reporters, for example, may use spoofing to conceal their number when calling potential sources of information or informants, to keep confidentiality intact. Domestic violence victims can use spoofing to hide their identity and whereabouts when making a call. I know someone who was stalked by her ex-husband, so she used software that concealed her number when she made outgoing calls to people he knew (and might be with).

It's also legal for someone from a business or organization to call you from what appears to be the company's main or 800 number, not the direct line of the person making the call. For example, if you get a call from AARP's national headquarters, your caller ID will give you the main number, not the number of the individual staff member.

Your number can be spoofed, too. If you get calls from people saying your number is showing up on their caller ID, but you never called them, that is an indication that your number has likely been spoofed. Just explain that your number is being spoofed and that you didn't make any calls. Consider placing a message on your voicemail letting callers know that your number is being spoofed. Scammers are known to switch numbers frequently, and it's likely that within hours they will no longer be using yours.

BLOCKING CALLS

So how can you block robocalls and other nuisance calls before they get to you?

Illegal robocallers often simply call (or program in) sequential numbers with no idea of who, if anyone, might be on the receiving end. Many of these calls are made for a single purpose: to see if someone will answer the phone. That way, the scammers know the phone is "live"—that is, there is a real person on the other end to potentially entice with their pitch. Your number can then be sold to other robocallers as a hot prospect—and you'll get even *more* such calls. Here's what you can do to curb those nuisance calls.

The first thing you want to do is register on the Do Not Call Registry to block sales calls. Add your phone number for free by visiting www.donotcall.gov or calling 888-382-1222 (TTY: 866-290-4236) from the phone you want to register. You can register up to three numbers. After you register, other types of organizations may still call you, such as charities, political groups, debt collectors, and pollsters, as well as companies you've recently done business with or given written permission to call you. But the truth is, the registry only helps with companies that are legitimately trying to sell you something, not scam artists.

The best way to avoid scam calls and reduce your chances of receiving them in the future is to simply not answer the phone if there is a number you don't recognize on your caller ID. By letting these calls go to voicemail, you'll often find that no message has been left; this is a sign that the caller was simply looking for a live number.

If you've gotten a call from a number you want blocked on your iPhone, tap on the number and you'll typically see an icon next to the number (an *i* inside a circle). Tap on that and a list will come up, usually lower on the page, with "Block Number" or "Block This Caller" on it. Tap on it and the number is blocked. For Android smartphones, tap the number that called, select "Details," and then hit "Block Number." The problem with this, of course, is that it blocks only callers who have previously called you, and you have to go through the tedious process of blocking each call individually.

Depending on the kind of mobile phone you have, you may be able to program it to automatically block anonymous callers. Many Android phones let you block all unknown callers. Go to "Settings," click on the phone icon, and look for call blocking. It allows you to block all incoming unidentified numbers.

On many iPhones, you can go into your settings, turn on "Do Not Disturb," and limit who can call you to "Favorites" or "All Contacts." Anyone not on your contact list won't get through. You can also download a silent ringtone from the App Store and set it as your default. Then go to Contacts and set a different ringtone for those on your contact list. You will hear the phone's tone only when someone on your contact list calls. You'll need to add people you want to hear from to your contact list.

Several free and fee-based applications for iPhones and Android phones allow you to block anonymous numbers. Some flip phones allow for call blocking, but the technology is not as advanced as call blocking for smartphones; there is also often a limit on how many numbers you can block, and everything must be done manually.

But here's the problem with these apps: Putting a blanket block on all unknown numbers and anonymous numbers can block legitimate callers as well. What if, for example, someone in your family has to call you from a friend's, neighbor's, or medical provider's phone that isn't on your contact list? Also, some professionals, such as doctors, block their numbers on outgoing calls. If you are expecting a call from someone important whose number might be blocked because of the technology you use, you can temporarily disable the blocking feature. But carefully consider the pros and cons before blocking all but known callers.

SERVICES FROM YOUR CARRIER AND THIRD PARTIES

Because nuisance calls are such a, well, nuisance, providers—whether for mobile, Internet, or traditional landline phones—offer systems to block unwanted calls. And, of course, there are apps for that. Do an online search to look for the cost (some are free) and reviews from experts and other users. Here are my suggestions.

A freebie for virtually every landline user is *77. Press *77 to block "anonymous" and "private" numbers, then deactivate it anytime with *87. Note that *77 works only on callers who block delivery, not on spoof callers.

Many phone services will now tell you when a call is possibly a nuisance or robocall. The caller ID can often say something like "Spam?PotomacMd" or "Scam Likely." Here are additional services provided by the major phone companies. Contact your provider for specifics and costs.

- AT&T offers Call Protect, designed to stop fraud calls before they reach the phone and warn you of potential spam calls.
- Sprint offers Premium Caller ID, which identifies callers who are not already in your contacts. The Sprint Premium Caller ID app displays callers' category and fraud risk level—low, medium, and high. Then you can decide whether to answer, block the number to prevent future calls, or report the call, to help Sprint identify spam.
- T-Mobile offers Name ID, Scam ID, and Scam Block. Scam ID tells you if the call is likely a scam. Scam Block allows you to block all likely scammers before they reach you.
- Verizon Wireless provides Call Filter with spam detection, with alerts if an incoming call is likely spam; spam reporting, allowing you to report a phone number to help Verizon improve its spam detection service; and spam blocking, which lets you set up your spam filter and personal block list to automatically send unwanted calls to voicemail.

You can also use third-party apps that filter calls. Most of these collect a sort of blacklist of scammers' numbers and block them before the call comes through. Here are some you may want to look into: Hiya, Mr. Number, Nomorobo, RoboKiller, Truecaller, and YouMail.

One last option is a call-blocking device attached to traditional landlines. Brands include CPR, Digitone, Mcheeta, Sentry, and Tel-Lynx. These boxes, generally under $100, block thousands of pre-programmed known nuisance numbers from reaching your phone and allow you to add more numbers.

Phone technology is always changing, of course, so when you purchase a new phone or provider, be sure to ask about and understand call-blocking technology that may be new or updated.

"YES" SCAMS

It's been reported that scammers record what you say and then use your words against you when you try to say you never ordered that magazine or service. Here's how it works: The caller will ask you to confirm your billing information, which he says he already has. He reads it to you and asks you if it's correct. Once you say "Yes," he or she has gotten your consent. Or he or she will simply ask, "Can you hear me?" and record you saying "Yes," then use that voice recording to authorize fraudulent charges by telephone. It's not clear how ubiquitous this scheme is or if there have been actual victims with money lost, but the FCC took it seriously enough to issue a warning about "yes" scams in March 2017.

The service, gift, or trip offered by the scammer or robocall, it turns out, isn't really free at all. There's postage and handling to pay to deliver the gift to your door; there are registration or processing fees. In addition, to obtain the "free" item, you must hand over your credit card information, name, and address. (And remember: "Free" means free. Anything that is labeled "free" but costs you one penny or more is not free.)

SPOIL THE SPOOF! HOW TO CURB THE CREEPY CALLS

While law enforcement scrambles to thwart illegal robocalling—and it's especially hard when many call centers are halfway across the world—let's review the steps you can take to cut back on the number of calls received.

- **Use robocall-blocking services.** Check with your carrier, third-party apps, and call-blocking boxes.
- **Ignore it.** Just don't pick up if you don't recognize the number. That might kick your number off the list or to the bottom of the list. Sometimes, though, they'll just keep trying.
- **Be tight-lipped.** If you do pick up a call from an unknown number, say nothing. Your voice launches

robocall recordings or transfers to call centers, where a live operator will try to get your personal and financial information. Saying nothing usually disconnects robocalls within seconds, and generally you won't get a call back from this number. If the call is from an unsolicited "live" caller, let the caller break the silence. If you don't recognize the voice, hang up. And, of course, never give incoming callers information about your accounts, your Social Security number, PINs, address, or account numbers, or the names or routing numbers of your financial institutions.

- **Check it.** If you feel the call may have been legitimate, call the business by using the number you have in your records, on a bill, on the back of your credit card, in the phone book, or on the company's legitimate website. You will most likely learn that your instincts were correct and that the call you received was an attempt to steal from you.

- **Know which calls to avoid.** The most common calling cons are pitches that promise to reduce your debt and credit card rates or get you preapproved loans; offer free or low-cost vacations, timeshares, home security systems, or medical supplies; get you better and cheaper health insurance; or come from government and utility company impostors. Hang up. If you think it may be legit, call back on a number you find independently.

- **Ask: Is it one of those days?** Research shows that robocalls tend to be made more frequently on Fridays and Tuesdays. Be on heightened alert on those days.

- **Consider whether it's time for a change.** The most frequently targeted area codes are in Atlanta, Dallas,

New York City, Los Angeles, Houston, Chicago, Baltimore, Phoenix, Newark, and the San Francisco Bay Area. If you have a number in one of these area codes, changing your number within the area code might not be enough to reduce the number of nuisance calls you get. Consider calling your carrier and asking to have your number changed to another area code called less frequently by robocallers. (You may even be able to keep your seven-digit number.)

- **Report them.** Report the call to the FTC and the Do Not Call Registry. It might not do anything about the call you just received, but it will help in the future by adding the number to the blacklist.
- **Sue them.** There is a provision in the U.S. Telephone Consumer Protection Act of 1991 that gives consumers the right to take illegal robocallers to court—if you can identify who they are. I'm not sure suing a robocaller is practical for most people, but it's an option for those who feel they are being harassed by robocalls and cannot find any other way to relieve themselves of the annoyance.

Suing the caller is what Paul DeMuth, of Harmarville, Pennsylvania, had to resort to. He fell behind on his student loan payments due to extenuating circumstances, and Navient, the loan company, started robocalling him relentlessly—even after DeMuth told the company to stop calling him. Audio recordings from the calls made by Navient to DeMuth back up this claim. In one instance, after DeMuth received a robocall, spoke to a live person, and asked the company to stop, Navient called again six hours later. Again he asked the company to stop calling because the calls were now bordering on harassment. But the calls kept coming. An independent arbitrator found that Navient had placed two hundred unauthorized robocalls to DeMuth over two years. The company was ordered to pay DeMuth nearly $300,000, less the amount he owed on the student loan, $15,700.

BEWARE OF ONE-RING CALLS

One-ring calls are a common ruse to prompt you to call the number back to find out what the call was about. Be especially aware of one-ring calls from area codes 268, 284, 809, and 876, which originate from Caribbean countries with high per-minute phone charges. If you get a one-ring call, don't call back.

As long as predatory sales practices and scammers exist, so will robocalls. Technology continues to try to stay one step ahead of criminals whose weapon of choice is the phone. But until phone systems are developed to the point that only the calls you want are allowed through, we can look forward to some level of annoyance from unwanted calls.

11

Great Real Estate Ruses

Getting your home ripped away from you is traumatic, because it's so personal—and especially because for many people, their home can represent their largest and most important asset. Con artists target not just the homes we own but rental property, short-term vacation homes, and home improvement schemes. In this chapter, we'll look at how these scams happen and how to recognize them before you become a victim.

When it comes to home scams, the goal is to get your money or property, and while that is a constant, how it's done tends to reflect trends in the housing market. Like prices, real estate scams shift with supply and demand in any given market. During a housing bubble, like the one that peaked in 2005, common scams involve fraudulent brokers who issue predatory loans—an unscrupulous practice that entices borrowers to take out loans that carry high fees and interest rates.

When the bubble bursts, swindlers change their game. Homeowners can find it difficult to keep up with payments and taxes. Fraudsters prey on people underwater on their mortgages (when the amount of the home mortgage exceeds the market value of the home) with phony refinancing and loan modification schemes. Predators looking for homeowners unable to keep up try to fraudulently take over deeds. Con artists take advantage of renters pushed out of their homes, offering apartments that don't exist in exchange for exorbitant security deposits.

Running parallel to these schemes are vacation and timeshare fraud and home improvement rackets that plague consumers. These frauds can also mirror what is going on in the economy. When the economy is healthy, more people take vacations and purchase timeshares, which can lead to more vacation scams. Likewise, more people renovate during economic booms or after a natural disaster, and that is when shady contractors come out of the woodwork.

Today, even as state and federal governments have done more to try to combat fraud, and as the market recovers, housing and vacation schemes of all types haven't abated. It can be hard to know whom we can trust. This chapter can help you figure it out.

Hall of Shame: Leonard and Jack Rosen and the Gulf American Land Corporation

"If you believe that, I've got some swampland to sell you in Florida." Most old sayings are rooted in the truth, and this one is no exception— it seems to have originated with fraudulent deals to sell swampland in Florida in the 1920s. Flash forward to 1958, when the Rosen brothers, Leonard and Jack, formed the Gulf American Land Corporation to sell Florida land to buyers from New York, Chicago, Detroit, Baltimore, and even overseas.

The land, like that in the 1920s, was unbuildable swampland. (Today we call these areas wetlands, and they are often protected.) The brothers would often sell land by mail order, to people who never saw it. They used engaging ads that imagined a Florida home as a tropical paradise right on or next to the beach. Other buyers toured the property from small planes chartered by the brothers, never getting close enough to see the muck that would never hold a foundation, let alone an entire house.

In 1967, the Florida Land Sales Board charged the Gulf American Land Corporation and the Rosens with deceptive and misleading promotion and sales methods. The brothers had defrauded 1,300 buyers by selling them partly drained wetlands—land the company claimed would one day be developed neighborhoods and rural country estates but that, in actuality, could never be built on. The business was suspended, and much of the land in the area remains vacant to this day. That puts them in our real estate fraud Hall of Shame.

CLASSIFIED CONS

Internet ad fraud costs consumers millions of dollars. I was in a restaurant not long ago when a young man who worked there asked if he could speak to me in private. "Of course," I said, thinking he wanted some advice or maybe an autograph (it does sometimes happen!). Instead he showed me a check and asked if I thought it was real.

First I asked him how he had come to possess the check. "Well, I listed a car for sale on Craigslist for $10,000, and a fellow in Canada wanted to buy it," he told me. "He sent me a check for $13,000, with $3,000 to use to transport the car. He asked me to deposit the check and send him the $3,000 back for the transportation." That explanation of the overpayment seemed reasonable on the face of it, and the check looked authentic. But it was indeed a scam. The young man's bank would have deposited the $13,000 check and quickly discovered it was fraudulent, and had he followed through with sending the con artist $3,000 and the car, the young man would have been on the hook for the $3,000—and he would have been out his $10,000 car, too.

In most cases, selling your unwanted but perfectly good items on Craigslist, Facebook Marketplace, and similar websites can be a good way to make a little cash. But today's scammers scour classified ads to find targets for the bad-check scam—and they often succeed. There do not seem to be tracking numbers on how many people get taken by these scams, but it's likely in the hundreds of thousands annually. It generally works just like it did with my friend in the restaurant: The scammer contacts the poster and asks if the item is still available. The phony buyer then makes arrangements to send a check to the seller, which is usually for more than the amount of the item, and asks for the extra money to be returned. The checks look so authentic, even banks are fooled—especially when a regular customer brings one in for deposit. The fraud is revealed once the check is processed, and the person who deposited the check is on the hook for any of the money already spent.

RENTAL RIP-OFFS

"I had never looked on Craigslist for a rental," said Hillary, a New Jersey resident who is planning a move to Kissimmee, Florida. "But my friend sent me a listing that was so perfect I had to pursue it." The apartment was the right size, in the right location, and at the right price. She responded to the ad and received a prompt reply. "The guy seemed professional . . . and we had several email conversations," said Hillary. But her suspicions began to rise when, as part of her application process, he asked for a security deposit and one month's rent—before Hillary had been approved or had even seen the apartment. "I politely asked him for proof he was who he said he was (the homeowner), and his response was basically, 'You can trust me, I'm a Christian, I give you my word.'" Once Hillary asked to see a copy of the title of the property and a utility bill, he stopped responding. "That's when I knew it was a scam," she said. Hillary quickly reported the fraudulent listing to Craigslist as well as to the complex where the alleged apartment was located.

Real estate agent Toni Patillo tells a story about a couple of different rental scams. In one, scammers broke into a vacant house, changed its locks, and took out ads on Craigslist and in the *Los Angeles Times* saying it was available to rent. They were able to write up a fraudulent lease and take money from unsuspecting renters. Only later—when the actual buyers who were in escrow to purchase the property drove by the house and discovered it was occupied—was the scam revealed. Another time, one of Toni's employees found a house to lease and met the current tenant, who claimed to be related to the landlord and authorized to collect applications and deposits for it.

Toni's employee gave him the application and a check for deposit. Feeling that something was fishy, the employee went back to his office to do some additional research on the property and discovered that it was in fact listed for sale and the current tenant he had just met and given a deposit check to was being evicted for nonpayment of rent. The listing agent for the sale confirmed that the lease was a scam and encouraged the employee to go back and get his check. At which point, he raced back to confront the tenant and eventually got his deposit back.

All these ads look convincing because scammers use the same sorts of language that legitimate landlords use to advertise properties. Often, fake rental ads use photos of properties that are not for sale or rent or images simply stolen from other real estate listings. This is such a common scam that you have to scrupulously check any rental listing you see that might be of interest. Over 141 days of tracking rental ads on Craigslist in twenty cities, a joint university study found 29,000 rental ad scams, with two-thirds of the ads originating in Nigeria.

Here are my best defenses for avoiding rental rip-offs.

Look it up. Research unknown properties with an online search of the address, as well as any names, emails, and phone numbers associated with the supposed landlord or agent. If the search results show that the property is for sale—that is, not for rent—beware. Of course, nonexistent addresses or addresses belonging to other nonresidential properties or to a business are likely a sign of a scam. Your online search may also reveal social media postings by people who fell victim to this particular scammer.

Make sure it's as advertised. If you can, see the property. You should do this to check to make sure the neighborhood is as advertised, the house or apartment complex is in good repair, and so on. Even though the apartment may actually be for rent, deceptive landlords and property owners can fudge descriptions of the condition of the property or claims about the safety and nature of the area it's in. So see it for yourself. Don't rely on promises or pretty pictures.

Read critically. Copy the descriptive text for the property and paste it into a search engine to see if you can find other listings using the same copy. While real estate agents often use the same words and terms to describe houses, large swaths of verbatim copy right from another listing is a sign of a scam. Also check for what is called "scammer grammar"—a poor command of the English language and frequent misspellings, particularly in any follow-up communication you may receive concerning a well-worded (and likely copied) advertisement.

Go face-to-face. If the person with the listing says he can't meet you or he's out of the country and won't be back until after the rental period begins, this could be a scam. Go local, and go face-to-face. According to Craigslist, follow this one rule and you'll avoid 99 percent of scams. The caveat is that there *are* honest owners who live in one place and own properties in another place. In this case, the rental could be legit, but the person should have a local representative who can show you the apartment or house. You should also be able to have a video call with the owner via Skype or FaceTime. Which leads to my next tip.

Get on the phone. Email is the preferred communication of scammers. (Hillary found this out the hard way—she could not get the alleged landlord on the phone.) Request a phone number and put it into a search engine to see if there are any complaints related to it. Arrange for a video call via Skype or FaceTime so you can see the person.

Ask for proof. If you are dealing with a property owner, ask for proof of ownership, such as a copy of the title or utility bill, and identity, such as a driver's license. Remember: When Hillary asked for this information, the scammer disappeared. You can cross-check ownership with the property assessor's office or the recorder of deeds in the community where the rental is located. When speaking with a manager or agent about the property, request proof that the person has a right to sign a lease on behalf of the owner. Then check the information with the owner. Now, I did say that deeds can be forged, so checking on a deed is not definitive proof; but it is one of many tips you have to follow to ensure a legitimate rental.

Don't pay anything before you sign a lease. Avoid rental companies that require up-front fees or monthly membership dues to access listings of low-cost rentals, pre-foreclosure rentals, or rent-to-own properties. Most are scams. Moreover, if the landlord or agent wants a fee to show you the property, it's a scam. If you're asked for a security deposit that exceeds the limits set by your state, that's a scam. Some states have limits on how much a landlord can ask for in security deposits—often equal to one to two months' rent. Check your state's attorney general's office or consumer protection department for laws about rental security deposits.

Don't click on links to credit reports. A common way to defraud renters is by instructing them to click on a link to purchase and forward their credit report to the renting agent. This won't get you an apartment, but it will get the scammer a referral commission from the credit-reporting site, along with your personal information, which could be used for identity theft.

Be wary if they aren't interested. While you should not click a link to buy a credit report in a real estate ad, you also have to be wary about landlords who don't seem to have much interest in your credit history or background at all. Think about it: Would you rent to someone whose background you haven't checked out? No, and I wouldn't either. Landlords have legitimate reasons for knowing your credit score. They may also want to run a criminal background check and employment verification. If a landlord appears eager to have you sign a lease and hand over a check, with no interest in obtaining any information about you, proceed with caution.

Don't rent without a lease. Whether yearlong or month to month, leases offer both renters and landlords certain protections. While you do not legally need a lease to rent an apartment, if a landlord tells you that you don't need a lease—you can just pay him the rent— it could be because the landlord doesn't actually have a property to lease.

Do a double take. Use Google Images or https://tineye .com to search by image, making sure the photo of the property isn't taken from a legitimate source.

WHAT TO DO IF YOU'VE BEEN SCAMMED BY A RENTAL

Here's what to do if you believe you've been scammed.

- **Report the incident to local law enforcement.** The information that you provide can help track down a scammer and get your money back. You're likely not the only person to be scammed by this person, so reporting it is helpful to police.
- **Tattle.** Contact the customer service department of the company or entity that published the fraudulent ad. The

publication or website will want to know that the people it accepts money from are honest and legitimate. In my experience, both print and online publishers take scams seriously. Craigslist has a form to fill out if you think a poster on the site has scammed you.

- **File a complaint.** Call 877-FTC-HELP (877-382-4357) or visit the FTC's online Complaint Assistant.

- **Share your story.** Tell your friends and family about what happened. Sharing helps others avoid similar scams—and helps you work through the pain and frustration of getting scammed.

VACATION VICTIMIZATIONS

Who doesn't anticipate holiday breaks and summer vacations each year? We imagine the fun we'll have in the sun or on the slopes, exploring new places or visiting family and friends. Unfortunately, vacation seasons are also scammer seasons. Just as with the conventional long-term rentals described earlier, scammers steal photos and descriptions from other listings to advertise phony properties. Once you've agreed to rent the fake place, they take your deposit money and are never seen or heard from again. Follow the rules I laid out for avoiding rental scams when you are considering renting a vacation property. Here are a few more tips to avoid scams that are especially pertinent to holiday renters.

- **Don't click on deal links.** When making too-good-to-be-true hotel reservations, don't rely on links in online advertisements or social media, because those can lead you to copycat websites or high-pressure call centers. I recommend going directly to the hotel or booking website by typing its name into a search engine and checking for deals firsthand. In my experience, dealing directly with hotels can often get you the best hotel room rates, especially if you add in membership discounts (like AARP or AAA). Travel aggregators like Groupon, Kayak, Travelzoo, and TripAdvisor are also reliable and legitimate ways to find travel deals. If you're using a site like Airbnb or HomeAway, be sure to type in the location's address yourself instead of clicking on a link that might take you to a copycat or clone site.

- **Read reviews.** Always read what others have said about a property. Was the actual property "as advertised"? Did the neighborhood vibe match the description in the listing? Did renters say the owner was responsive to needs and problems? When a reviewer complains about something in the review, does the owner respond, and are they gracious and apologetic or are they defensive? Defensiveness could be a red flag for an owner who is unconcerned about repeat customers or good property management.

- **Question flexibility.** You should be skeptical if a rental deal seems too flexible during peak rental times. During high seasons, many owners of vacation rentals require a weeklong stay starting on Saturday or Sunday, so question a rental that lets you rent for less than a week or from Tuesday through the following Wednesday. This isn't as much of a red flag during the off-season, when landlords may just want to fill rooms.

- **Never wire money for short-term rentals.** Never pay for a vacation rental with a wire transfer or prepaid debit card—the preferred methods of scammers. When using a site like Airbnb or HomeAway, for example, always pay through the website with your credit card. Remember: A credit card is your best protection, because you are using the bank's money until you determine the product or service you bought is legitimate. Don't leave the site to pay or communicate with a property owner or manager—if you do, sites like Airbnb and HomeAway cannot help you.

TIMESHARE RESALE SCAMS

If you own a vacation timeshare and want to sell it, you could be contacted by a company that claims to have interested buyers. (We talked about this in chapter 1.) The caller might even provide the name and number of buyers whom you can call yourself—and the people on the other end of the line will confirm their interest in purchasing the share.

If you pursue this, the caller will often fax or send you legitimate-looking paperwork, along with a request for a credit card number for escrow and title services or an up-front payment—often by wire transfer—to cover sales commissions and services, closing costs, taxes, or other fees. After you send the money, the buyer and the agent vanish, along with your money. Some victims are hit with follow-up fraud: another business (usually run by the same scammers or their cohorts) that claims to help recover funds lost in resale rip-offs—for a moderate up-front fee (also never to be seen again).

If you're interested in selling a timeshare, follow these tips.

- Check with your resort about resale or buyback programs. Expect to pay 10 to 30 percent in commission.
- Deal with reputable, well-known local real estate agents who have a demonstrable track record of resales.
- Never go with a company that charges up-front fees.
- When listing a timeshare yourself, stick with a legitimate website like RedWeek or TUG (Timeshare Users Group).

HOME REPAIR RIP-OFFS

There's a knock on the door. When you answer, a man tells you he's a handyman or contractor and offers to fix things around the house. He can fix that dented gutter or power-wash your vinyl siding. He can even repaint your bedroom and stop that faucet from leaking. All for a very reasonable price. In another scenario, a couple of well-dressed fellows turn up to tell you how you can make money from the electric company by installing solar panels on your home—for only $5,000 down—and you'll never pay a high electric bill again. In a third scenario, after a very bad storm, someone who calls himself a roofer might turn up and say he can fix the damage to your roof for $1,500. All he needs is one-third of the total amount to buy materials.

Should you write a check to any of these people? Not a chance.

Home improvement scammers often use storms and the damage that results as an excuse to ring your bell and offer their services. Likewise, a change of season is a time when many of us do home repairs and major maintenance jobs, so this is when door-to-door home repair solicitations reach a peak. These scams often begin with the person telling you the repairs must be made immediately or you will suffer the dire consequences of putting it off. These people often speak very quickly to confuse you, and they apply pressure to get you to sign a contract without giving you time to read it. Maybe they'll tell you they are doing work on other homes in the neighborhood; perhaps they have leftover material that can save you money—but only if you sign on the dotted line *today*. If people come to your door selling a home improvement product, ask for literature you can read when you have time. If they refuse, shut the door.

You can also unknowingly invite home improvement scammers in when you contact them through an ad or post. Paula and George found this out in a costly way.

"We needed our roof done," Paula told me. "It didn't have a leak, but the shingles were curling and it was just a matter of time before the roof would fail. We had gotten a couple of estimates but wanted a third estimate." Her husband, George, found the biggest roofer ad in the paper and called the number. (He's not alone; many people assume that companies that can afford sizeable ads are successful, and therefore trustworthy.) They got an estimate from Joe, a relatively young man, and his price was about $1,000 less than the other two estimates they got. He was also local, unlike the other companies.

Paula and George did everything right after contacting the roofer: They contacted the references Joe provided. They checked to make sure he was a member of the National Association of Home Builders. They asked for his insurance, and then called the insurance company to verify that he had an up-to-date policy. They found out he was licensed. Paula said that her husband liked

Joe but that the contractor would not look her in the eyes—her first red flag. "He immediately told us a sob story about his daughter," she said. "That made me uneasy."

As the couple was coming closer to making a decision, they talked about it over dinner with relatives. "My cousin's husband, who was a contractor . . . advised us to ask if we could get a better price if we paid cash. And we did," recalled Paula. "The whole job was originally quoted at $5,800, and [Joe] asked us for $3,600 cash for the materials and the rest of the money would be for labor. I was hesitant, but we gave him the money, and within a week he delivered shingles to our house and put a tarp over them."

Then they heard nothing. Paula called. At first, Joe said he was doing another job and would be over as soon as he could. She kept calling, but her messages went unanswered. Then she bumped into him at her local Walmart.

"'Joe, what's going on?' I asked. He said he would get it done before winter." At this point, it was early December, but Paula said she wasn't worried, because the weather was still warm and lots of people were still doing construction.

Still, Joe never showed up. In late December, a storm hit and an ice dam formed under the shingles of the roof. The roof started to leak.

"We knew from checking with Home Depot that the shingles we bought from Joe were worth $1,800, which meant half of our money was out under a tarp. I was upset and I went to the courthouse to file a complaint," said Paula.

"It cost us $525 to file a complaint in civil court. During our court date, Joe showed up with receipts for lumber, underlayment, all sorts of items—$2,400 above the quoted cost. He handed them to the judge, and they were all dated the day before the court date. The judge laughed at him."

Joe also claimed that the weather had prevented him from doing the work, but Paula went online to obtain the weather reports for the months she had been waiting for a new roof. Most all of the days had been perfect for outside construction: clear, sunny, and dry.

The judge easily decided in their favor. "But as we were leaving, the judge said, 'Good luck getting it.' I asked what he meant, and the judge explained that we could put a lien against his house. However, unscrupulous contractors often put everything they own in their spouse's name. They are notorious for doing that." It's hard to collect simply because people do not pay—even if you put a lien on their business, scammers will often shut the business down and start a new one.

Paula and George were out $3,600, but they did have the shingles, most of which were still usable. By summer 2009, contractors were required by law to have a license in Pennsylvania—which Joe eventually got. Because of this law, if you have a judgment against a contractor, you can go to the courthouse and, for about $100, put the judgment on the contractor's record until it's paid. "So I sure as hell did that," said Paula. "As soon as it went on his record, his lawyer called us and asked if we would settle for $800. We declined. It was either going to be the full $1,800 owed to us or nothing."

Eventually, Paula and George found another contractor. Luckily, they could still use the shingles that were sitting on their front lawn, but they had to buy additional supplies to finish the job. Overall, the ordeal ended up costing the couple an additional $6,000 over and above the $3,600 they had originally spent.

HOW TO AVOID HOME REPAIR RIP-OFFS

- **Don't believe the hype.** As Paula and George learned, just because a company places a large or impressive ad doesn't mean it is honest or does quality work.
- **Be skeptical of unsolicited advice.** Don't engage strangers who ring your bell unsolicited and tell you that you need work done on your house. Either don't answer the door, or tell them no thank you and good-bye.
- **See for yourself.** Paula called references, but they could have been phony. She advises consumers to ask references if you can come by and see the work: "Inspect it yourself, and ask the homeowners, 'Are you satisfied with the work? How long did it take?'"
- **Check for a license and insurance.** Avoid unlicensed contractors, even in states where it's legal to operate without a license. Always make sure your contractor is licensed to work in your state, bonded, and insured. Verify that insurance is up to date, and avoid contractors who are not insured.
- **Sign a contract.** Don't hire a contractor who tells you there's no need for a written contract. Legally, contracts for $500 or more must be confirmed in writing, but it's a good idea to have a written contract for smaller projects, too.
- **Look for a real address.** Avoid contractors who have just a post office box or a cell phone number. Look for a street address and a business phone number.
- **Don't pay cash.** Never give a contractor cash for a job. If a contractor balks at the surcharge that credit card companies add, I offer to pay the 3 or 4 percent. That is a very

inexpensive insurance policy against poor workmanship or no-shows—if the arrangement falls through, you can go to the credit card company and get your money back. Credit card use by contractors is increasing, but if yours doesn't accept plastic, even an alternative like PayPal tied to a credit card is better than cash, even though there may be a fee attached.

- **Have the contractor pull permits.** Don't use a contractor who requires you to pull permits for a job. This is a sign that the contractor is unlicensed or has had run-ins with the building inspector. If permits are necessary for the project, obtaining them should be part of the contractor's job. Always check with your building department to verify that your contractor has gotten all necessary permits.

- **Don't pay for materials up front.** Be wary of contractors who ask for money to buy materials before starting the job. Reliable, established contractors can buy materials on credit. Don't work with a contractor who demands full payment up front.

- **Withhold final payment.** Don't pay for the job in full until it is completed properly, necessary inspectors have signed off, and you approve of the work done.

- **Sue in criminal court.** If you do get ripped off by a shady contractor, civil court judgments are difficult, if not impossible, to collect. Talk to your local law enforcement or district attorney's office to see if criminal charges can be applied to your problem.

NOT SO USER FRIENDLY: UTILITY SCAMS

Here's a common utility scam: Swindlers claiming to be from the county or city water department ring your doorbell and tell you they need to check the water supply, fixtures, and fittings and test the water quality. When you let them in, they take a look at some pipes, put some water in a test tube, swish it around, stick in a dipstick, and then tell you that the water doesn't test well, so you'll need to get a water filter. As luck would have it, the scammers just happen to have a water filter in the back of their truck, and they can leave it for a utility installer, who will come later to put it in, but the unit must be purchased and paid for today. This scenario has played out all across the country for years. Of course, these people are not from your municipal utility, and no installer will ever come to put the filter in.

How can you know it's a scam? Because county and city utility companies don't show up unannounced to sell you a product (though a private company might). If a public utility company has to do any work on your home, like testing the water supply or changing an electrical meter, it will contact you in advance, usually by conventional mail or email. Moreover, utility company staff must carry official photo IDs. Check IDs carefully and if there's any question, don't worry about insulting the person who is there by calling the utility and asking if the representative is legit. Most of all, never let people into your home unless you have scheduled an appointment with them and know who they are.

Dorothy in the classic film *The Wizard of Oz* got it right when she said, "There's no place like home." "Home" to me is where my family is, and where I feel safe and comfortable, surrounded by loved ones. Keeping our homes, even temporary ones, safe and secure as we move through life is important to our financial, physical, and emotional security. Never let anyone make you feel you're being too careful, then, when it comes to finding, establishing, or maintaining your home.

RULE #5

Shelter Your Heart

12

It's Personal: Fraud That Hurts More Than Just Your Wallet

Family-related fraud is heartbreakingly common. Today, I hear reports of harder-hitting crimes: family impostors, ancestry and family history scams, inheritance cons, and adoption fraud. In this chapter, I talk about some of the various ways family-related fraud is committed, so we know what to look for and prevent it from happening.

When people ask what motivated me to turn my life around, I have one answer: family. I attribute my rehabilitation as an adult and my continued success as a contributing member of society to my wife of more than forty-two years and our three sons. They have been a powerful source of strength and love for me. But, as a budding con artist, one of my first victims was my own father.

My parents had split up when I was twelve, and it shattered me. The confusion and anger caused by the breakdown of their relationship was one of the events that propelled me down the wrong path. When I was fifteen, I used my father's credit card to buy car parts and then resold them for cash. This put my father into debt to the tune of about $3,400 (a lot of money today, and a great deal of money in 1963). When he received the credit card statement, let's just say my father was not pleased. I was severely punished and can only imagine the betrayal he must have felt. I left home shortly after, when I was just sixteen.

VIRTUAL KIDNAPPING

I've found no national statistics on virtual, or fake, kidnapping, but it's bad enough that the FBI has issued warnings about it and says that in four states alone, virtual kidnapping cost eighty victims more than $87,000 in total. This frightening new scam takes one of two forms. The first is when a scammer calls and pretends to be a relative or friend in peril because he or she has been kidnapped. The kidnapper then takes over the call and demands ransom money to release the person from captivity. In the second scenario, the alleged kidnappers call directly, saying they are holding your loved one and demanding money. In neither case has an actual person been abducted—but that doesn't make these episodes any less traumatic.

Fake kidnappers can call from anywhere. They collect as much personal information as they can about a target, using social media sites to obtain all sorts of details, including nicknames, hobbies, family members, and pet names. These scammers use hacking techniques to obtain even the unlisted cell phone numbers of their marks. When the kidnappers make the call, they usually have someone screaming the name of the target in the background, or "Mommy" or "Daddy," in the case of a child kidnapping ruse. They then try to keep the target on the phone for as long as possible, threatening to do harm to the loved one if the target hangs up. Scammers try to convince the person to wire money to a bank account—and, unlike in real kidnappings, where the sums requested can go into the millions, the amounts are smaller, in the thousands of dollars. Ransom demands can drop quickly, as scammers will do anything they can to get you to send money.

NOTORIOUS G: THE GRANDPARENT SCAM

You may have heard of the grandparent scam, in which scammers demand the target send substantial amounts of cash, pretending to be their grandchildren. Unfortunately, people seventy and older who pay a scammer in cash rarely report the crime to the Federal Trade Commission. We do know, however, that 25 percent of people seventy and older who have reported fraud to the FTC said they sent the scammer cash. The average loss from impostor fraud for people from all age groups was about $2,000. For people over seventy who sent cash to scammers, it was much worse—median individual losses were $9,000.

Rich, a target of such a scam, picked up his office phone one day and heard an innocent-sounding voice on the other end say, "Hi, Grandpa."

"Who's this?" he asked.

"Don't you recognize my voice? It's John. I'm in Chicago."

Rich thought the voice certainly sounded like someone his grandson's age, but he wasn't positive it actually was his grandson, who lived in Los Angeles, not Chicago. But John's sister, Louise, had a job in the Windy City, so Rich figured maybe John was visiting her.

"Can I tell you something in secret that you won't tell anybody else, please?" the young man asked. "Louise and I went to a White Sox game last night," he said. "We were on our way back to our hotel when our cab was pulled over by the police. They found pot in the trunk and arrested us. I'm at the police station now with a lawyer." *Weird,* Rich thought, since Louise was renting a cute little apartment. Why would they need a hotel room?

"Were you carrying any drugs yourselves?" he asked. "No," came the answer. Rich wondered why his grandson would be arrested if the drugs were in the cab's trunk, not on the young man's person. It's possible he could have been detained temporarily as a witness, but since a cab is a service available to the public, passengers would not be held accountable or liable for anything the cabdriver had in his vehicle.

"The police say I have to stay in Chicago for four to six weeks, until the cabdriver's trial. If they release us, they want $2,000 to make sure we'll come back," the young man said, and asked Rich to talk to his lawyer. "He's right here next to me." Rich then asked the young man why he'd called him, hundreds of miles away, instead of relatives who lived in Chicago.

"Please, Grandpa," came the emotional response. "Please help."

Skeptical still, Rich asked, "John, can you tell me your address in Los Angeles?" With that one question, the phone went dead.

After the call ended, Rich emailed his family members to tell them about what had happened and heard from two of John's other grandparents, who told him they'd received similar calls.

One identified it as a scam right away and hung up. But another grandparent was a victim. He had received a call claiming that his grandson Mark had been arrested in Arizona after getting into a bar fight and needed $1,500 bail. The grandfather, shaken, asked, "Can I speak to Mark?" A young man got on the phone and explained to the grandfather that he did indeed need bail money. When the grandfather mentioned that the caller didn't sound much like his grandson, the young man, sounding distraught, said his nose had been broken in the fight and it was affecting his voice.

"Mark" explained that there was a Western Union near the grandfather's home, and he could go there and wire the needed money right away. So the grandfather went there and wired $1,500. A short time after arriving home, the phone rang again, and the caller, again identifying himself as his grandson, thanked him for the money . . . and asked for more. It was then that the grandfather realized it was a scam. He immediately called his daughter (the mother of his grandson) to ask where the boy was. "At work," she replied, and nowhere near Arizona. He was deeply embarrassed about becoming a victim, and refused to report the incident to the police.

It's not clear in this case whether the scammers even knew the child's name until the grandfather said it. Sometimes scammers call numbers at random, searching for a person who is old enough to have a grandchild. They mention that the grandchild is in trouble and improvise from there. Other scammers buy lead lists of people who've been scammed before or people who are older and have grandchildren. They also garner information through social media sites, genealogy pages, and even obituaries. Another ploy, as in Rich's case, is having someone acting as an authority figure, such as a lawyer, available to step in to add credibility to the story.

Here's what to do if you get a call from someone claiming to be a family member in need.

- **Hit the pause button.** Calm yourself, be skeptical, and say you will have to consult another family member before taking any action.
- **Check it out.** Call family members or the person who the caller claims to be at a known number to check on the person's whereabouts. If the emergency is real, you can respond accordingly. If it's not, you've avoided a scam.
- **Call back.** Generally, you won't want to ask for a callback number, since a scammer will give you a fake number and have a co-conspirator answer the phone. But if you do get a callback number for a purported police station or lawyer's office, for example, verify it online. Better yet, ask where they are and then look up the phone number for that place. If it's legit, you can call back after you've checked with other family members.
- **Probe.** Question the callers without giving up any information—expect *them* to provide it. In Rich's case, he asked for his grandson's address, which the scammers didn't know, so they hung up. Asking for details without providing any is a good way to find out if it's a scam. Eventually scammers will run up against a detail they do not know.
- **Don't post bail.** If you get a phone call asking you to post bail, don't pay anything over the phone or by wire transfer. Again, call any law enforcement office back on a

number you locate independently and find out exactly where the person is detained and the booking status. You can also use the court's website to determine whether an arrest was actually made.

- **Follow the money.** Pay close attention to how the person wants you to provide money. If it's by wire transfer via Western Union or MoneyGram, a prepaid debit card, or cash or check sent via courier, that's a red flag.
- **Report it.** If you're a target of a grandparent scam or receive a scam call, even if you don't become a victim, report it to the FTC at www.ftc.gov/complaint or by calling 877- FTC-HELP. You can also call AARP's Fraud Watch Network hotline at 877-908-3360; all that data is uploaded into the FTC consumer data. The FTC tracks scammers to help other victims.

THE FAKE INHERITANCE SCAM

Recently, I received a letter that claimed to be from a lawyer representing a long-lost and now dead wealthy relative who left me millions of dollars. I've gotten these before and have seen many others in my work at the FBI. They explain that all you have to do is contact this lawyer, often representing the "Royal Bank of Grenada," for example. If it's a letter sent to your home or business address, it might be on heavy paper stock with an impressive bank seal in gold or platinum. It looks official—and important. Except, of course, it's a scam.

The author of the correspondence will provide detailed instructions on how you can access this large sum of money if you reply. But if you do, you will receive directions to wire a fee to the attorney's account—just a mere percentage of the millions that will allegedly be coming to you. Your bank routing and account numbers are required, too—so that the lawyer representing the deceased relative can make sure those millions reach you safely. With this payment and information, your surprise inheritance can be processed.

Phony inheritance scams have existed for decades (see "Hall of Shame: Baker's Dozens," page 257). They were first spread by classified ads in newspapers looking for victims—the supposed "rightful heirs" of someone with an often common-sounding last name. Today, inheritance scams are more often done via email. They are an iteration of the phony lottery-winning scam (page 35), which says you have a large sum of money coming to you if you wire a modest fee to the author of the email or letter to complete the transaction.

If you receive any kind of correspondence about an inheritance, do the following.

- **Cut the wire.** Never wire money to strangers.
- **Verify.** Check any correspondence you receive about inheritances to make sure names and addresses are legitimate. Run an Internet search on names and check companies with consumer protection agencies to discover any pattern of abuse or complaints.
- **Understand your rights.** If you think any correspondence about an inheritance looks legitimate, consult with an attorney specializing in estate law before proceeding.

Hall of Shame: Baker's Dozens

In 1839, a man named Colonel Jacob Baker died, leaving a tract of land in Philadelphia worth billions of dollars. Or so the legend went. Many years later, in the 1920s, a man named William Cameron Morrow Smith formed a legal association and placed ads in newspapers asking people with the Baker last name to join in the fight to recover their fortune. All that was required was a small fee so that Smith and his associates would have the money to fight the legal battle for the inheritance—which participants would split once the fortune was recovered.

The problem was that Colonel Baker existed only in the mind of William Smith. It was a scam perpetrated on thousands of people drawn in by the possibility of claiming their share of a lost fortune. The government finally learned of the scam, and after a twelve-year investigation, Smith was arrested in 1936, but not before what is known as the Baker Estate Fraud had netted him and his colleagues close to $25 million from more than fifty thousand Bakers, Barkers, and even some Beckers from all over the United States and Canada.

STOLEN INHERITANCE: FAMILY ESTATE FRAUD

Far worse morally than scams involving nonexistent inheritances, in my view, is when relatives, friends, or trusted professionals work to steal real inheritances that heirs legitimately deserve. In this crime, there are several victims: the person whose money is being misdirected and the true heirs.

My friend John was a victim of inheritance fraud. John is in law enforcement and incredibly savvy and experienced. His story demonstrates just how clever fraudsters can be.

John grew up in Arkansas, one of four children in a happy and close family. "My mom passed away in 2001, my dad received her money, and after that he reconnected with an old college girlfriend, Joan." The couple got married and moved about thirty miles away from John's home in Virginia. "I was not happy about it, but that's okay. My father seemed content, and he and his new wife lived only thirty miles from me. That was a blessing."

But things changed when John's father was diagnosed with leukemia in 2009. "He fought that very hard," John told me. Joan had a daughter living in Brooklyn who was pregnant, so in April 2012, she and John's father moved to New York (about three hundred miles away), without John or his siblings knowing it. "It was only after they had moved that he let us know," John said. "Yet we remained in close contact with him and his wife."

After his father died, that summer, John went to New York, and Joan gave John a copy of his father's will.

"I saw he had signed this will just a few months prior to his death," he said. Bells went off. "There are a hundred reasons why a seventy-nine-year-old man with a terminal illness would change his will, and I would put elder financial abuse on the top of that list," said John, who believes that as his father got sicker, it was easier for his second wife to manipulate him.

Fast-forward to February 2013. Joan was the fiduciary of John's father's estate, and she submitted the inventory of the estate to probate court, claiming that his estate was worth around $70,000. But John believed the estate to be worth between $200,000 and $500,000. Joan also presented John with a statement that claimed the estate was worth far less than John believed. "She asked me and my siblings to sign it. We declined because . . . we had a strong hunch that the document she was asking us to sign was a lie," according to John. If John and his siblings were to sign the document, it meant they would be potentially handing Joan (and her attorney) tens of thousands of dollars. "My siblings and I felt we had a serious civil matter on our hands," John said. "We contacted a civil attorney, who went back and forth with my stepmother's attorney, who was the very same attorney who wrote my father's new and last will."

In July 2013, a year after his father's passing, John and his siblings still had not received any inheritance money. John sent a letter to the county's commissioner of accounts, asking only for a list of expenses for the adjudication of the will. Shortly after, John received a check from his father's wife, acting as his fiduciary, in the amount of $5,831.79, dated the same day he'd sent his letter to the commissioner of accounts. His three siblings received similarly dated checks for the same amount, which in total represented just over $23,000.

John investigated and believes he was the victim of a con. "I strongly suspected that the commissioner of accounts was running a trolling operation with my father's wife's attorney and another elder lawyer." (Trolling means conspiring to find someone to defraud.) "The only way my siblings and I received any money was because I had sent that letter. You see, the letter I sent didn't ask for money, so what caused these checks to be sent? I suspect [the commissioner] called the attorney who had generated the final will and warned him to get in touch with the fiduciary, Joan, to tell her to send the money."

In this type of trolling operation, fraudsters locate vulnerable and wealthy older people. These con artists often work as financial advisers and trusted professionals in the field of elder care and elder law. They are involved in country clubs, churches, senior centers, or friendship centers, where they troll for potential candidates. In John's case, it turned out the attorney who rewrote his father's will was a member of his father's church. (See page 115 for more on what's called "affinity fraud.")

"They often look for people with savings of at least $100,000, who live alone, or who are in diminished health," John told me. Once a target has been identified, the predators must gain access to their financial accounts. "These people win trust because they have excellent social skills and are able to apply undue influence over older people, gaining power of attorney, the transfer of titles to property, and the ability to shift heirs in wills and trusts," said John. In this situation, he believes that his father's second wife was also part of the inheritance scheme, aware of and complicit in what the attorney and the commissioner of accounts were doing.

It's been several years since John's father died, and the entire estate is still being adjudicated. Where the money went will likely never be known. "My father's wife has probably spent it all by now," John said. "He did not discuss these matters with us. The sway his new wife had over him was very powerful." The commissioner and the lawyers no doubt got their piece, too, John suspects, while John and his siblings received almost none of the money they deserved.

Other ways an inheritance can be stolen or fraudulently changed are just as insidious. A child can overreach and exert undue influence over a parent to change a will, insisting that he deserves more than other siblings. This often happens when one child feels that he has taken on more of his fair share of caring for a parent than the other siblings have provided. Outsiders could also gain the trust of a person and convince her to change her will or transfer property into their names. All a scammer has to do is get an individual to sign a revised will or hand over power of attorney and then the scammer has control of the money.

These scams happen frequently, but there is legal relief for people who feel that they or their family members have been taken advantage of: the Elder Abuse Prevention and Prosecution Act, which became law in 2017. It aims to help stem the tide of what its sponsor, Senator Chuck Grassley of Iowa, called "financial exploitation of America's seniors . . . the crime of the 21st century." The bill mandates increased penalties for fraud against people fifty-five and older, comprehensive training for FBI agents, elder justice coordinators in federal judicial districts and the FTC's Bureau of Consumer Protection, a working group to provide policy advice, a resource group to assist U.S. prosecutors in pursuing elder abuse cases, and more. I think this is good news.

Estate planning can be a complicated legal issue, so be sure to consult a trusted professional. To prevent inheritance theft, consider these tips.

- **Talk about it.** Have the conversation about what will happen to your money and property sooner rather than later. "Having lived through this, and if I could do it again, I would say talk to your parents when they are still young," John advised me. "My siblings and I should have gone to my father when he was sixty, or he to us. It would not have hurt my feelings if he had gone to one of my brothers or my sister and not me to discuss his will . . . Keep the lines of communication open. That way, if a disease does strike or someone gets hit by a car and dies, you've had the conversations. You've all reviewed the financial information."

- **Have a plan.** After you have a conversation, make a plan. Review that plan periodically—every five years or so.
- **Think like a predator.** Talk with your loved ones about the potential for people to take advantage of you or them. Think about how people might get in your good graces through community and other organizations, and be aware of the games they play to get you under the ether.
- **Identify trusted financial and legal advisers.** The best attorney might not be the person you meet at your house of worship or community center. Remember: John's father and his new wife met their lawyer at church. Check credentials and make sure professionals you're considering have no complaints against them.
- **Don't go it alone.** Never sign paperwork without consulting with your family or trusted advisers.

FAMILY HISTORY FRAUD

While you're trying to build your family tree and track down relatives you've never met, genealogy scammers are trying to get your money. Here are the most common scams.

Family name sites and books: Before you sign up for a lineage site or genealogy book online or from a mail solicitation, check out the offers and the companies very carefully. Scam sites compile information from public databases in an effort to deceive consumers into thinking they have detailed information about their family lineage. The goal of these sites is to convince you to register using your credit card so that they can steal that information or sign you up for recurring payments. The goal of family name books is to convince you that they have done extensive research on your family surname and will provide a book that is filled with generic information you could have found for free in a quick Internet search. One such company, called Halbert's, was prosecuted and shut down for running such a scam in the 1980s and '90s. Do an Internet search on the site name with "reviews" and "scams" and see what comes up.

Scam genealogists: Just about anyone can set up a website, claim to be a family historian, and then charge a fee for tracing your ancestors. That's okay as long as the person doing it represents herself or himself honestly. It's not even necessarily a bad sign if a person doesn't have any certifications in genealogy—many of you probably know at least one person in your family who is really good at constructing accurate family histories going back generations. But before giving your money to a researcher, know what you are getting for the fee and whom you're hiring to provide the information. The names of professional genealogists, both certified and uncertified, can be obtained from the Association of Professional Genealogists (www.apgen.org). Read the fine print of any agreements, and make sure you are not signing up for recurring fees for information you may never receive.

Phony coats of arms: You may have seen products emblazoned with your family name and a coat of arms at tourist or gift shops, online, or in newspaper ads. That's okay, if you want to have some fun. But most family names don't actually have a coat of arms—so, while it's not illegal to sell these products, they aren't authentic. Sure, I could create an Abagnale family crest, but it would not be officially recognized by any government or historical society.

ADOPTION FRAUD

The phone rang around 11 a.m. That was the time Darlene usually called. Mary picked up the phone to talk to the woman who was six months' pregnant with the baby that Mary and her husband, Jay, would eventually adopt. Mary and Darlene usually engaged in a lot of awkward small talk: Darlene detailed arguments with her family, the nice time she'd had with a friend at the movies, or her problems getting to and from work. Mary had already sent Darlene's mechanic $500 to help her fix her car—an amount that was well within the legal limits of what adoptive parents can give birth mothers in New York State, where Mary lived. On this call, Darlene mentioned that she needed $200 more to replace the battery in the car, and the cost of that also seemed within the limits prescribed by the state.

After Mary hung up with Darlene, she called her adoption attorney to double-check that it was okay to send the money. Her lawyer okayed the amount. Later that day, though, the lawyer called back. "Have you sent the money yet?" she asked Mary. "Yes, I sent it to the auto body shop. Why?" It turned out that Darlene had been talking to at least one other adoptive couple and asking them for money as well—to get her rent and utilities paid.

Promising your baby to more than one family is fraud. Darlene was exposed because she had answered an ad placed by another prospective couple in a local newspaper. Unfortunately for her, the number went straight to the office of Mary's lawyer, who was representing those prospective parents as well. An associate who answered the phone recognized the young woman's name and story. When Mary's lawyer confronted Darlene, she was never heard from again, and Mary and Jay had to start their search for an adopted child from scratch.

Placing classified ads and using the lawyer's contact information was common practice in some states back in 2006, when this incident happened. Now prospective parents and pregnant women who want to put up a child for adoption often use the Internet. Either way, the adoption process absolutely can and does work, but you can still be scammed.

Mary and her husband were the victims of a common form of adoption fraud: when women who are pregnant commit to or attempt to commit to more than one family to get money from each of them, said Suzanne Nichols, an adoption attorney in New York and New Jersey with more than thirty years of experience in the field. In situations like this, Nichols told me, the woman often has no intention of placing her baby for adoption. All states have a window of time within which a birth mother can change her mind after the birth of a baby, and that time frame varies from state to state.

Another adoption fraud involves women who are not even pregnant faking documents to show that they are. "That's why you need someone who can interpret medical records, because people who say they are pregnant are not necessarily pregnant," said Nichols. A professional will never let you get involved until medical records prove beyond a doubt that the woman is pregnant, along with a projected due date. "The due date is important because a woman can be pregnant and say she is due in three months, but the actual pregnancy records say she is due in six months. That date can affect many things, including expenses paid to the mother by the adoptive parents."

Technology has made pregnancy fraud somewhat easier, which is why Nichols said she does not accept anything but original paperwork from potential birth mothers. "Taking pictures of documents and then emailing or texting them is not good enough. Scanning documents is also not acceptable, because photos and scans of documents can hide tampering or changes. Never accept anything but an original ultrasound and medical paperwork," she told me. "I also had a birth mom tell me the name of her doctor, and when I checked online, there was no doctor by that name in her area. In that sense, the Internet can be a positive; it allows you to do quick information verifications."

A CHANGED MIND IS NOT NECESSARILY A SCAM

As I mentioned, the time period in which a birth mother can change her mind after the birth of a baby, and can take her baby back from adoptive parents, varies from state to state. Birth moms can and do change their minds for legitimate reasons, so be prepared. Adoptions happen every day, but they are emotional roller coasters. Mary and Jay relinquished one baby when the birth mother changed her mind within her state's seventy-two-hour window. It was not a scam; she just changed her mind. It's understandable, since placing a child can be a heavy-duty act of selflessness. "You never know," Suzanne Nichols told me. "I had a birth mom change her mind because the adoptive parents brought a nanny to the birth. The birth mom had raised four children as a very young mother and without help, and the idea of a nanny bothered her."

DNA TESTING: FRIEND OR FOE?

In June 2018, a genealogy and home DNA-testing company called MyHeritage announced that the email addresses of more than 92 million of its clients had been found sitting on a server outside of the company. The files contained clients' email addresses and "hashed" passwords—that is, passwords that are scrambled using some high-tech formula. That meant that clients' DNA results and other information could potentially be accessed by anyone who obtained those email addresses and deciphered the passwords. MyHeritage's announcement of the breach noted that "the hash key differs for each customer," suggesting a fairly sophisticated security measure where an additional and usually unique value was added to the password before hashing, to make the hash itself more resilient to cracking—but not impossible. Fortunately, I've yet to hear of anyone who has been defrauded as a result of this breach.

While it's fun and fascinating to learn about your background and potential medical future using DNA testing—and many people have constructed amazing family trees and connected with formerly unknown relatives using these kits—privacy concerns are something to take seriously. A 2018 FTC probe into DNA testing was prompted in part by U.S. Senator Chuck Schumer, when his office expressed concern that DNA test kits could put consumers' privacy at risk, since DNA-testing companies may sell or share information with third parties.

Schumer stated: "Putting your most personal genetic information in the hands of third parties for their exclusive use raises a lot of concerns, from the potential for discrimination by employers all the way to health insurance. That's why I am asking the Federal Trade Commission to take a serious look at this relatively new kind of service and ensure that these companies have clear, fair privacy policies and standards for all kinds of at-home DNA test kits. We don't want to impede research but we also don't want to empower those looking to make a fast buck or an unfair judgement off your genetic information."

In December 2017, Lesley Fair, senior attorney for the Bureau of Consumer Protection at the FTC, also expressed concern to consumers about the testing kits, and offered some advice about protecting the privacy of the sensitive information that DNA tests reveal.

- **Be proactive about privacy.** While several companies offer similar testing services, check to make sure the one you choose has strong privacy guidelines in place. What does the company do with your personal data? Don't buy a kit until you know your information will be kept private.
- **Know the risks.** Hacks happen every day, and in all kinds of ways. Before you swab your cheek or spit into a test tube, think about the risks associated with DNA testing and the fact that hackers could gain access to your information in a data breach.
- **Be cautious about website options.** Similar to social media websites, testing companies allow you to customize, to a certain extent, how and if your contact information or "profile" can be accessed by outsiders or fellow site members. However, the default settings of testing sites may not be the most private. Do you want your profile to be public, available only to other users, or completely private? Think about this before setting up your account. Do you want other users to be able to send you a personal message? This might be desirable if you are trying to connect with family members. But someone who seems to be connected to you may not be who they say they are, and even if they are related to you, that doesn't guarantee good intentions. Once you set your privacy options, revisit and potentially revise them until you are comfortable with the way the site works.

- **Speak up.** If you signed on to a genetic-testing company but feel it is not living up to its stated promises about confidentiality, tell the FTC. They've brought dozens of cases challenging deceptive or unfair practices related to consumer privacy and data security, including a settlement with a business that sold products based on at-home genetic testing but allegedly failed to provide the promised security of consumers' personal information.

Family is special, and family-related fraud can be just plain greed. Or it can be very personal—like the relative who manipulates a loved one into rechanneling a financial legacy. Those frauds could be the result of pent-up anger, hurt feelings, or ongoing disputes. That is why the best advice I can give you— and it is advice I try to live every day—is to keep the lines of communication open between your loved ones. Discuss matters when they arise; don't wait. Settle disputes quickly and fairly, and be willing to compromise.

And for those frauds committed by your garden-variety con artist, I hope the tips provided in this chapter help you spot them—and walk away.

13.

Charity Scams: Giving Back, or Dodgy Donations?

C on artists set up all sorts of phony charities and claim to help all sorts of groups and causes—from veterans to disaster relief to animals and more. That's because scammers know there is money to be made from generous donors—Americans gave more than $410 billion to charities in 2017. In this chapter, I go over some traditional scams as well as social media and "crowdsourcing" charity rip-offs. More important, I provide tips on how to avoid getting taken when you're just trying to help.

REGULATIONS AND SCAMS

The regulation (or lack thereof) of charitable organizations makes it easy for fraudsters to set up phony charities. It's not difficult to obtain 501(c)(3) designation, the tax-exempt status a charity needs to operate. For example, a charity could give as little as one-half of 1 percent of what it takes in to its cause and remain within the boundaries of the law—as long as it does not mislead donors or lie to them about where money goes.

"That's the unfortunate part of the regulation," said Paul Streckfus, who worked in the IRS's Exempt Organizations (EO) Division and is editor of the *EO Tax Journal*. "A charity can't engage in politics according to law, but if a charity for orphan children, for example, has a million dollars in the bank and holds a picnic for these orphans once a year, they are legitimately operating as a charity, because they are doing *something* for orphans."

The Internal Revenue Service regulates these charities on the federal level, but, because of short staffing, keeping charities in line can fall on state regulators, according to Streckfus. Even when scam charities do get caught running afoul of regulations and are forced to shut down, many simply start over again under new names. That's why you have to be extremely vigilant about the charities you give to.

So how do you make sure the charity you're considering is really doing good? Several organizations rate and review charities to ensure they are fulfilling their stated mission and identify the percentage of donations that go to that mission. I have provided a list of some of the best ones in Resources, page 321. This list includes Charity Navigator and Give.org, which have easy research tools. Charities giving minimal amounts to a cause may be just barely on the right side of the law, but by spending the lion's share of their proceeds on salaries, fund-raising, and other administrative costs, they are also diverting money away from the people or groups they purport to serve and away from the very best charities, those who use the majority of donations to make a difference.

You can also check lists of the worst charities. These lists generally call out charities that allocate 4 percent or less of the donations they receive to direct cash aid. Over a ten-year period, one charity raised $14 million but distributed only $10,000 to in-need diabetes patients, the population it was meant to serve. Six charities offered no direct cash aid at all. Do you really want charities like that to have your money and personal information?

MAKE A LIST, CHECK IT TWICE

Consider writing up an annual giving list and providing it to everyone in your family and, if you own a small business, your employees. If you are solicited by an organization that isn't on the list, simply explain that you have given to your selected charities, and then politely decline to contribute.

VETERANS CHARITY FRAUD

I find fake charities that pretend to support vets to be particularly egregious. The money doesn't get to injured or emotionally or financially distressed vets and instead goes to criminals who benefit by falsely associating themselves with heroic people.

Travis Deloy Peterson ran veterans charities, including one called Veterans of America—a credible-sounding name—which promised that donated cars, boats, and other items would be picked up and sold, and the proceeds used to help veterans.

Peterson employed aggressive and illegal robocalling tactics, falsely claiming that donations would be tax-deductible when in fact his charities were fictitious and did not even have tax-exempt status, according to the FTC. Between May 2014 and July 2018, Peterson received numerous donations of cars and boats, which he sold, using the proceeds for personal gain.

Peterson was part of a larger government crackdown on phony veteran charities. The shutdown of Peterson's operation, anounced in July 2018, was a joint effort of the FTC, attorneys general from U.S. states and territories, and sixteen additional state agencies that oversee charities. The coordinated effort to target fraudulent and deceptive fund-raising for military and veteran causes resulted in one hundred actions against phony veteran groups.

Before giving to any veterans group, do your research (see page 284 for tips on how) to make sure you're giving to an organization that matches your vision of how a charity should spend its money.

Hall of Shame: Kai Brockington

Georgia fraudster Kai Brockington had an unusual and lucrative approach to charity fraud. He didn't steal from individual donors. Instead he convinced and sometimes even paid people to lie to their employers about donating to a phony charity he ran so he could pocket the funds companies gave in "matching" programs (when a company matches a donation you make to a nonprofit). "He created a real charity on paper, but it never actually did anything other than line his own pockets," said Special Agent James Harter of the FBI's Atlanta Division, who worked on the case.

In 2013, Brockington set up a charity known as Our Genesis Project. It claimed to fund community medical clinics to serve needy populations. He even registered the organization as a charity with the state of Georgia and the Internal Revenue Service. Next he tricked his own employer into matching his donation and enlisted several friends and associates to tell their employers that they had donated money to the cause. The companies matched the donations, most of which went to Brockington, although he sometimes paid the donors a percentage of the money he took in. He received $668,000 in donations over about four years. He spent all of it on himself and his family.

A bank noticed suspicious activity on the faux charity's account, and when they looked into Our Genesis Project, they saw that the charity's website was constantly "under construction" and that there was no evidence of anything charitable happening. The bank tipped off the FBI, and in May 2018, Brockington pleaded guilty to tax and mail fraud. He was sentenced to forty-one months in federal prison.

According to the FBI, the donating businesses never checked into the charities, and that was a significant factor in Brockington's swindle working for as long as it did. Moreover, many of the donations that some employees claimed they made far exceeded their salaries. "If the employee's income wouldn't reasonably cover a charitable donation," said Special Agent Harter, "the employer should probably ask where that money is coming from before matching the donation."

DISASTER RELIEF FRAUD

I wrote this chapter in October 2018, as Hurricane Michael barreled toward the Florida Panhandle, its eye focused sharply on Panama City and Mexico Beach. The monster storm was expected to do maximum damage to the area, and, unfortunately, it didn't disappoint. Michael's 155-mile-per-hour landfall winds were only two miles per hour short of Category 5 status. That made it the strongest storm to strike the United States since Hurricane Andrew had plowed through South Florida in 1992. No storm of this magnitude had ever touched down in the Florida Panhandle in recorded weather history.

When it was all over, at least forty-three people had died, entire blocks of homes and businesses were completely obliterated in Mexico Beach, and many other parts of the Panhandle suffered devastating property damage. Roughly 1.5 million people lost power, from Florida to Virginia.

Many groups and individuals came together to help, from FEMA to the Red Cross. People from all across the United States asked how they could help. With pictures of homes flattened by a hurricane and children looking hungry and lost, who wouldn't be moved to help?

But some people take advantage of disasters for personal gain. In fact, this is a prime time for scammers who prey on your charitable instincts. Beware of calls or social media posts from charities or individuals asking for money right after a national or global disaster. Do your research, or, better yet, make your donations to long-standing, reputable organizations so that you can be confident it is being used for its intended and stated purpose.

These campaigns are overseen by experts to ensure that donations of money, goods, and services are used properly and go to the people who need them most. One example is attorney Kenneth Roy Feinberg, who was the court-appointed special master overseeing the September 11th Victim Compensation Fund. Later, Feinberg served as the government-appointed administrator of the BP Deepwater Horizon Disaster Victim Compensation Fund, and in 2013 he became administrator of a fund to help victims of the 2013 Boston Marathon bombings. Giving to a compensation fund that is administered by an expert like Feinberg is one way of knowing your money is being distributed and spent appropriately.

ANIMAL RESCUE RIP-OFFS

Americans give a lot of money to animal charities. Nonprofits that focus on the environment and animals received $11.83 billion, or 3 percent of all U.S. charitable donations, in 2017. It's important to me on a personal level as well. Growing up, my family always had pets. Dogs, cats, fish, birds, minks—you name it. My wife worked in a veterinary clinic in Houston during high school and college. My wife and I also had pets that our boys loved and learned how to care for. So animals and animal rescue mean a lot to us as a family.

Unfortunately, animal rescue fraud is a big problem. According to the Humane Society of the United States, collecting accurate data on animal populations found at shelters and rescue centers is extremely difficult, because there are no real reporting requirements for these organizations. The ASPCA reports that about 6.5 million pets enter shelters each year, while the Humane Society puts the number at six to eight million.

Even more challenging is figuring out which rescue centers and shelters are reputable and which ones aren't. Images of sweet kittens and soulful puppies stuck in cages touch most of us on a deep emotional level—I can't think of a person who is not moved by the suffering of an innocent animal. As a result, animal lovers donate a great deal of money, as well as goods (food, blankets, towels, feed bowls) and volunteer hours, to shelters and rescue missions. Many of these organizations are legitimate, but scammers also prey on the compassion and generosity of animal lovers, either by pretending to rescue animals or by running animal shelters that are crowded and filthy.

Oftentimes, animal shelter or rescue scams start with pictures posted on fraudulent rescue websites or posts on social media sites like Facebook and Twitter. The bad guys will post pictures of animals and claim that they are being kept at "high kill" shelters and are next on a list to be euthanized. The pleas threaten imminent death unless money is sent to rescue these adorable animals and move them to no-kill shelters or private homes. Time is always a factor in these scams (as it is in real situations, where animals really *are* high on kill lists). This is a very effective strategy, since there are, in fact, legitimate rescue services that alert people about animals who are about to be put down. But in kill-list scams, the money collected by scammers does not go to save an animal, nor does it go to any legitimate rescue groups or shelters, according to Teresa Chagrin, the Animal Care and Control Issues Manager for People for the Ethical Treatment of Animals (PETA). "There's often not even an animal involved, and the picture attached to the plea was probably stolen," she notes.

Sometimes, when there is a real shelter involved, it will be in deplorable condition. At some shelters that have been raided, law enforcement agencies have found live dogs stuffed in cages alongside others that have died, and hundreds of cats wandering around covered with sores and in pain. These animals are often starving and injured. Adrienne Gonzalez, a reporter who investigates animal fraud and heads up a watchdog website called GoFraudMe, says that some rescue groups are run by hoarders who tell people they will take their unwanted animals and care for them—but the rescuers are quickly overwhelmed by the number of mouths to feed and care for, and disaster ensues. Donations to these groups may go to buying a little bit of pet food, but mainly they are collected by the people running the sham shelters and used for personal benefit.

IF YOU SEE SOMETHING WRONG, TELL SOMEONE

Strong animal welfare laws in the United States are designed to protect both domesticated and wild species. These laws apply equally to mammals, reptiles, amphibians, and birds. If you believe an animal is being harmed or in danger, especially because of fraudulent activity, call 911. It is extremely important to report crimes, and calling 911 about a crime against an animal is legitimate, legal, and appropriate. Be ready to answer, to the best of your ability, where, who, what, when, and how. Remember: Law enforcement cannot stop animal cruelty and fraud if they do not know about it.

Here's how to make sure you're helping pets and protecting yourself.

- **Contribute to spay and neuter clinics.** "If you care for animals, animal homelessness, and unwanted animals that end up in shelters, donating to a spay and neuter clinic means your money is going to prevent animals from becoming homeless in the first place," said PETA's Chagrin. "Donating to these groups saves thousands of puppies and kittens just by spaying one dog or cat." Chagrin also points out that spay and neuter clinics are rarely, if ever, scams. Of course, you should always check to make sure the clinic actually exists if you do donate to one. Visit local clinics if you can, and research others online.

- **Make sure the animal exists.** Before sending money or committing to take an animal (and pay for any shots or medical care it might need), verify that the animal actually exists and is in need, or in danger of being euthanized. You can do this by setting up a video call to see animals and calling the shelter where they are staying.

- **Check conditions.** If you plan on helping a shelter or rescue group in your area, visit! I cannot stress this enough—if a shelter or rescue center refuses to let you on the grounds or take a tour, that is a major red flag.

- **Don't give to individuals or organizations you cannot check out.** If you see a posting on social media about an animal on a kill list, or a plea from a "friend of a friend" about a need for money to help a shelter or rescue you are unfamiliar with, first verify the legitimacy of this claim.

- **Volunteer!** If you are able, volunteer at a local shelter or rescue mission. Giving your time and love to animals in need is one of the best ways to help.

CROWDSOURCE AND SOCIAL MEDIA GIVING

Kate McClure was driving in Pennsylvania one night in October 2017 when her car's fuel warning light came on. She kept driving, hoping to make it home, but eventually ran out of gas. She had no choice but to pull over, get out of her car, and start walking toward the closest gas station. That was when she ran into a homeless man, Johnny Bobbitt, sitting by the side of the road. He looked pretty scruffy, but when he asked Kate what was wrong, she didn't feel threatened. Kate told him she had run out of gas, and Johnny told her to get back in her car and lock the doors. He soon came back with a red gas can filled with fuel. Johnny said he had used his last $20 to buy the gas so Kate could get home safely. Kate was so struck by his generosity and the fact that he was homeless that she and her boyfriend, Mark D'Amico, decided to raise money for Johnny through GoFundMe, an online resource for soliciting and receiving money for charitable causes.

"Johnny did not ask me for a dollar, and I couldn't repay him at that moment because I didn't have any cash," Kate wrote on the GoFundMe page. "But I have been stopping by his spot for the past few weeks. I repaid him for the gas, gave him a jacket, gloves, a hat, and warm socks, and I give him a few dollars every time I see him." The page sought to raise money so Johnny could rent an apartment and start to get back on his feet again.

The story went viral, and the couple raised more than $400,000 on Johnny's behalf from people around the globe. More than fourteen thousand donors pitched in. Kate and Mark's tale of wanting to help Johnny get back on his feet—by helping him kick his addiction to drugs, secure him an apartment and living expenses, and, eventually, find a sustainable job—was pure media gold.

But it was all a scam, and all three people were in on it from the get-go. The so-called hero homeless man, the woman he "saved" with some gas, and her boyfriend were all colluding to create the fund-raising scam. In fact, they had known each other for a month before the scam went into action. They had come up with the plan to create, first, the heartwarming story, and then the fund-raiser to dupe unsuspecting people out of their cash.

This case shows that, as worthy as many social media fund-raising campaigns can seem, if you don't know the fund-raiser personally, you really don't know where or to whom your money is going or how it will be used. These donations are usually not tax-deductible, either—which is not a reason not to give, but it is something to keep in mind. In theory, Internet fund-raising is a great concept—since you can give money directly to the person who needs it. But I'm sure that the people who gave $10, $50, or $1,000 to the Johnny Bobbitt campaign didn't want their money to go toward a new BMW or a trip to Europe for the couple who started the GoFundMe account.

The problem with online fund-raisers is that anyone can set one up for any reason, real or imagined. "It was not that long ago that people were ashamed to go to the Internet to ask for help, and now they have become quite bold about it," said Gonzalez. "When I started to track Internet fund-raisers in 2015, the most popular were for funeral expenses. Today, it seems as if you can't die without a GoFundMe page."

"GoFundMe claims to deploy round-the-clock observation of the platform and best-of-class monitors," she adds, "but my argument is, if the platform is so good, why is there no shortage of GoFundMe scams to write about? I have been monitoring the GoFundMe platform for four years, and the fact is, anyone with a sob story can establish an account."

Gonzalez is right. We decided to set up an account to raise money for a house that had supposedly burned down, and it took a matter of minutes. It was very straightforward—though a lie. We took it down immediately, of course, but it proves Gonzalez's point that it's easy, and required no verification or proof that my house had actually burned down. Fund-raising sites are businesses, and it is "donor beware"—as is true of any free market transaction.

There are other ways online funding scams prey on people's sympathies. "Not long ago, I saw a Twitter account of someone claiming to be a gay teen whose ultra-religious parents were throwing her out of the house. She created a GoFundMe account that day and had collected $4,000. The next day the account—and the money—was gone," said Gonzalez. Whether this was real or made up, we'll never know.

Unless you can confirm that the stories are true and you know the money will be well spent, it's better to decline to give, no matter how tragic the situation sounds. A friend of mine, for example, donated baby clothing to a local woman in need whom she read about on her Facebook News Feed. A few of her Facebook friends seemed to have connections to her. It seemed legitimate, so she dropped off new and nearly new baby clothes at the woman's house. Later, several people saw the woman selling the donated clothes to a resale shop. Once you give something to someone and it is theirs, they can do what they want with it. Make sure you are okay with that.

The bottom line, said Gonzalez, is to give to a regulated charity that helps the groups and causes you care about. This is not to say there are no legitimate causes helped by GoFundMe and other for-profit online funding groups. There are. Discerning between good and bad, real and fake, is what can be challenging. Although crowdsourcing websites like GoFundMe or CrowdRise by GoFundMe do try to monitor what goes up on their site, keep in mind that these are businesses, not nonprofits. "An IRS-regulated charity may be a better bet," Gonzalez said.

CHARITY BEGINS WITH HOMEWORK

There are many ways you can determine whether a phone call, pitch letter, or social media post claiming to solicit aid for those in need for any reason—police, firefighters, veterans, children, animals, the environment, important research, or historical and cultural preservation—is legit. Here's how.

Verify legitimacy. The organization or individual soliciting funds should be a legitimate 501(c)(3) charitable group. Ask to see an official letter from the IRS showing that it is registered and tax-exempt. The organization or individual should also be able to show you a copy of the IRS Form 990 or 990-EZ showing its financial reporting for each year. Or you can look it up on the IRS website. If the 501(c)(3) organization takes in more than $20,000 per year, it would also have, and be able to produce upon request, annual returns and applications of exemption. If it is incorporated, articles of incorporation and bylaws should be available.

Find out how much of the money is going to the stated mission. How many of your dollars actually get to the cause? The percentage you feel comfortable with is up to you. Charities know the exact percentages of dollars spent on fund-raising, salaries, and the cause itself. See Resources, page 321, for a list of websites that provide the percentage a charity spends on its stated mission versus administrative costs.

Find out about the charity's specific good deeds. Don't accept answers like "We educate the public" or "We raise awareness"—alone, those are empty and meaningless phrases. Look for specific projects that have quantifiable results. In some cases, you can actually check up on the response. For instance, if a charity claims that it provides school supplies to needy children in your local district, call the school administrator to verify that claim.

Check the name twice. Some deceptive charities mimic the names of well-known charities by changing a single word. In March 2018, four people were indicted on charges of creating the Wounded Warrior Fund and Wounded Warrior Foundation, tricking donors into believing they were giving money to the Wounded Warrior Project (which has also come under fire for misappropriation of funds). Instead of putting the money toward clothing, school supplies, and food baskets, the alleged fraudsters were accused of using donations worth more than $125,000 for personal gain. Similarly, a former New York stockbroker with ties to organized crime allegedly set up several bogus nonprofit organizations with legitimate-sounding names—the American Cancer Society of Washington, American Cancer Society of Seattle, American Red Cross of Seattle, American Red Cross of Washington, United Way of Seattle, and United Way of Washington—and by doing so obtained donations fraudulently. He kept donations for himself.

Check your mail. Experts say that old-fashioned paper mailings are less likely to be scams than email. Still, it pays to be suspicious of mail from groups you've never donated to. You may have gotten this mail because the sender bought your name and address from a marketing company or another charity that sells its donor list. Always authenticate the organization before donating.

Go local. "I always advise friends and neighbors to work with or give to charities they know or are working to serve their communities," said Paul Streckfus. That way you can see firsthand how they operate, get to know the people involved, and actually witness the good they are doing.

Don't let the pressure get to you. No reputable charity insists that you make a gift immediately. Telephone solicitors for legitimate good causes *can* be high-pressure, telling stories that are designed to tug at our heartstrings with a sense of enormous urgency. However, they *will* take no for an answer and give you time to check them out before donating.

Check registration. Check to see if your state or the state where a disaster happened requires charities and fund-raisers to be registered with the state by visiting the National Association of State Charity Officials (www.nasconet.org). If a state requires registration and the charity is not registered, seriously consider passing along your donation to another charity.

Double-check "text to donate" numbers. Before you text a donation to a charity, confirm the text number with the charity. The donation will show up as a line item on your mobile phone bill, but this could take a billing cycle.

Designate your donation. If you know the charity is legitimate and you are ready to donate, you might want to designate exactly where you want your money going—for example, a disaster relief, rather than a general fund the charity could use for any of its work.

Don't get taxed by donating. Personal appeals for money on crowdsourcing sites are typically *not* tax-deductible, which is different from donations to nonprofits like Goodwill, the Red Cross, or the Salvation Army. If you are concerned about the tax implications of your donation, do your homework on the tax status of the charity.

Pay safe. Be careful in the way you make a donation. Personal money transfers can be untraceable if the money is lost or stolen in transit. Cash is always untraceable—a few dollars tossed in a Salvation Army kettle and similar types of donations are low-risk, but large donations should not be made in cash, unless you can afford to lose it. Checks can be stopped before they clear. As always, I believe that paying by credit card is safest—but offer up credit card information only if you have initiated the donations. Don't give credit card information to unsolicited callers.

Charity scams prey on people's finest instincts to help others, contribute to the well-being of society and the planet, and help those in need. You never want your hard-earned dollars to be misdirected to a scammer's selfish financial needs. That's why it is so important to be diligent before you write that check, type in your credit card information, or drop off food and clothing. Never lose sight of the value in helping your neighbors, friends, and, yes, even strangers. But now that you're aware of the red flags, do be cautious.

14.

Love You Knot: The Wild World of Dating Scams

In the past twenty-six years, the advent of online and digital dating has changed the way we meet people. Before smartphone apps and dating websites, we'd traditionally seek out romance at bars, through newspaper personal ads, or through introductions made by well-meaning friends and relatives. One of the first online dating sites appeared in 1993, created by Andrew Conru, a Stanford University graduate student looking for love after a breakup, according to technology and science multimedia publication Motherboard.

Since that time, online dating has exploded—and so have dating scams. A 2019 AARP survey found that more than one in four adults over eighteen said that either they or someone they knew had been victimized in a relationship scam. The survey found that targets experience more feelings of social isolation and report more negative life experiences than those who haven't been targets. Strong social ties are so important in fighting so many scams, and romance is no exception.

This chapter looks at the most common scams, how to spot them, and how to protect yourself while searching for your soul mate—or even just a coffee date.

JUST ONE TAP AWAY: PHONE APP SCAMS

"It happened several times to me," said Timothy, a friendly sixty-year-old former fashion executive. After breaking up with his longtime partner, Timothy moved from Manhattan to a small artsy town along the Delaware River in Pennsylvania. He'd been single for five years before he started online dating. "I want to have a relationship, and I want to be monogamous, so it's challenging when you combine that desire with living in a somewhat rural area," he said. "I am geographically undesirable for a lot of legitimate people."

Still, there was no shortage of men who said they wanted to meet Timothy, who is youthful, fit, educated, and good-looking. When Timothy heard from a "serviceman" overseas, he was intrigued.

The man contacted Timothy via the dating app Tinder. "He told me he was deployed all around the world and was currently in Africa. He said his mother and father had died and he was all alone in the world. He caught his boyfriend in bed with another man," said Timothy, who really felt sorry for the fellow—an orphan stationed far from family, discovering that his partner had betrayed him. "I didn't send him money, but I did send him a care package, about $100 worth of stuff including underwear, homemade cookies, and other everyday items he said he needed. I sent it to an address in Africa," Timothy explained. Bells went off when the man told Timothy that he could not get the package out of customs and he needed $100 cash to pay the fee. That was when he realized it could be a scam. "I didn't send him any money."

Other men followed, telling similar tales of woe, with slight variations. "One told me he had a daughter and asked me if I was near a Walmart so I could buy him an iTunes card," said Timothy. He later learned that fraudsters want iTunes cards to buy upgrades of free dating apps. Since membership levels are displayed on the apps, members can see who belongs for free and who paid the fee. "Once they have a paid subscription or premium membership (paid for on someone else's dime), they seem so much more legitimate to other paid members."

UNTRUE LOVE

Today you can identify a potential partner based on their interests, talents, and location, right on your computer or cell phone, within minutes or even seconds. Use of dating mobile apps and websites has tripled since 2013. In 2018, mobile dating applications accounted for almost a quarter of the industry's revenue, and their growth has outpaced other dating services. I'm sure you know at least one person who has met their match online; I know several.

Simultaneously, the use of dating and other social media to scam unsuspecting, sincere people looking for love has also skyrocketed worldwide. It's called catfishing, where scammers, using fake identities and profiles, befriend victims through online social platforms and trick them into thinking they're sincere people looking for a committed relationship. Romance scammers have stolen millions of dollars from unsuspecting people over the years. In 2016 alone, they stole $220 million from Americans, according to the FBI. The agency also said that complaints about dating scams tripled between 2011 and 2016.

When I speak to groups today, I hear many stories from women and men who tell me how they were dating someone for six months or so before realizing the guy was married, for instance, or they met someone who disappeared shortly after they loaned him money.

Like other clever fraudsters, matchmaking criminals are skillful at what they do. They know which buttons to push with sincere and trusting people who are predisposed to finding love. Indeed, scammers can be geniuses at manipulating targets into believing they have found a genuine soul mate, and consequently into parting with large sums of money to cover a pressing doctor's bill or to pay the plane fare to meet you.

The perpetrators can be members of criminal rings from other countries who operate out of Internet cafés. Nigeria, a country with a large cohort of educated young men who are fluent in English yet have difficulty finding legitimate employment, has given birth to some of the largest of these rings. Or they can be people in the United States and other parts of the world with few skills or options, who turn to dating sites as a source of potential income. It can also be someone like I used to be, people who are just looking for a way to survive from one day to the next any way they can.

While the FBI says that the most common targets are women over forty who are divorced, widowed, and/or disabled, it doesn't matter if you're male or female, old or young, gay or straight.

Every age group and demographic is a potential target of a dating scam.

You don't have to hire a private detective to check up on a potential mate—you can and should do some due diligence on your own, because it's fairly easy. You can usually find out if a person works where they say they work with a single phone call to that place; you can confirm where they live with a quick Internet search. In fact, a search of a name can reveal quite a bit about a person (which, of course, should give us all pause, because there's a lot of information about everyone on the web).

You need to verify because with many free dating apps and sites, con artists can easily make a fake profile. We tested this out. My team and I were able to create fake profiles on several dating apps. One colleague of mine, a sixty-year-old married mother of one, created a fake profile, complete with photo, of a forty-five-year-old gay man living in Florida. Many men responded, including several who claimed to be deployed overseas and in need of money. The person you are talking to might not even be the gender or age he or she claims to be. While paying for a premium membership protects you somewhat from scammers, it's clearly not a guarantee.

HE HAS AN AFFINITY FOR YOU

Melissa Trent, a forty-something single mother in Colorado Springs, Colorado, logged into her account on the dating website Plenty of Fish and was excited to see a new message from a user called "lovetohike1972." Wow. Melissa was outdoorsy, and she had such bad luck finding anyone nice who shared her love of hiking and the Colorado wilderness. The message lovetohike1972 sent was pretty flattering, too: "I can't believe a woman as pretty as you is on a site like this."

Melissa was eager to check out his account, and she was not disappointed by what she saw. Lots of photos showed a really nice-looking, fit, smiling guy in hiking clothes, engaged in various outdoor activities. His interests included hiking, biking, skiing, and craft beer—all the things Melissa liked, too. She thought this guy sounded perfect—and such a change from most of the men who contacted her on the site, who she thought looked unappealing or seemed interested only in sex.

She decided to respond, and after exchanging a few messages, she gave the man her mobile number. He reached out later that evening. His name was Jeff Cantwell, and he was soft-spoken but energetic-sounding. He sounded *nice*. Jeff was new in town, having just relocated to Colorado Springs from Kodiak Island, Alaska, where he was born, to study to become an arborist.

A couple of days later, Melissa agreed to meet Jeff for a date in a public place. The attraction she had felt on the phone was confirmed when she saw and talked to him in person. He *was* good-looking. He looked just like his photographs—that gave her a feeling of security. They talked about hiking, and he regaled her with stories about some of his adventures on the trail. He seemed like the real deal. And there was no argument over the bill—Jeff paid. A few days later, he asked what her two daughters liked to eat, and then came over to make spaghetti and meatballs for all of them. It was a fun, easygoing dinner.

For several days after that, the two were in constant contact, by phone and text. Each time, Jeff told Melissa more and more about his background: He had lost his parents in a car accident, an accident that had also claimed the life of his fiancée and their baby. He had been in Afghanistan, where he was injured. He had completed many difficult and challenging hikes.

Then, one weekend shortly after their conversations had started getting deeper, Jeff told Melissa that his bank card had stopped working. At issue were his VA benefits—whenever a military check was deposited into his account, his account would be frozen while the check cleared. It seemed plausible enough to Melissa, who really didn't know much about how the VA worked. And Jeff had asked her for only $100 to see him through the weekend, which he would pay back promptly on Monday. Then they decided to go to a casino, and that was when Jeff asked Melissa if she could instead withdraw $200 from her account—$100 to get him through the weekend and $100 more for them to gamble with. She consented, and they actually managed to stretch the gambling money for ten hours before it was gone.

During their time at the casino, she overheard Jeff talking to another customer about living in Alaska, and she heard him tell the man, "My mom is Inuit," in the present tense. But he'd told *her* that his parents were deceased. It was the only red flag she had noticed up to that point. Still, she told herself that just because she would talk about a deceased person in the past tense didn't mean that everyone would. She dismissed it.

The following Monday, Jeff said he needed to drive to his bank's branch in Denver, more than an hour away, since he was still having trouble with the money in his account. She agreed to let him take her Audi. He also asked her if he could use the credit card that she left in her car to fill up the tank. Melissa didn't recall leaving a credit card in her car, but she put it out of her head and said okay.

After some time went by and Melissa had not heard back from Jeff, she became increasingly worried. Where was he? She texted him, and he replied that by the time he had gotten to Denver, the bank was closed, and he'd have to stay overnight—in her car, in the bank parking lot. Melissa wanted him to send a picture of him in the bank's parking lot to prove he was really there, but he became angry at her questioning. He texted through the night, and the messages seemed to become increasingly fraught with emotion. As a result, she called the El Paso County Sheriff's Office, who called Jeff and spoke to him about the car. He assured the officer that he would return the car. The police called Melissa back and told her not to worry—Jeff hadn't stolen her car.

But the next day there was still no car and no Jeff. At that point, Melissa learned that the police had been able to use Cantwell's cell phone number to identify him as Jeffrey Dean Caldwell, a forty-four-year-old criminal from Virginia who had already been incarcerated in several states for seven felonies, including burglary and writing bad checks. He had been paroled in September 2016 after serving some time for identity theft in Colorado. But in April 2017, after he connected with Melissa, he had stopped checking in with his parole officer.

Eventually Caldwell was arrested in South Dakota. Melissa did get her Audi back, but it was in very bad condition. Apparently, Caldwell had gone on a craft beer tour and decorated the car with stickers from every brewery he had visited. It was also a mess inside, as he'd apparently used the car as his home.

"These con men are transient and move around a lot without any way to track where they are," said Lieutenant James Disner, of the Larimer County Sheriff's Office, which had also arrested Caldwell almost a decade earlier. "I have been successful in a few of these types of cases, but only by reaching out to the communities they prey on."

Community is the key here—Caldwell sought out women in the hiking community, and Melissa was not his first victim. This is a type of affinity fraud, the same kind that financial scammers often use to lure victims into investment schemes (page 115). Dating scammers use common interests and membership in groups to connect with people and establish a basic level of trust. Caldwell often trolled Internet dating sites for "like-minded" people or found victims through in-person Meetup groups for hikers, and he would spend time at trailheads, hostels, outdoor equipment stores, and other places where hikers congregate and hang out, according to Brendan Borrell, a journalist who wrote about Caldwell and communicated with him while he was on the run from the law. So be mindful: Just because someone seems to share your interests or belongs to the same groups as you does not guarantee that the person is trustworthy.

PROTECT YOURSELF FROM ONLINE DATING SCAMS

Here are some other simple things you can do to protect yourself and your heart when it comes to finding love online.

- **Reality show.** Verify that the person you're talking to is real. Do an online search to see if the things you read match up with his or her claims. Is what you read on the person's Facebook, Twitter, or LinkedIn pages consistent with what you're being told?

- **Be mysterious.** At least in the beginning, and until you're sure you're not being scammed (see my list of red flags on page 301). Don't provide your last name, phone number, address, or place of work until you've actually met. Guard against suitors who ask for any of this personal information too quickly. Tactfully say something like "I have a policy not to disclose that information until we know each other better and have met in person."
- **Don't get tracked.** If you use a mobile app for dating, turn off your location settings so cons can't figure out where you live or where you go.
- **Photo finish.** Dating scammers tend to fraudulently use other people's photos and assume their identities or a made-up identity. Before you engage with anyone on a dating site, use https://tineye.com or Google Images to "search by image" and see if that person's photo shows up in other places using a different name.
- **Check out love letters.** If you get a suspicious message, check it out. Timothy says many of the messages he received from scammers used similar language, as if they were copied from a script. Cut and paste suspicious wording into a search engine and see if the same words pop up on any romance scam sites.

PRISONER OF LOVE

Lisa is a retired lieutenant from the Pennsylvania Department of Corrections. For many years she worked at the State Correctional Institution at Muncy, a state women's prison. She was perplexed by the number of prisoners who lure in people from the outside world with the promise of romance once they were no longer incarcerated—part of a scheme to extract money from innocent and well-meaning people. It is a subject that people who have been in contact with prisoners and scammed by them are reluctant to discuss. Being seduced by someone already in prison for committing a crime can be deeply embarrassing. Lisa wants to change that, by telling people who may be drawn to reach out to someone in trouble how to protect themselves.

Why do people communicate with prisoners? Most people who decide to become pen pals with people behind bars feel lonely, Lisa said, and "it comes from an altruistic impulse to reach out to someone in trouble and to help them change."

Inmates in state prisons can receive newspapers and periodicals, as long as they come directly from the publisher. They can also write and receive letters. While mailings are checked for contraband and letters can be read by guards, written romantic exchanges between prisoners and those on the "outside" can and do happen.

Lisa said that a small but popular community newspaper published near Muncy, *The Valley Trader,* had a section called "Look Before You Leap," which was made up of personal ads. Prisoners would use the small amount of money they received at prison jobs to place ads looking for pen pals and romance, and they would also answer ads from people looking for companionship, especially those with sad stories—for example, "My wife died recently and I am looking for a companion." These kinds of ads are common and appealing to prisoners looking for targets who may be vulnerable.

"The inmate would respond and basically tell the person

whatever they wanted to hear," said Lisa. The deception extends to physical appearance as well. "There are situations where a very heavy, middle-aged woman would send a photograph of a much younger, thinner, and prettier woman. Remember: Many women in prison are cons and they are used to conning people."

How do prisoners get photographs of themselves for the ads? They can be stolen or borrowed from other inmates, as I mentioned. But prisons also have programs that allow them to have pictures taken, usually by another inmate, in the visiting room or some other public area. "They are wearing prison garb, but there is often a backdrop like a nature scene or something else more attractive than cinder-block walls," said Lisa. These photos are ostensibly meant for the family members of prisoners, she said, but they are often used in romance schemes. Inmates also borrow or steal photos from younger or better-looking prisoners. The one thing prisoners are honest about is being in prison—which can be a lure for the lonely.

Once the prisoner has earned a victim's trust, the conversation eventually turns to money. "Prisoners usually ask for any money to be sent to their inmate account," Lisa said. They can use money to purchase coffee, cigarettes, and other items that are not provided by the prison.

In one situation, a man called the prison, sobbing. "Apparently, the woman he was corresponding with had asked for bail money, which he sent. Bail money is generally fairly substantial, if it is legitimate. But he never heard from her again," Lisa said. He was hoping she would post bail and meet him when she was released. Unfortunately, there is no "bail" in state prison. "You do time until you make parole or are released. Many people who are unfamiliar with the prison system don't understand this," she said. You also cannot get probation from the state prison; that applies only to people in a county jail. Bail is extremely rare in federal prison as well. "Anyone in the state prison system who is asking you for money to post bail is scamming you," said Lisa. "The number-one red flag when communicating with a prisoner is a request for money."

Many times, inmates will tell their pen pals that they are getting out a week after their actual release date. Once they have your money and they get out of prison, you don't hear from them again. Lisa recalls one story: "A man had come to prison and he was crying—'She promised me that she was going to come and take care of me,' he told me. 'I sent her a couple of thousand dollars,' he said, which represented his savings. But she was long gone, having been released a week earlier. I told him he can press charges and she can be found and prosecuted. But he refused, telling me his family would be upset to learn he had been communicating with someone behind bars, and that he had sent her money." This is one reason why prison love scams (as well as other dating scams) are underreported or not talked about at all: People feel ashamed and embarrassed.

I'm not going to tell you not to write to someone who is serving time in jail. The impulse to reach out to troubled people is admirable. I was in jail, and I turned my life around. Today I am a happily married man, father, and grandfather. I do my best every day to repay the hurt I inflicted on my victims through service to my community and country. So I do know that prisoners and people who commit crimes can change. I also know that many do not. Career con artists rarely change. Proceed with caution, and never send an inmate money.

DATING SCAM RED FLAGS

While dating scammers who take advantage of people at their most vulnerable times—when they are hoping to make a connection with a potential soul mate—is not entirely avoidable, being vigilant in how you assess potential dates is key for avoiding heartbreak.

Language counts. Carefully examine the words that suitors use. Those who make spelling and grammar mistakes are often scammers in foreign countries, where English isn't their first language. They could be using translating software, which is imprecise and, at times, awkward and ungrammatical. Timothy noticed that scammers claiming to be American can give themselves away through colloquial speech. "A lot of them use the term 'mum' instead of 'mom' or 'mother'—more common U.S. expressions. That's another giveaway someone may not be who they claim to be," said Timothy. Excessive use of religious terms like "God-fearing" can be a red flag, too, according to Jules Hannaford, who wrote about being scammed by an Internet date in her book *Fool Me Twice*. Likewise, as Hannaford found, someone with an accent that doesn't match their culture or country may be suspect.

The deploy ploy. "Anyone who says they are deployed overseas should send up a red flag," said Timothy. Be skeptical of claims that your suitor is working overseas for the military or the government. "Any job that requires them to move around is a red flag," said Hannaford.

No gift, no go. If someone asks for a gift card, iTunes card, or straight-up cash for travel, medical emergencies, hotel bills, hospitals bills for a child or other relative, visas or other official documents, or losses from a financial setback, it's a scam. As soon as Jeff Caldwell asked Melissa for $100 and then increased the request to $200 when they got to the ATM, she should have politely declined and walked away. Good riddance.

Glamour shots. If the person's photo looks like something out of a magazine, it very well may be. You can use https://tineye .com or Google Images to upload an image and find out whether it appears in other places on the Internet.

Love bombing. That's when your suitor showers you with endearing terms right away. "One of the keys to a scammer is that he will call you 'babe' almost right away, and become very affectionate—that lets me know something is fishy," said Timothy. Hannaford also raised the red flag of instant intimacy. "It made me very uneasy when 'Truman' said 'I love you' very shortly after we started chatting, before we even met," she said.

Won't meet face-to-face. Scammers will often make excuses about why they cannot meet you in person. Some won't even talk to you by phone, Skype, or FaceTime; they'll only text or email.

No-shows. They tell you they are just about to travel overseas, so they cannot meet you. Likewise, they constantly make plans to visit but cancel at the last minute because of a traumatic event, family emergency, or business deal gone sour.

Dislocation. If a profile photo looks like it was taken in a country different from the one they say they're living in, it could be a sign of a scammer.

Family tragedy. Claims of being a widow or widower, with or without a child, accompanied by a sad story, like a partner who has recently died of cancer, should set off alarm bells. In Melissa's case, Caldwell had told her that his parents, fiancée, and child had died in a car accident. This was to build up sympathy and an intimate bond, which might have been part of the reason she was inclined to give him money and the keys to her car.

Name game. While not always the case, people using two first names as their full name can indicate an alias.

Funny numbers. If the person you're chatting with gives you a phone number from a country other than the one you expected or the one they say they are from, it could be a scam.

Moving details. Scammers will often claim to have been in your country or area in the past and say are planning to move back in the next few months, or they'll claim to be seriously considering a move to your area.

Social media problems. Scammers' social media pages have few photos and few, if any, posts about their personal lives. They also have few friends or connections, and the ones they do have seem to be of the same sex.

Off-site offers. Beware when a suitor asks to leave a dating site immediately and instead communicate using personal email or instant messaging (but also refuses to use any platform that offers live, face-to-face communication).

MATCH POINT

One of the other common questions I get when I speak to people is this: How can scammers avoid developing any feelings for the people they scam, especially in a love scheme, where emotions must become entangled with a target? Don't scammers have a soul, a heart? How can they take advantage of someone they've met, spent time with, and perhaps even been intimate with?

Well, it's actually very easy. Many of them are thinking only about themselves, and since many are sociopaths or just doing this to make money, selfishness and a lack of empathy come naturally.

I can tell you from experience that many of the scammers who are like the people in the stories I've told in this chapter are living hand to mouth. They are simply trying to figure out how they can get their next meal, their next room for the night, or, in the case of inmates, some extras while on the inside or money to live on after they're released. They simply do not have the capability to think about other people. When Lisa asked the prisoner, who had bilked several men out of thousands of dollars, why she had done it, she simply said, "They are willing to give it up, and I am willing to take it." Her statement sums up perfectly the philosophy of the narcissistic criminal. It seems they really can't imagine why you'd even be upset with them.

I know this from personal experience. It took me a while to realize how much I had hurt people. After I was caught as a young scammer, I wondered why so many people I had spent time with were saying such nasty things about me. After all, many times I was the one taking them out to dinner, and entertaining them. The funds I was using may have been ill-gotten, but I was picking up the tab, wasn't I? I hadn't stolen anything from *them*. It didn't occur to me until much later that I had taken advantage of their emotions and feelings, and that in many ways is much more hurtful than taking money or possessions from someone, for our greatest possession is really our heart. Keep yours safe.

Epilogue

Fraud, Fast Forward

Six hundred billion dollars. That's the global cost of cybercrimes, including the malicious scams, malware, phishing, ransomware, and records lost to hacking that we've been talking about, according to security company McAfee. Tack on the emotional toll that fraud takes on individuals and communities. Then add consumer, property, and other kinds of scams, and the impact is staggering. Whether it's one individual cheating another out of money or large organized groups of criminals stealing identities from millions of people with robocalls, fraud has the potential to upend our lives. It's one of the reasons I get up every morning and do what I can to educate people about fraud.

When people ask what keeps me up at night, here's how I answer. First, I tell them that fraud will become more sinister, broader, and more destructive. Second, I tell them that our identities have to become more secure, sooner rather than later. Third, I tell them that knowing what to watch for and what to do—the core of this book—is the key to protecting yourself.

What follows is a look at how fraud could play out in the future and what we can do to protect ourselves and our families.

IT'S PERSONAL: PRIVACY BREACHES

I'm always concerned that the next big privacy breach will be individuals' search engines or personal search histories. The number of vulnerable searches is potentially in the billions. Internet World Stats estimates that more than 4.2 billion people—about 55 percent of the world's population—have ready access to the Internet through either a personal or public computer or a mobile phone. People of notoriety, politicians, public figures, and even private citizens could be held up by hackers and other cybercriminals for huge ransom demands with the threat that potentially embarrassing search histories would be made public. That could include searches of controversial political opinions, pornography, your own personal health issues. As I was writing this epilogue, the IT Governance Institute reported that in January and February 2019 alone, there were nearly 2.5 billion data breaches—about thirty thousand breaches per minute. And I believe that this already large number can explode exponentially if criminals find new ways to access what we do on the Internet.

Whichever web browser we use, it is tracking our web searches and downloads. In some ways, it's a benefit: It automatically knows where you've been and takes you there easily. But you might not want other people to have access to your search and download histories, no matter how benign they may seem, especially since cybercriminals are always advancing the ways they can access this information.

So how can you keep yourself safe? Be vigilant about reviewing and erasing your web activity. Most browsers make it easy to remove your browser history. You may also want to erase your download history (not the downloads themselves), cookies (small bits of data that websites want to store on your computer), and your computer's cache (which holds copies of graphics your browser uses to load pages quickly). With most browsers, you can do all three by opening your history tab and then clicking "Clear history." With one click, whatever you choose is gone. In addition, most computers allow us to open browser windows in what is called "private" or "incognito" mode—it's generally the option under "File" in the browser bar—and doing so means that searches done in these private windows won't be saved and therefore can't be tracked.

FRAUDS OF THE FUTURE—WAR WITHOUT WEAPONS

Today, from fifty feet away, a knowledgeable hacker can shut off someone's pacemaker. In a few years, criminals will be able to shut off thousands of pacemakers from even longer distances, maybe thousands of miles away. From fifty feet away you can also take control of a car. I can envision a future where all cars are autonomous and networked, and entire fleets could be commandeered from thousands of miles away, to create maximum chaos and destruction.

Cyber fraud could become an important part of weapons systems used by rogue nations as a way to push entire economies into bankruptcy and economic and social chaos. All accomplished without firing a single missile or shooting a gun. But make no mistake: Cyberwar is not, and will not, be perpetrated only by bad actors. Legitimate governments, like our own, also employ cyberattacks, the same techniques criminals use to destroy institutional networks, to defend against our perceived enemies.

In one widely reported story, for instance, Stuxnet, a sophisticated virus, targeted Iran's nuclear centrifuges, destroying a fifth of them. Ralph Langner, a control system security analyst who has done extensive research and analysis of Stuxnet, wrote that "it proved to be the most sophisticated piece of malicious code known to man." It made the centrifuges self-destruct. "Stuxnet didn't act like any previous malware before. Its objective was not the theft or manipulation of data. It was the physical destruction of gas centrifuges in the Natanz fuel enrichment plant, the crown jewel of Iran's nuclear program."

One of the problems with complex malicious codes is that they can be studied and adapted for use by bad actors. I guarantee that this is already happening and that some sort of cyberattack will be used in an attempt to destroy integral parts of the government—fraud of the highest and most dangerous order. It's just a matter of time. There is a lot of money in fraud, so paying coding experts who care only about themselves and their own selfish aims is a lucrative investment. I have seen evidence of this firsthand in my work with the FBI.

Most industrial manufacturing facilities use standardized industrial control systems, Langner said, so "if you get control of one industrial control system, you can infiltrate dozens or even hundreds more of the same breed." The Stuxnet virus spread mainly through the very simple use of flash drives, not via networks. Langner wrote in *Foreign Policy,* "The sober reality is that at a global scale, pretty much every single industrial or military facility that uses industrial control systems at some scale is dependent on its network of contractors, many of which are very

good at narrowly defined engineering tasks, but lousy at cybersecurity."

That is a huge concern, since attackers may set their sights
on civilian infrastructure to do maximum damage—things like
large industrial plants and factory floors, traffic-signal and transit
systems, water treatment facilities, and nuclear power plants.
Criminals will find ways to disrupt connectivity to infiltrate orga-
nizational networks, take over electrical grids, and shut down
banking systems. We can prevent some attacks, and we'll get better at detection as technology advances—but we will never be able
to prevent the evils of war. What we *can* do is learn to recognize
breaches and prevent fraudsters from doing harm and, when we
can't prevent it, minimize it. We have to hire the best and bright-
est to stay one step ahead of those cybercriminals wishing to do us
harm—an expensive prospect, likely costing trillions of dollars.

TODAY'S IDENTITY, TOMORROW'S DIGITAL FINGERPRINT

I worry that the common ways we use to confirm the identities of
individuals are extremely basic and therefore easy for fraudsters
to steal, replicate, and use. A friend and colleague, Larry Benson, the director of Strategic Alliances for LexisNexis Risk Solutions and the creator of Fraud of the Day, a daily online fraud
publication, also marvels at the fact that so many institutions and
organizations still rely on birth certificates and Social Security
numbers to verify identities.

"Take a look at a contemporary birth certificate," he suggests.
Compare it with an old one if you're able—they look quite

similar. "Does the birth certificate have a picture or a description of the person on it? No. Current birth certificates give only the most basic record of a human birth on a particular day and hour at a particular location, plus gender: female, male, and, in a few states, X [for non-binary people]." Not nearly the information needed to confirm that we are, in fact, who we say we are.

Yet birth certificates, which we can use to claim identity, are simple to obtain. Benson has the proof: "I have birth certificates for actor Johnny Depp, director Steven Spielberg, athlete LeBron James, former Speaker of the House John Andrew Boehner, astronaut Neil Armstrong, famed boxing legend Cassius Clay Jr. (the birth name of Muhammad Ali), my mother, and a bunch of regular people. I also have the death certificate of Colonel Sanders—they are easy to obtain as well."

The second most basic form of ID is a Social Security card. A Social Security card has a name and number on it, but no other information. There are many ways to create a fake Social Security card—in fact, a simple search on the Internet brings up many businesses willing to make one for you. These companies are periodically shut down, but others pop up to replace them just as quickly. Relying on such a simple piece of paper for ID verification is a real problem for the future.

LOOKING FORWARD

If scammers can get around all these modes of checking your identity, and they have all the tactics we've talked about throughout this book, what can we do to stop fraud in its tracks?

The technology of facial recognition, a type of biometric (that is, applying statistical analysis to biological data), is one possible answer, and this technology will become more advanced (and commonly used) in the future. Even as it stands now it is better than a Social Security card or a birth certificate. Facial recognition software uses algorithms of an individual's facial characteristics to compare driver's license or ID photos with other images that the department of motor vehicles has on file. This technology will become increasingly difficult to fool. If recognition analysts see an image that is associated with two or more identities, they try to determine whether it was a clerical error— for instance, from a name change due to marriage or divorce—or willful fraud.

As of this writing, thirty-nine state DMVs use facial recognition software. "You have an opportunity, using this technology, to find people who are trying to skirt the system," said Geoff Slagle, director of identity management for the American Association of Motor Vehicle Administrators. "It has really helped to identify fraudsters."

In Massachusetts, self-service license renewal kiosks use biometrics to ensure that people are who they say they are—and raise the alarm if there's a problem. Colorado, Idaho, Iowa, Maryland, and Washington, D.C., have all begun testing digital driver's licenses (DDLs), which are encrypted and app-based, with remote reader technology—including facial recognition—to access the app.

I anticipate that eventual cost savings and security features will prompt widespread adoption not just in the United States but globally. Slagle agrees. "It is not a question of whether or not this happens; it's a question of when," he said, noting that similar efforts are ongoing in Europe, Asia, and southern Africa.

Another biometric, fingerprints, can also be used to make birth certificates and Social Security cards—and our identities—more secure and harder to steal. "There is no reason why a birth certificate cannot be issued, at birth, that contains a chip with the child's fingerprint, since fingerprints are fully developed at birth," said Benson. A patent for this technology was issued a few years ago, he said, but states and governments in general take a long time to adopt anything new. It costs money and time. "Such a birth certificate would be more expensive, perhaps by a dollar or so. Until the technology becomes more widespread and people feel more comfortable with it, many states will hold off implementing the system. But the states who do adopt it will be ahead in terms of ID protection."

Many groups are concerned about privacy violations with biometric facial recognition software, since it could be used to identify people at political protests and rallies or in other public places, like shopping centers, sports arenas, and even city sidewalks. Some, but not all, state DMVs have taken steps to limit the software usage to license plate reconciliation. But in the future, privacy *could* be jeopardized in an effort to stop identity fraud. We have to continue to develop ways to establish identity without violating individual rights.

BITCOIN BUSTS

Bitcoin is a digital and global currency that can be thought of as cash for the Internet. It allows people to send and receive money over the Internet, even to someone they don't know or don't trust. It is unregulated, operating outside of the traditional banking system. Since the currency has gained popularity and has increased in value over the past few years, it's become a target for scammers looking to take advantage of people's interest in it as an investment. Because its value is determined by software that very few people actually understand, there are several ways you can become a victim of bitcoin fraud.

Some of the most prevalent bitcoin scams include online fake bitcoin "wallets" that, when downloaded, install malware onto your computer that can steal personal information. Another virtual currency scam is people falsely representing real bitcoin companies. When they gain the trust of an unsuspecting buyer, they gain access to the buyer's online "bitcoin wallet," spending what's in it. There are also classic pyramid schemes using bitcoin, with fraudsters selling phony currency at ridiculously low prices.

Bitcoin scams lure victims with promises of low prices and high profits. For instance, a promise from an impostor posing as a legitimate bitcoin dealer, complete with a professional-looking website, offers to set up an account for bitcoin trading or selling in exchange for a traditional currency fee, like the U.S. dollar. Once you set up the account, your bitcoins are stolen and can never be retrieved. That's because bitcoin transactions cannot be changed or reversed—a feature of the currency, not a bug. I expect cryptocurrency scams to increase as cryptocurrencies like bitcoin become more popular.

BLOCKCHAIN

Blockchain is the way of the future. It is the best way to secure information, and to secure it 100 percent. In simple terms, blockchain assigns a name, date of birth, and blood type—to create "verifiable claims" that cannot be hacked. It is in essence a record or block of information (or a transaction) that is added to other blocks of information, creating a chain of data. That means every block of information or data or transactions is connected to all the other blocks before and after it. This "chain" makes it difficult to tamper with any single block of data because a hacker would need to change the block containing information as well as information in the blocks around it, in order to avoid detection.

Permission to access and share these verifiable claims and data is stored on the blockchain's "ledger," which can record transactions between two parties efficiently and permanently. Communication occurs between peers instead of via a central authority like a bank, and every transaction—though no sensitive data—is visible to anyone with access to the system. Blockchain technology can also be used to protect and validate other vital records, including healthcare files, academic credentials, financial information, property deed records, and energy credits. You cannot break or hack into the blockchain. You cannot change anything on the blockchain. Proponents say it's a technology that will eventually be adopted by all types of governments, businesses, and corporations.

I strongly believe that blockchain is the future of secure data processing and storage and that it will greatly minimize and even potentially eliminate identity theft. It is the best way to secure information.

WHAT WE CAN DO

The most important step you can take to prevent fraud is to educate yourself on the latest threats and frauds using the many resources available, including AARP's Fraud Watch. Sign up at www.aarp.org/fraudwatchnetwork. Then follow the suggestions I've provided throughout this book.

- Freeze your credit.
- Clear your computer's browsing history regularly or use private windows when searching on the Internet.
- Keep track of your finances by reading bank and credit card statements carefully.
- Use a major credit card for all major transactions—and even small ones. Track your account regularly and question suspicious transactions.
- Use two-step authentication for passwords until the time comes when we can eliminate the need for passwords.
- Never share personal information with people you don't know, or on social media.
- Don't leave your smartphone unlocked.
- Shred sensitive documents using a micro-cut shredder.
- Read the fine print and understand what you are signing before making a financial commitment, whether it's an investment opportunity, property transaction, or charitable donation.
- When in doubt in considering a financial commitment, get a second opinion.

- Don't be embarrassed if you are a victim of fraud; report it to law enforcement and the AARP Fraud Watch Network.
- Vote for politicians who advocate for investment in national security systems to prevent "weaponless war" and other mass cyber scams and crimes.
- Advocate for local and state governments to institute technologies like biometrics and blockchain to protect identities.

Finally, I believe we have to get back to forming strong communities where people know and look out for one another. A lot of fraud happens in isolation and online. If we look up from our electronic devices and limit our online time to specific tasks and goals, we will be less prone to scammers online. We'll also feel happier and less isolated. A 2018 study from the University of Pennsylvania found that using social media for more than thirty minutes a day may lead to depression. Depression, in turn, can lead to risky or careless behavior, which makes you more susceptible to fraud. Community engagement can help keep us all safer. This may seem simplistic, but we have to get out from behind our screens and understand who our neighbors are. We can form neighborhood watch groups and prevent door-to-door scam artists and other criminals from sweeping through a neighborhood. When we are in doubt about something—a financial opportunity, for instance—we can hash it out with a friend, relative, or neighbor. Of course, even well-connected people with loads of friends can be victims of scams. If you are approached by a scammer or are a victim of a scam, report it to AARP's Fraud Watch Network.

So, for all of us: Stay vigilant, stay informed, and keep in touch.

Acknowledgments

Many people helped prepare this book for publication. I would especially like to express my gratitude for the many people who shared their stories of fraud in this book, the law enforcement and government agencies that shared insights into identifying and fighting fraud, and everyday citizens who provided their stories and lessons. Some of these people are mentioned by their real names in this book; others, especially those who have been victimized by criminals, chose to remain anonymous or share their stories under assumed names.

I am also indebted to the men and women of the Federal Bureau of Investigation, for supporting me and affording me the opportunity and privilege to teach at the FBI Academy and assist with FBI field office programs.

I owe a debt of gratitude to my partners at AARP who participated in the creation of this book, including Jodi Lipson, director of AARP Books; Karen Horrigan, of the AARP Brand team; Kathy Stokes, Amy Nofziger, and Kristin Keckeisen, who are part of the Fraud Watch Network team and who reviewed drafts of the manuscript; and Laurie Comadena Edwards, Gena Wright, and Mark Bagley, who worked on promotion of the book.

I also want to thank the AARP fact-checking team—Karen Font, Kris French, Michelle Harris, and Chuong Trang—and Tom Miller, literary agent.

At Portfolio, I would like to thank publisher Adrian Zackheim; marketing expert Taylor Edwards; publicity professional Alyssa Adler; Chris Sergio, for his amazing cover design; Olivia Peluso, who helped keep the book organized and moving; copy editor Will Palmer; and, of course, my editor, Leah Trouwborst, for her keen eye and creativity.

I personally want to thank Karen Kelly, who without a doubt is the most talented writer and researcher I have ever had the opportunity to work with. Karen has the incredible ability to make the most difficult subjects easy to understand so the reader can easily implement solutions to these very serious problems. Karen has had the opportunity to write numerous books, conduct interviews, and research the most complex subjects, and it was an honor and a pleasure for me to have the opportunity to work with her on my book. You meet very few professionals in your lifetime; Karen Kelly is one of the few. I am sincerely grateful for all of her hard work.

Selected Sources

AARP. *The Con Artist's Playbook: The Psychology Behind ID Theft, Fraud and Scams.* Washington, DC: AARP Fraud Watch Network, n.d. www.aarp .org/content/dam/aarp/money/scams_fraud/2017/07/The-Con-Artists -Playbook-AARP.pdf.

————. "Scams and Fraud." Alerts, articles, and other resources. https://www .aarp.org/money/scams-fraud/.

Abagnale, Frank, and Will Johnson. *The Perfect Scam.* AARP podcast series. www.aarp.org/podcasts/the-perfect-scam/.

Choi-Allum, Lona. *401(k) Participants' Awareness and Understanding of Fees.* Washington, DC: AARP Research and Strategic Analysis, February 2011. www.aarp.org/work/retirement-planning/info-02-2011/401k-fees -awareness-11.html.

Equifax. *A Lasting Impact: The Emotional Toll of Identity Theft.* Atlanta: Equifax, 2015. www.equifax.com/assets/PSOL/15-9814_psol_emotionalToll_wp.pdf.

Federal Bureau of Investigation. *2017 Internet Crime Report.* Washington, DC: Internet Crime Complaint Center, Federal Bureau of Investigation, 2018. https://pdf.ic3.gov/2017_IC3Report.pdf.

Internal Revenue Service. "Tax Scams—How to Report Them." Last updated April 23, 2018. www.irs.gov/businesses/small-businesses-self-employed/tax -scams-how-to-report-them.

Kircanski, Katharina, Nanna Notthoff, Doug Shadel, Gary Mottola, Laura L. Carstensen, and Ian H. Gotlib. *Heightened Emotional States Increase Susceptibility to Fraud in Older Adults.* Stanford, CA: Stanford Center on Longevity, Stanford University, May 5, 2016. http://longevity.stanford.edu /2016/05/05/heightened-emotional-states-increase-susceptibility -to-fraud-in-older-adults-2/.

Pascual, Al, Kyle Marchini, and Sarah Miller. *2018 Identity Fraud: Fraud Enters a New Era of Complexity.* Pleasanton, CA: Javelin Strategy and

Research, February 6, 2018. www.javelinstrategy.com/coverage-area/2018 -identity-fraud-fraud-enters-new-era-complexity.

Sauer, Jennifer, and Alicia Williams. *Online Relationship Scams: Protect Your Heart and Your Wallet: Online Relationship Scams: An AARP National Survey of Internet Users Ages 18+*. Washington, DC: AARP, February 2019. https://doi.org/10.26419/res.00277.001.

Shadel, Doug, and Karla Pak. *AARP Investment Fraud Vulnerability Study*. Washington, DC: AARP Research, February 2017. https://doi.org/10.26419 /res.00150.001.

———. *Under Fire: Military Veterans and Consumer Fraud*. Washington, DC: AARP Research, November 2017. https://doi.org/10.26419/res.00182.001.

Resources

AARP Fraud Watch Network

877-908-3360

www.aarp.org/fraudwatchnetwork

Sign up for free watchdog alerts; get tips to spot and avoid scams like identity theft, investment fraud, and holiday scams; review a scam-tracking map that provides real-time alerts from law enforcement in your state; and call the toll-free fraud helpline to report fraud or speak with fraud counselors.

Abagnale & Associates

800-237-7443

www.abagnale.com

Frank Abagnale Jr. speaks widely about fraud. Contact him to learn more about hosting him for speaking engagements.

Federal Trade Commission

600 Pennsylvania Avenue NW

Washington, DC 20580

202-326-2222

www.ftc.gov

You can report fraud at www.ftc.gov/complaint. Try to provide specifics, such as a copy of any letter or email you receive and the date and time of any calls, along with what the caller said and the phone number of the caller. Even though scammers use spoofing to simulate real numbers, or create fake ones, law enforcement agents can still potentially track numbers to identify the caller. For any type of identity theft, begin by making a report at www.identitytheft.gov.

Financial Industry Regulatory Authority (FINRA)
1735 K Street NW
Washington, DC 20006
301-590-6500
www.finra.org

FINRA is an independent organization that upholds standards for broker-dealers. Its website provides resources for investors, including a way to file a complaint against a broker-dealer.

Internal Revenue Service (IRS)
800-829-1040
www.irs.gov

The IRS provides information on federal taxes, tax fraud and prevention, and related financial crimes.

Medicare
800-MEDICARE (800-633-4227)
TTY: 877-486-2048
www.medicare.gov/fraud

Contact Medicare to find out how to spot and report Medicare-related fraud. Report suspicious calls regarding your healthcare or health insurance to Medicare's 800 number.

Each state has a Senior Medicare Patrol (SMP) that can give you reliable information and help with all your Medicare questions, including those about possible fraud or identity theft. You can locate your state's office at www.smpresource.org/content /what-smps-do.aspx, or call 877-808-2468. Staff will also help you determine whether fraud or theft has occurred.

If you have established that someone else is using your Medicare benefits, follow the same procedure as with any other kind of identity theft by making a report at www.identitytheft.gov.

National Do Not Call Registry
888-382-1222
TTY: 866-290-4236
www.donotcall.gov

Register your home and mobile numbers for free to stop unwanted sales calls from legitimate companies. You might still receive political calls, charitable calls, debt collection calls, informational calls, and telephone survey calls. Companies you've recently done business with may also call you, though if you ask them not to, they must honor your request. Once your number is on the registry, if you do get a sales call, it's likely a scam.

North American Securities Administrators Association Inc.
   (NASAA)
750 First Street NE, Suite 1140

Washington, DC 20002
202-737-0900
www.nasaa.org

NASAA is a voluntary association that helps protect investors from fraud.

Social Security Administration (SSA)
800-772-1213
www.ssa.gov
Social Security Fraud Hotline
P.O. Box 17785
Baltimore, MD 21235
800-269-0271 (10 a.m.–4 p.m. Eastern time)
TTY: 866-501-2101

Contact the Social Security Administration for tips on preventing fraud. You can report fraud directly to the Fraud Hotline.

U.S. Securities and Exchange Commission (SEC)
Division of Corporation Finance
202-551-3100
www.sec.gov

The SEC will answer questions about security transactions and verify registration of securities dealers and firms. The Division of Corporation Finance seeks to ensure that investors are provided with material information in order to make informed investment decisions.

CHARITY RATINGS AND REVIEWS

These organizations rate and review charities. With many, you can search the charity's name and get the percentage it donates directly to its stated mission.

Charity Navigator
139 Harristown Road, Suite 101
Glen Rock, NJ 07452
201-818-1288
www.charitynavigator.org

CharityWatch
P.O. Box 578460
Chicago, IL 60657
773-529-2300
www.charitywatch.org/home

Give.org (BBB Wise Giving Alliance)
3033 Wilson Blvd., Suite 710
Arlington, VA 22201
703-247-9321
www.give.org

Givewell
182 Howard Street, No. 208
San Francisco, CA 94105
415-689-5803
www.givewell.org

CREDIT-REPORTING AGENCIES

Go to www.annualcreditreport.com to get a free annual credit report from each of the three nationwide reporting services—Equifax, Experian, and TransUnion. For the most current results, request a report from each of the companies periodically throughout the year (for example, Equifax on January 1, Experian on May 1, and TransUnion on September 1). You can also set up credit freezes by contacting the three services.

Equifax
800-685-1111
www.equifax.com

Experian
888-397-3742
www.experian.com

TransUnion
800-888-4213
www.transunion.com

Index

Frank Abagnale is one of the world's most respected authorities on the subjects of fraud, forgery, and cyber security. A world-renowned consultant for more than four decades, he lectures at the FBI Academy and field offices. More than fourteen thousand financial institutions, corporations, and law enforcement agencies use his fraud prevention programs. He consults with major corporate clients such as AARP, Trusona, Experian, Intuit, and LexisNexis. He is the author of the bestselling memoir *Catch Me If You Can*, as well as *The Art of the Steal* and *Stealing Your Life*.